THE
RESCUE
OF BAT 21

★

Darrel D. Whitcomb

A Dell Book

Published by
Dell Publishing
a division of
Random House, Inc.
1540 Broadway
New York, New York 10036

The trademark Dell® is registered in the U.S. Patent and Trademark Office.

ISBN: 0-440-22654-6

Reprinted by arrangement with Naval Institute Press

Printed in the United States of America

Published simultaneously in Canada

February 1999

10 9 8 7 6 5 4 3 2 1

OPM

Many believe the war in Vietnam was a war without heroes. But that was not the case.

Richard Nixon, No More Vietnams

This story is dedicated to some of those heroes, the ground warriors and air warriors who saw the end of our nation's participation in that war. And to all of those who ever strapped into the seat of a jet or recip or helicopter and went out to try to rescue one of their buddies in that wasted effort, especially the Sandys and Jolly Greens.

Most of all, this book is dedicated to the brave crews of Blueghost 39 and Jolly Green 67. Ten men went forth to save one of their own; only one returned. They were brave men. God bless them all.

One of the reasons for the outstanding morale of the U.S. crewmembers was that in the event they were downed, they knew that every possible effort would be made to rescue them. This confidence was a vital factor in maintaining the esprit of air units.

Military Assistance Command Vietnam, Command History

When [the Vietnamese colonel] heard the rescue mission was for one survivor, he held up his finger, and meaning no disrespect said, "Just one?" We all understood his remark. . . .

Lt. Col. G. H. Turley, The Easter Offensive

CONTENTS

FOREWORD

In the classic Japanese novel *Rashomon*, a tragic incident is recounted several times, each from a different perspective, resulting in a much more comprehensive understanding of what actually occurred. In *The Rescue of Bat 21*, Darrel Whitcomb has written an American nonfiction version of that classic tale, recounting from several different vantage points the shootdown and rescue of Air Force Lt. Col. Iceal "Gene" Hambleton, call sign Bat 21 Bravo.

As in the case of the *Rashomon* incident, on the surface this incident also would appear to be a rather straightforward and well-known adventure story. In fact, such an account was written sixteen years ago by retired Air Force Col. William C. Anderson and made into a 1988 feature movie, *Bat 21*, starring Gene Hackman, Danny Glover, and Jerry Reed. As Michael Lee Lanning comments in his 1994 *Vietnam at the Movies* (New York: Fawcett), even though "the film is based loosely on the true experiences of LTC Iceal Hambleton . . . none of the actors is particularly believable."

One reason may be, as Colonel Anderson says in the

afterword to his 1980 book *Bat 21*, although the subtitle reads "based on the true story of Lieutenant Colonel Iceal Hambleton USAF," the fact was that for security reasons, "certain parts of the story which seemed important to me were still classified—particularly certain aspects of the Air Force escape and evasion techniques. Further, I was requested to protect the identity of certain individuals [and as a result] would have to replace them with certain fictions approximate to the truth."

Not only that, "taken in all, the actual rescue effort . . . was so complex, involved so many people, made use of such complex logistics and [in some cases] such exotic technologies that there was a real danger that the central narrative . . . might be swamped in peripheral detail." To avoid that, Anderson "interpolated into the story a fictional character who would perform the roles actually played by a rather populous cast of real people . . . a representative of all the heroic, unsung forward air controller (FAC) pilots who throughout the long, bitter struggle in Vietnam daily risked their lives for their service and their country."

Appropriately enough, one of those "heroic and unsung" FAC pilots, Darrel D. Whitcomb, has now written the honest-to-God true account of the Bat 21 rescue operation. From 1972 until 1974, he was a forward air controller in Southeast Asia, directing airstrikes in support of friendly forces in Vietnam, Laos, and Cambodia. Awarded the Silver Star for gallantry in action, two Distinguished Flying Crosses, and sixteen Air Medals for his wartime service, Whitcomb knows from firsthand experience the realities of the battlefield. Further, with the passage of time, many of the restrictions on use of classified information that hampered Colonel Anderson no longer apply. Rather than being constrained to avoid the complexities of the rescue operation, he has been able to incorporate those details into his account.

The first three chapters set the stage for this important episode in military history. The situation in South Vietnam in the spring of 1972 was not at all like the picture that most Americans have of the war. Gone was the massive American ground combat presence of the earlier years. Only two U.S. infantry brigades remained in the country, and they were restricted to defending their own base areas. "Vietnamization" was the watchword: the responsibility for the defense of South Vietnam had been passed to the Army of the Republic of South Vietnam (ARVN). The black-pajama-clad Viet Cong guerrillas were long gone as well, replaced by the regular military forces of the North Vietnamese Army (NVA).

Sensing that victory was at hand, the North Vietnamese Politburo ordered a major multidivision cross-border invasion of the south to administer the coup de grâce. In I Corps, the northernmost portion of South Vietnam, four NVA divisions attacked directly south across the demilitarized zone (DMZ) while another two divisions attacked to the east from bases in Laos. Simultaneous multidivision NVA attacks were also launched against Kontum in II Corps in the central highlands and An Loc in III Corps north of Saigon.

It was unlike anything seen in the war before. Not only were the advancing NVA forces equipped with tanks and heavy artillery, they were also accompanied by sophisticated air defense units armed with a variety of electrically guided surface-to-air missiles (SAMs). The ARVN defenders were hard pressed by this NVA blitzkrieg, and in response, the United States launched a major air campaign in support of these beleaguered forces, including B-52 bomber strikes against NVA troop concentrations. Accompanying the bombers were EB-66 electronic warfare aircraft to locate enemy SAM sites and to jam their missile-guidance-system radars.

On 2 April 1972, one such bomber strike force took off from its base in Thailand to attack NVA forces advancing across the DMZ. Coming under a heavy SAM barrage, one of their accompanying EB-66s, codenamed Bat 21, was shot down. Its navigator, Air Force Lt. Col. Iceal Hambleton, successfully ejected, landing, as Whitcomb describes it, "literally in the middle of one pincer of the invasion force coming down from the north and west." The subsequent attempts to rescue him set off the "biggest U.S. air-rescue effort of the war."

Therein lies the tale, and Whitcomb tells it well, weaving in its complexities to reveal what an immense task it turned out to be. The rescue story begins with the tragic efforts by the Army's 196th Light Infantry Brigade's "F" troop, 8th Cavalry, to use their Cobra gunships and "Huey" helicopters to make a "quick snatch" before the NVA could react. It continues with the intense Air Force attempt to use search-and-rescue techniques that had worked so well in many other combat situations to extricate Hambleton. But this time, the only result was more aircraft shot down, many more damaged, the loss of one Jolly Green HH-53 rescue helicopter and its entire crew, and two more airmen—FAC lieutenants Mark Clark and Bruce Walker—down behind enemy lines.

The heart of Whitcomb's tale, however, is the incredible odyssey of Lt. Tom Norris, a Navy SEAL, who, along with his South Vietnamese cohorts, infiltrated behind enemy lines to first rescue Lieutenant Clark and then Lieutenant Colonel Hambleton from the jaws of death. Sadly, Lieutenant Walker would be killed by the NVA before he too could be rescued.

Was it worth it? Whitcomb examines that question and the several controversies surrounding the rescue effort, including charges that in saving one man, it jeopardized the lives of an entire ARVN division.

That in turn leads to his retrospective on the mental and emotional condition of the Air Force in 1972. While not as exciting as the accounts of the rescue operation, these final chapters have far greater long-term implications. In 1972, says Whitcomb, the airmen "were a frustrated force." Since 1968 their main mission had been to "isolate" the battlefield by interdicting the Ho Chi Minh Trail, or, as one of my Air Force students at the Army War College in the early 1980s characterized it, "bombing holes in the jungle." But airpower is "primarily an offensive weapon," and such defensive operations are not the Air Force's raison d'être. Besides, the strikes were not working. NVA infiltration continued apace. And when Gen. John Lavelle, the Seventh Air Force commander, tried, albeit surreptitiously, to concentrate on NVA air defenses, he was relieved from command. Ironically, it was precisely those air defenses that later led to the shootdown of Bat 21.

Accordingly, "by 1972, search and rescue was about the only mission that meant anything to the aircrews," an attitude that explained the enormous effort expended to rescue "just one man." But there was a darker side to this as well. "Unfortunately, by 1972, 'their own' for the Air Force aviators did not include those fighting on the ground."

The emphasis on the Ho Chi Minh trail "intensified an ugly side of the Air Force psyche. . . . Since its separation from the Army in 1947, its aircrews had shown little interest in land battles. . . . Consequently, the American aircrews did not feel the loyalty to one's own toward the South Vietnamese ground troops that the ground advisers felt for the southern soldiers and Marines. Their loyalty was reserved for their fellow airmen. . . . By April 1972, U.S. air units that were covering the U.S. withdrawal from Vietnam were emotionally separated from their allies on the ground."

As Whitcomb concludes, the Bat 21 story "is part of the larger timeless one of men in combat and the bonds between warriors and their nation." Yet, he continues, "the story is also a warning about the dangers of alliances and pitfalls of coalition warfare in wars that are too drawn out, with objectives not clearly defined." It is a warning we ignore at our peril.

Col. Harry G. Summers Jr., USA (Ret.)

**It's a hell of a story. I just hope that
it is told someday.**

Capt. Harold Icke (O-2 pilot), Bilk 11, letter to his wife

PREFACE

This is a work of military history. It is a story about a specific act that took place in northern South Vietnam in the spring of 1972. In the process of writing it, I made two very interesting discoveries. First, I discovered that the story of this rescue is much larger than just the saving of one person in a long and bitter war. It is really a story about how we Americans fight our wars.

Second, I discovered that writers of military history are faced with an unavoidable dilemma: whether or not to use standard military jargon. Either the terms can be simplified so as to make them understood by the casual reader, or the real words can be used, along with attempts to explain them satisfactorily—at the risk of becoming tedious and boring. I have chosen a middle course by trying to homogenize most military terms for clarity and including a glossary for reference.

One other explanation is called for: that of call signs. Every aircraft that flew in the war had a call sign that the crew used on the radio to identify itself when talking with other agencies. Generally, a specific call sign would belong to a particular unit (squadron or battalion) or be assigned for a particular operation. Some units assigned call signs to individuals to be used whenever they flew.

If an individual was shot down, he would maintain his call sign while on the ground. If the aircraft had more than one crewmember, the individuals would be referred to by the call sign with a suffix designating their place in the crew. For example, if an F-4 with a call sign of Boxer 22 went down, the pilot would be referred to as Boxer 22 Alpha, and the backseater, or weapons-systems operator, would be referred to as Boxer 22 Bravo (Alpha and Bravo are the phonetic alphabet replacements for A and B—see the glossary). Indeed, this could become very confusing. In March 1972, an AC-130 gunship went down in Laos. All fifteen crewmembers bailed out and reached the ground. Each was called by the mission call sign of Spectre 13 with his proper suffix, Alpha through Oscar. All were successfully rescued. Bat 21 was an aircraft with a crew of six. Only one, Bat 21 Bravo, survived.

The various call signs—Sandy, Jolly Green, Nail, Covey, Blueghost, and so on—are proud vestiges of the war, clung to zealously by the men who used them. For some, even to this day, their call sign for their tour or even for one particular mission is part of their persona, as important as their name. This is a very important part of the story of this rescue.

ACKNOWLEDGMENTS

I gratefully acknowledge the help and enthusiasm of all of the participants. The reason is simple: it is their story. I could not tell it honestly or accurately without them.

When I resolved to write this story, I determined that I would try to include every guy who was involved in it. My efforts were considerable—and I have the phone, airline, and postal bills to prove it. But ultimately I fell short of my goal. There were two reasons for this. First, many of the participants have disappeared. They came back from the war and just melted back into society without a trace. Second, an equal number of those I did find refused my inquiries. They did not want to talk about the war. They had washed these experiences from their memories and no longer wanted to think about or deal with them.

Those who were willing to give the time and effort filled me with rich narratives of their exploits. Indeed, it is remarkable how clear their memories are after so many years. They helped me to capture much of the story and most of the flavor of the air and ground battles in Quang Tri, South Vietnam, in the spring of 1972. These battles were some of the most intense and brutal of that war. With an old expression in mind—"History is not what happened but what is written"—I have tried to write it right.

I have so many people to thank for their help in this effort: Douglas Pike at the Indochina Archive, Berkeley, California; Dale Andrade, Alexandria, Virginia; Dick Boylan at the National Archives, Suitland, Maryland; Lynn Gamma, Joe Cavers, and M.Sgt. Barry Spink of the Air Force Historical Research Agency, at Maxwell Air Force Base, Alabama; Lt. Col. Mark Clodfelter, professor of aerospace science at the University of North Carolina; Earl Tilford at the Army War College, Carlisle, Pennsylvania; Col. Jon Bear, Col. Gary Weikel, and Col. Al Feldkamp (Ret.) for their patient reviews of my work and their "been there" kind of comments; Lt. Col. Tony Willis (Ret.) of the Jolly Green Giant Association; Lt. Col. Mack Brooks at the U.S. Army Casualty and Memorial Operations Center, Alexandria, Virginia; Dick Long at the Marine Corps Historical Center, Washington, D.C.; Jack Matthews at the Marine Corps Staff College, Quantico, Virginia; Jeanne Lafontaine and Lt. Col. Larry Norman at the Air Force Military Personnel Center, Randolph Air Force Base, Texas; the patient librarians at the Pentagon library; my three children, Jenny, Matt, and Sarah, who let me use the computer; my wife, Chris, who patiently read all of my manuscripts and made constructive comments and corrections; the participants themselves who put up with all the questions. Finally, my bud, Nail two and a quarter—and he knows why.

THE RESCUE OF BAT 21

Prelude

It was June 1995, and the news was riveting. A young American pilot, Capt. Scott O'Grady, had been shot down in his F-16 by a lethal surface-to-air missile while flying an operational mission over the skies of Bosnia-Herzegovina, a place most of his countrymen could not even find on a map.

He was part of an American force sent as an element of a larger UN contingent dispatched on a "peacekeeping" mission, something not clearly understood by the majority of Americans. For days, his countrymen and women wondered about his fate. Then came the exciting news that he had been located and rescued by a daring U.S. Marine helicopter team under the cover of a massive armada of fighters and other supporting aircraft.

The American people welcomed the young captain home as a hero. In what appeared to be developing into a dismal quagmire threatening to engulf the United States in a land war in Europe for reasons unclear to the American people, O'Grady's rescue was a bit of good news. Across the nation, the successful operation was celebrated. One of our own had been rescued. As all this transpired, though, I was reminded of similar events in an earlier conflict, daring rescues amid what had become a long and divisive war. It was, as Yogi Berra used to say, "déjà vu all over again," because it spoke of a timeless bond among warriors. That is what this story is all about.

1

★

The great opportunity to end the U.S. aggressive
war has come.
Appeal by North Vietnam

We are going to do everything we can to protect
our people and keep our casualties down.
The only assistance we're going to give the
South Vietnamese is air.
Gen. Creighton Abrams

Hide and Seek

I T IS ALMOST LEGEND now—the saga of Bat 21. It is
the personal story of Air Force lieutenant colonel Iceal
"Gene" Hambleton, who, as a fifty-three-year-old navigator on an unarmed EB-66 electronic jamming aircraft,
was shot down on 2 April 1972, just south of the demilitarized zone (DMZ) in South Vietnam. The only survivor of a crew of six, he landed in the midst of one of the

pincers of an invading North Vietnamese force of over thirty thousand troops and was trapped behind enemy lines. In an act of unparalleled personal bravery, he evaded enemy forces for twelve days before being rescued. His is a heroic and inspiring story that has been highlighted in several books, in magazine and television articles, and even in a Hollywood movie starring Gene Hackman and Danny Glover.

But there are many more parts to the story. Hundreds of individuals in many different units and services worked day and night to recover Lt. Col. Hambleton. Drawn from every U.S. military component, including the Coast Guard, they were ceaseless in their efforts to rescue one of their own. Several of them paid with their lives to bring him out. The story has a happy ending, for today Hambleton lives in retirement under the warm skies of Arizona.

And the story is not really that simple. The Bat 21 rescue, which *Stars and Stripes* called the "biggest U.S. air rescue effort of the war" (23 April 1972, p. 1), took place in northern South Vietnam, in the middle of a massive conventional land and air battle between South Vietnamese ground forces, supported by American air and sea power, and invading North Vietnamese ground and air defense forces. The rescue was only one of many that occurred during a period of almost three weeks. These were all part of the larger U.S. Air Force efforts that took place in the area to support the South Vietnamese before they stopped and partly repelled the North Vietnamese offensive. The battles that actually lasted until the cease-fire in 1973 were some of the most intense and sustained of the war.

Some ground veterans of that massive 1972 battle

have questioned the propriety of the Bat 21 search and rescue (SAR), occurring as it did in the midst of a momentous clash between the two armies. They claim that the overall effort interfered with and actually had a disastrous effect on the Army of the Republic of South Vietnam's (ARVN) efforts to stop the invading North Vietnamese Army (NVA). These are serious charges, worthy of review.

But none of these controversial aspects could be anticipated as events began to unfold on a wispy morning in the early spring of 1972. The young American pilot could not believe his bad luck. "Damn this miserable weather!" he thought as he cruised at three thousand feet and nervously eyed the almost solid layers of clouds both above and below him. They stretched as far as he could see. This was a problem, because he had to get down to see the ground. Rumor and intelligence were telling him that enemy units were moving about—not Viet Cong, but hardcore NVA units. He had to check that out.

Spotting a good-sized hole in the clouds below him, Maj. Dave Brookbank eased back the throttle on the small O-1 spotter aircraft and began to descend. He finally cleared the clouds at about one thousand feet above the ground. Visibility below the clouds was good. He and his Vietnamese observer were just south of the DMZ, which separated North and South Vietnam. It was almost noon on 30 March 1972.

Quickly orienting himself to his location, Brookbank did not need binoculars to be able to tell that the roads and trails in the area showed heavy use. But he was looking for artillery, NVA artillery. All morning long, his forward unit outposts had been reporting sporadic incoming fire. He wanted to see if he could spot the enemy guns and perhaps attack them with friendly artillery, or, if possible, call in airstrikes.

And then he saw the flag. It was a huge one, a North Vietnamese flag raised on a flagpole on the north side of the Ben Hai River, which was the actual line between the North and South. Usually the enemy was not so brazen. Such a visual display was an open act of defiance to pilots such as he. The young pilot was considering firing a marking rocket at it when he noticed something else. Not too far away, an enemy soldier was standing in the open next to a clump of trees.

Dave banked the aircraft toward him to have a closer look. The soldier was wearing a pith helmet and the standard North Vietnamese light green uniform, and he had a field pack on his back. Dave dropped the nose of the O-1 to shoot a rocket at him, but the soldier ducked into the trees. A game of hide and seek. Dave pulled his craft back up to altitude, and the soldier reappeared. Dave tried the pass again; same result. So Dave continued to circle. As he did, the soldier slipped from tree to tree, never giving a clear shot.

Mesmerized by the hunt, Brookbank decided to change tactics. He opened his left side window, pulled out his CAR-15 folding stock rifle, and began shooting at the lone figure. After three long bursts, he had to change bullet clips. As he did so, the soldier stepped clearly into the open, aimed his AK-47 at the small aircraft, and fired an entire magazine of bullets. Brookbank saw the flash of the rifle and both heard and felt the bullets pass by. Some found their mark on the O-1, fortunately in noncritical areas of the aircraft. Coming to his senses, Dave sharply banked the aircraft away from the senseless encounter. Only then did he realize that several other larger guns were also firing clip after clip of high-explosive shells at him. Jinking to avoid the fire, and moving farther south, he happened to notice numerous large muzzle flashes to the north. Almost immediately his tactical radio came alive with excited voices. His Vietnamese backseater informed him that several friendly locations were reporting heavy incoming large-caliber artillery fire. Dave looked at his watch; it was high noon. Dave Brookbank was in the exact spot to witness the beginning of the overt North Vietnamese invasion of South Vietnam—what would come to be known as the Easter Invasion.

Like that lone soldier, the NVA were coming out into the open to fight. Like the two men in that small O-1, they would be met by a combined American–South Vietnamese force. The majority of the American effort would be airpower. Dave was in exactly the right place at the right time to observe the beginning of the next-to-last chapter of the long U.S. involvement in Vietnam. In a little less than a year, all American forces except for a handful of individuals would be out of South Vietnam. In a little less than three years, South Vietnam would no longer exist. That same flag that Dave Brookbank saw north of the Ben Hai River would fly over Saigon.

But none of that was evident as the battle opened in the eighth year of nearly nonstop American aerial combat operations in the war, and the eleventh year since Washington had first sent advisers. It had become the United States's longest war. And to an increasing number of Americans, it was a war that had gone on too long. The United States likes its wars to be quick and with clear purpose. Vietnam violated those principles. By

1972, the American people were tired of the killing and dying.

For the first several years of the war, U.S. strategy was attrition warfare—attempting to wear down the enemy by destroying the Viet Cong, and attacking targets in the strategic heartland of North Vietnam. But this had not brought victory. After the great battles of Tet 1968, the strategy shifted from attrition to pacification. The air-strikes against North Vietnam were halted. Negotiations were begun with the North Vietnamese as President Lyndon Johnson began to look for a political settlement to the war. Defeated by the conflict, he refused to run for a second term.

His successor, President Richard Nixon, supposedly had a "secret" plan to end the war. After taking office, he announced that his overall objective was to leave South Vietnam as "a free, independent and viable nation which is not hostile to the United States, functioning in a secure environment both internally and regionally."[1] His plan was to "Vietnamize" the war. The airpower that was no longer being used to attack North Vietnam was instead being used to support U.S. allies in the field and to create a shield behind which South Vietnam could build up its military, pacify areas of Viet Cong influence, and stabilize its society. The primary effort was directed at cutting the North Vietnamese supply routes in Laos known as the Ho Chi Minh Trail, which North Vietnam was using to funnel men and materiel into the South.

Based on this new political guidance, the commander of the Military Assistance Command Vietnam (MACV), Gen. Creighton Abrams, was given an updated mission for his command. He would take actions to "enable the

South Vietnamese forces to assume full responsibility for the security of South Vietnam." He would do so with American forces rapidly being reduced by domestic political pressure.[2] It would be a race to see whether the South Vietnamese could build up fast enough to rapidly replace the departing Americans. By 1972 the race had almost run its course.

The leaders of North Vietnam saw the conflict differently. To them it was not a war, but a struggle—"Armed Dau Tranh," they called it. But throughout the period of the American involvement, a great debate raged within the North Vietnamese politburo, centered around how best to engage the Americans and their South Vietnamese allies, who were so superior in firepower and mobility. Both guerrilla war and open confrontation were tried. The open confrontation, which became known as the Tet Offensive of 1968, brought the Viet Cong and North Vietnamese forces into the open, where they were engaged and decimated by superior American firepower. The commanding general of the North Vietnamese Army, Gen. Vo Nguyen Giap, learned from that mistake. He could not expose his forces to raw American airpower without proper defenses.[3] In the interim he directed his forces to avoid large-unit confrontations and operate as "super guerrillas," stinging here, slashing there, but never offering the Americans a chance to really hurt them. It was a game of hide and seek. North Vietnam was prepared to wait until the United States tired of the war and went home. Time, they felt, was on their side. Ho Chi Minh preached that time was the perfect trade-off for superior enemy size and strength. He bragged that his people were prepared to struggle fifty years to drive the United States out.

Whether or not that was true was not important; what was important was that the United States believe it.

From 1968 to 1971, General Giap slowly formulated another strategy for engaging the superior force. Abandoning the primacy of small-unit guerrilla (hide-and-seek) operations, he determined to engage his enemy with a superior, high-technology force. It would be a force heavy with tanks and artillery, conventional in every sense of the word, and as modern as his suppliers, the Soviet Union and China, would make it. Anticipating a strong American response with airpower, he planned for an air defense of massed antiaircraft guns, sophisticated tracking radars, and both radar-guided and heat-seeking surface-to-air missiles.[4]

North Vietnam realized the critical significance of this moment in history. North Vietnamese leaders felt that the antiwar movement was so strong in the United States that it would preclude any significant American reaction. Additionally, they believed that spectacular battlefield victories would inflict losses on those American forces remaining, destroy the Vietnamization program, and undermine President Nixon's stature at home. They wanted to drive a wedge between the alliance of the United States and South Vietnam. They also wanted to counter the increasing successes of the pacification program, which was steadily rallying the South Vietnamese people to their government.

The North Vietnamese strategic goals were straightforward: demonstrate to the South Vietnamese government the determination of the North Vietnamese and Viet Cong to fight and defeat the ARVN in the field, gain new territory to place under the North Vietnamese flag on Ho Chi Minh's eighty-third birthday on 19 May, and end the war. The timing was critical, for the leaders in Hanoi could see the success of the pacification and Vietnamization programs in the South. If both were allowed to continue uninterrupted for another year, the Viet Cong might be completely finished as a force, and South Vietnam might become the strongest military power in Southeast Asia. Then it could turn its power against North Vietnam.[5]

In the northern part of South Vietnam known as Military Region I, the North Vietnamese tactical objectives were simple: seize Quang Tri and Hue, liberate Quang Tri and Thua Thien Provinces, and establish local governments to control the population.[6] Hanoi knew that the United States would not commit ground troops to the battle, but would retaliate with airpower. The North remembered the pounding that its forces had taken during the attacks of Tet in 1968. Consequently, invading columns were covered with multiple air-defense regiments equipped with antiaircraft guns, tracking radars, and radar-guided and shoulder-fired heat-seeking missiles in large quantities, procured by General Giap. They would create a "meat grinder" that would achieve localized air superiority over defending ARVN units.[7]

This invasion through the DMZ and Laos was coordinated with a second, near-simultaneous NVA attack, also from Laos, into the highlands region northwest of Pleiku, ostensibly to cut South Vietnam in half. A third major offensive was launched three days later out of Cambodia, against Tay Ninh and Binh Long Provinces. Its objectives were to seize the towns and airfields of Loc Ninh, An Loc, and Quan Loi; establish a regional government; and prepare for possible follow-on operations against Saigon itself. These attacks also featured large formations of infantry, armor, and artillery.[8]

Strategically, the NVA attack in Military Region I did not come as a surprise. Both South Vietnamese and American commanders had been monitoring the North Vietnamese buildup north of the DMZ and throughout Laos. The recently ended dry season along the Ho Chi Minh Trail had been the worst on record. Vehicle sightings and kills were the highest ever. To protect their convoys and road network, the NVA had flooded the trail with all types of antiaircraft guns, and even with SA-2 surface-to-air missiles.[9]

Tactically, though, it was a different situation. Military Region I was defended by the South Vietnamese I Corps. Its commander, Lt. Gen. Hoang Xuan Lam, had also been monitoring the enemy buildup. But he did not believe that the enemy would attack through the DMZ. It had never happened before; the terrain was flat and exposed and unfavorable for maneuver by armor units. Besides, North Vietnam would not violate the 1954 Geneva Accords that had established the DMZ, or the 1968 "understanding" with the United States that had led to the cessation of U.S. bombing. Consequently, he placed his newest division, the 3d, along the DMZ. He expected the attack to come from the west, out of Laos. Therefore he placed the highly experienced 1st Division west of Hue facing the Ashau Valley, and the 2d Division west of Chu Lai. Additionally, General Lam had been reinforced by two Vietnamese Marine brigades from the national strategic reserve. These two units, the 147th Brigade and the 258th Brigade, were placed under the operational control of the 3d Division.

The 3d ARVN Division was the newest in the Vietnamese Army and was commanded by a promising young officer, Brig. Gen. Vu Van Giai. It was organized in October 1971 and consisted of the 2d, the 56th, and the 57th Regiments. But its newness was misleading, since its battalions had been recruited from the area and had already fought many battles along the DMZ. The units enjoyed good morale and were generally well equipped. The division deployed its regiments in an arc, generally from along the DMZ north of Dong Ha west to around Cam Lo and Camp Carroll.[10] The 57th Regiment was located on Fire Support Bases Charlie-1, Alpha-1, and Alpha-2. The units of the 56th were located on Fire Support Bases Charlie-2 and Alpha-4; those of the 2d were located at Camp Carroll and fire support bases Khe Gio and Fuller.[11]

Brigadier General Giai also expected any major enemy attack in his area to come from the west. Therefore he placed the two Marine brigades facing the western approaches, to forestall this threat. The two Marine brigade command elements were placed at Fire Support Base Mai Loc and Fire Support Base Nancy, with their battalions at forward locations: Nui Ba Ho, Sarge, and Holcomb. Both units were at full strength and well equipped.[12]

Additionally, the division had operational control of various small regional force units between Route QL-1 and the coast, north of Dong Ha. But General Giai was also worried by the buildup north of the DMZ. Those were hardcore NVA mainline units, not Viet Cong cadres. His troops were used to fighting against guerrilla-type formations, not line units. They were stationed in fire support bases and patrolled only their own local areas. They were not prepared to man and hold battle lines.

To prepare his troops for the possibility of more conventional warfare, General Giai directed that the 2d and 56th Regiments swap locations. This would accomplish two objectives. First, it would put his best regiment forward along the DMZ. Second, it would increase the area knowledge of his officers and soldiers and eliminate the entrenched "fire base syndrome" among his troops. The rotation was scheduled to take place on 30 March.[13]

The American ground-force presence in Military Region I was a shadow of what it had been in earlier times, reflecting the general American withdrawal from South Vietnam. Gone were the huge Marine and Army divisions with their large support organizations. The only ground maneuver unit remaining was the 196th Brigade. It was headquartered just outside of Da Nang Air Base, with detached units up at the Hue/Phu Bai Airfield, and it was restricted to defensive perimeter patrolling only.[14] American public opinion, and policy, was such that in the case of any heavy combat, the South Vietnamese would have to go it alone on the ground. That was the new reality of the war.

The 196th also had attached to it a cavalry troop, F Troop of the 8th Cavalry. This unit of approximately twenty-six helicopters and one platoon (forty soldiers) of infantry was the last unit of its type remaining in the northern portion of South Vietnam. Its mission primarily was reconnaissance, to find and fix the enemy so that larger, more powerful units could then engage them. It could do just about any type of aviation mission —including lift, attack, rescue—but on a smaller scale than its larger predecessors. It was one of the last remnants of what had at one time been the huge American fleet of helicopters that had swarmed all over South Vietnam. Under the command of Maj. Jack Kennedy, the unit was based at Marble Mountain Airfield, just two miles east of Da Nang. Its helicopters flew over the entire area and routinely supported whichever unit, U.S. or ARVN, that needed it. When flying such missions, the crews would stage out of whatever airfield was nearest, such as Quang Tri or Hue/Phu Bai. The unit even kept a small detachment at Quang Tri, under the command of a young warrant officer named Ben Nielsen, a Danish citizen who had joined the U.S. Army to learn to fly.[15]

The ARVN forces in the area still had American advisers assigned. They generally served from the regimental level up, with a heavy concentration on the divisional staff. With few exceptions, all battalion advisers had been removed as part of Vietnamization. The advisers consisted of both U.S. Army and Air Force officers. Those assigned to the 3d ARVN Division made up MACV Advisory Team 155. Administratively and operationally, they reported to the First Regional Assistance Command in Da Nang, which was commanded by Maj. Gen. Frederick J. Kroesen (U.S. Army). He also served as the senior adviser to General Lam.

The U.S. Marines still assigned advisers down to the battalion level. Administratively, they reported to their commanders in Saigon. Called *covans* by the Vietnamese Marines, they developed a strong attachment to their battalions and men.

The U.S. Air Force had also reduced its presence in South Vietnam. Most major air units had been returned to the United States or moved over to Thailand. The large air bases at Cam Ranh Bay, Phu Cat, Phan Rang, and elsewhere had been turned over to the South Vietnamese. In late March 1972, the Air Force had only twenty-three A-37s at Bien Hoa and sixty F-4s and five AC-119 gunships at Da Nang. They were under the command of Seventh Air Force, headquartered in Saigon close to its superior command, MACV.

But fighter, bomber, and attack forces in Thailand were still considerable. As of the same date, there were still ten AC-119s and fifteen A-1s at Nakhon Phanom Air Base; ten B-57s, seventy-four F-4s, and thirteen AC-130s at Ubon Air Base; thirty-five F-4s and sixteen F-105s at Korat Air Base; fifty-two F-4s at Udorn Air Base; and fifty-two B-52s at U-Tapao Air Base. These numbers included one F-4 squadron from Clark Air Base, the Philippines, and thirty-seven B-52s from stateside locations that had been moved to Thailand in February in response to the increased activity along the Ho Chi Minh Trail.

Tactical air support could also be provided by naval attack aircraft. In March 1972, the U.S. Navy had two aircraft carriers on station in the Gulf of Tonkin. These were the *Hancock* and the *Coral Sea*. Each had an air wing of approximately seventy aircraft. The U.S. Marines had withdrawn all of their attack aircraft from the theater.[16]

The U.S. Navy also maintained several destroyers and occasionally a cruiser off the coast to provide gunfire support. This was coordinated by U.S. Marine officers and men assigned to Sub Unit One of the 1st ANGLICO (Air and Naval Gunfire Company) of the Fleet Marine Force, Pacific, which had small detachments attached to various Vietnamese headquarters throughout the country.[17]

Even though it was slowly reducing forces in the theater, the Air Force continued to maintain a considerable SAR force in Southeast Asia. It consisted of the 3d Aerospace Rescue and Recovery Group, with several squadrons of HC-130 command-and-control aircraft (call sign King) and HH-53 helicopters (call sign Jolly Green). Its motto was "That Others May Live," and its mission was to search for and recover downed personnel in friendly or hostile environments throughout over 1.1 million square miles of area in Southeast Asia. When necessary, it could directly task the remaining U.S. Air Force A-1 strike aircraft (call sign Sandy) for direct support of SAR operations and could call upon any assets needed for a particular rescue through Seventh Air Force.[18]

The Air Force also maintained several squadrons of forward air controllers (FACs) in the theater. FACs had first been used in World War II. They provided critical liaison between ground and air units. Later, in Korea, they were initially used for the same purpose. But as that war dragged on, their use was expanded to also include visual reconnaissance behind enemy lines. They would fly out beyond the battle lines to search for enemy combat and logistical units. When these were found, fighters would be dispatched that would rendezvous with the FACs. Under the FACs' control, the fighters would attack the enemy targets.

But their use in Southeast Asia dwarfed these earlier conflicts. FACs ranged far and wide over the skies of the entire region. They provided tactical intelligence, targeting, and command and control. Once again they were the critical forward link between airpower and ground power. In many cases, they were also the eyes of commanders at several levels.

One squadron, the 20th TASS (Tactical Air Support Squadron), was located at Da Nang and was commanded by Lt. Col. Abe Kardong. His pilots flew the O-2 and OV-10 aircraft and patrolled Military Region I of South Vietnam and portions of the Ho Chi Minh Trail in Laos.[19] Generally using the call sign of Covey, the 20th TASS also controlled detachments that at one time had worked directly with American units and had used call signs such as Bilk, Mike, Trail, and Helix.[20] Previously, it had also provided FACs directly for ARVN units in the area. But as part of the drawdown of American forces, this had been discontinued. The Vietnamese Air Force now provided FACs for its own units. The American FAC missions still being flown in Military Region I ranged out beyond the ARVN units. Thus the remaining U.S. Air Force units in Vietnam had no direct link with the ARVN ground combat elements.

Another squadron, the 23d TASS, was located at Nakhon Phanom, Thailand. It was commanded by Lt. Col. Lachlan Macleay; its FACs exclusively flew OV-10s and patrolled the rest of the Ho Chi Minh Trail as well as portions of northern Laos and Cambodia. Generally, its call sign was Nail. It also maintained a sub detachment of aircraft at Ubon Air Base, Thailand. These aircraft patrolled over Cambodia and the southern tip of Laos and used the call sign Rustic.

The 23d TASS also had fifteen specially modified OV-10s. Called Pave Nails, these aircraft were equipped with a low-light laser designation device tied to a highly accurate LORAN D navigational system. The laser system was operated by a second crewmember in the backseat. It was boresighted to a night low-light observation scope that extended out of the bottom of the aircraft.

This device gave the crew the ability to guide highly accurate laser-guided bombs or to precisely locate positions or people on the ground. The system was also tied into the navigational system of the aircraft, so that once a position was noted and stored into the computer, the aircraft could be flown back to that point or lead other aircraft to it.[21] Originally the system had been designed to be used along the Ho Chi Minh Trail in the interdiction campaign against NVA trucks, supplies, and logistic centers. But the system's applicability to SAR operations and the youthful enthusiasm of the crews had become readily apparent, and increasingly the Pave Nails were diverted for rescue operations.[22]

As the American drawdown continued in South Vietnam, the Vietnamese Air Force (VNAF) took over the responsibility of providing FACs for the ARVN units and the staffing, direction, and running of the tactical air control system (TACS) at the divisional level.[23] This system was designed to integrate the targeting, control, and use of airpower into the overall operations of the ground combat units. This was the case with the 3d Division. When it was formed, the VNAF provided personnel for the TACS element, but it still had U.S. Air Force officers assigned as advisers—members of Advisory Team 155. As the offensive started, Air Force major Dave Brookbank was the adviser to the air liaison officer (ALO) who commanded the element. On paper, Brookbank's job was to work with this individual, Captain Tu, and help him develop the element into a smooth-running team that could support the division.[24]

Major Brookbank had arrived in Vietnam in early March. A B-52 pilot, he had been picked for this tour because he had flown fighters early in his career. But upon arriving at the division, he did not like what he found. The VNAF FACs were not providing the division the direct air support it needed. Most important, they were not responding to requests for visual reconnaissance being called in by the forward ground combat units. Indeed, because of the lack of response, the division had stopped asking.[25] This was unfortunate, because the U.S. Air Force had dropped a series of electronic sensors along the DMZ designed to detect enemy movement. But to be of optimum use, the sensor activations had to be verified by FACs, since the NVA had learned to deceive the sensors. The FACs could have verified the sightings. Following through, they could have reported the enemy activity and then called for airstrikes or artillery to destroy the enemy elements. That was how this version of hide and seek was played. In late March the sensors were indicating heavy enemy movement. But the reports were not visually confirmed, nor was the enemy attacked. That was unfortunate, because these reports were the heaviest ever recorded, and they were happening during the day.[26]

New to Team 155 and the 3d ARVN Division, Major Brookbank faced a myriad of problems within the division, and, if the rumors were true, he had little time to solve them. So Dave Brookbank decided to fly on the morning of 30 March. He wanted to set the example for his VNAF FACs and observe their performance in the air. He got to see a bit more than that.

2

★

Believe me, there is a real war
going on over here now!
Capt. Harold Icke, Bilk 11

The Battle

AT ABOUT THE SAME time that Major Brookbank
was trying to find his way down through the
weather over the DMZ, lunch was being served at the
officers' mess at the 3d ARVN Division headquarters at
Ai Tu Combat Base, a few miles south of Dong Ha.
Several of the Army advisers were entertaining a guest
who had come up for the day to see the division area—
Lt. Col. Jerry Turley, USMC. Like Brookbank, he had
just arrived in Vietnam and was slated to serve a tour as a
covan/adviser to the Vietnamese Marines. Since two of
their brigades were under the operational control of the
3d ARVN, he had come up to observe the operation.

They had just finished their meal and walked outside

when they began to hear the boom of the big guns to the north. Turley watched as the shells began to slam into the Quang Tri Airfield just across the road to the east. Then shells began to fall around the headquarters. He and his hosts quickly bolted for the command bunker. Inside, the group was greeted by the sounds of radio reports coming in from all forward positions indicating that they too were under heavy fire from an estimated three regiments of long-range 130mm guns.[1] Turley did not realize then that he was about to observe and take part in some of the most unusual actions of the war.

Unfortunately, the ARVN positions and fire support bases were not hard to locate, since they had been fixed for several years and were designed more for counter-guerrilla operations. Consequently, they were easy targets for the NVA guns. Everyone immediately sensed that these were preparatory attacks for the infantry and tanks of the three NVA divisions thought to be north of the DMZ and west of the Khe Sanh area.[2]

The NVA had planned their attacks to take full advantage of the seasonal weather. This was the monsoon season, which meant that the normal weather pattern for this area of Southeast Asia was low clouds and poor visibility. Having just arrived in South Vietnam, Brookbank did not realize at the time that the weather would remain like this for several days and seriously affect U.S. Air Force operations.

The opening NVA moves caught the 3d Division off guard. As directed by Brigadier General Giai, his two infantry regiments, the 2d and the 56th, were in the process of switching their areas of operation. Both units had their elements strung out along the road at the same time. Many of the moving units were caught in the open by the artillery and suffered grievous casualties.

The attack did not really come as a surprise to 1st Lt. Mickey Fain. He was a young FAC flying as Bilk 35 out of Hue/Phu Bai. The DMZ region was his assigned area of operations; he had been watching it closely for a few months and had personally seen the NVA buildup. He had duly reported it and put in airstrikes when available—which was not often enough, by his book. But even he was amazed at the size and intensity of the NVA attack. As it unfolded, it occurred to him that what he was seeing was a whole new kind of war.[3]

The follow-on armor attacks were not long in coming. T-55 and PT-76 tanks were seen that afternoon spearheading four attacks out of the DMZ. One spearhead was directed against a battalion of the 2d Regiment at Fire Support Base Fuller. It had been scheduled to be relieved by a battalion from the 56th. But in the confusion of the onslaught, the relieving battalion never arrived. The 2d Regiment battalion stayed in place. Another spearhead struck Fire Support Base Alpha-4, the old Marine base at Con Thien. There, the swap-out had been completed and another 2d Regiment battalion suffered through this attack. But the NVA thrust took a heavy toll on the 56th. The battalion that was supposed to move into Fire Support Base Fuller disappeared, surfacing in the rear areas several days later. The regimental trains were cut off from the combat units and were not able to fight their way back to friendly lines until 1 April. The headquarters element and one battalion of the 56th Regiment did make it to Camp Carroll, and their 3d Battalion did relieve the 2d Regiment at Khe Gio. But that regiment was never able to fight its way up to Fire Support Base Charlie-2.[4]

Another two combined-arms spearheads were coming south along Route QL-1 to hit the 57th Regiment at Fire Support Bases Alpha-1 and Alpha-2. Concurrently, the enemy also launched coordinated assaults against the westernmost fire support bases at Sarge, Nui Ba Ho, and Holcomb. The North Vietnamese onslaught began to overwhelm the disorganized and surprised ARVN. As Turley noted: "South Vietnam's entire northern boundary lay open to the largest enemy attack of the Vietnam War. Over 30,000 men from elements of the 304th and 308th Divisions, along with three separate infantry regiments of the B5 Front, two tank regiments, and five artillery regiments, entered the ground campaign of the Nguyen Hue Offensive in a decisive struggle for control of the South."[5]

He did not mention that these forces were covered by the heaviest, most sophisticated air defenses yet seen in the war. The NVA were prepared to fight for control of the air as well as the ground. But perhaps their best weapon against airpower at that moment was the weather. Low thick clouds and limited visibility made intense visual bombing impossible, because the pilots could not see the targets. Consequently the initial air response was limited. FAC coverage was immediately increased. As weather permitted, the 20th TASS began orbiting three FACs at a time along the DMZ. Fixed-wing gunships tried to work through the weather with limited success. The Air Force did begin round-the-clock operations with B-52s (code-named Arc Light missions) and fighters bombing under Skyspot radar control. Air Force reconnaissance RF-4s were also diverted into the area to lead blind airstrikes using their LORAN for precise navigation.[6]

The next day, 31 March, enemy attacks increased in intensity. By now all ARVN and Marine units were in heavy contact with the enemy. That evening it appeared that the Marines might have to evacuate the two westernmost outposts at Nui Ba Ho and Sarge and fall back toward Mai Loc. Elements of the 56th and 2d Regiments that had been manning the forward fire support bases at Fuller and Khe Gio respectively did begin to fall back toward the south and east.[7]

Capt. Harold Icke, Bilk 11, flew a four-and-one-half-hour mission that day. He took off in his O-2 with a VNAF FAC on board to check him out in controlling American fighters. They flew west as far as Khe Sanh and contacted the Vietnamese Marine units that were getting hit at Fire Base Sarge and Nui Ba Ho. But the weather was so bad that they could not get in and actually spot targets or put in airstrikes.[8]

The enemy pressure on the two remote outposts was unremitting. After almost nonstop artillery pounding and human wave attacks, the commander of the defending 4th Vietnamese Marine Battalion, Major De, directed that his men abandon their positions and escape and make their way back to the nearest friendly position at Mai Loc. In the early morning hours of 1 April, the Vietnamese Marines and their two American advisers, Maj. Walter Boomer and Capt. Ray Smith, moved off of the sites and attempted to elude their NVA pursuers.

But the escape from Sarge and Nui Ba Ho would not be that easy. Radio contact was lost with the 3d ARVN Division. The Marines and their Vietnamese were on their own, deep in by-now enemy territory, running and fighting for survival. Unsure of their whereabouts, the American advisers at Division in turn notified the First Regional Assistance Command that the whereabouts of Major Boomer and Captain Smith were unknown at that time.[9]

As the sun came up over the DMZ, Bilk 11 was airborne again and attempting to get out over the units. For a second time he had a VNAF FAC in his right seat for certification. But the weather was still terrible—thick clouds whose bases reached well down into the valleys. It kept the pilots from getting in over the fire support bases or the escaping Marine columns to direct airstrikes or search for enemy troops.

Captain Icke found this very frustrating. He wanted to do so much more for his lost countrymen. But even though two Americans were known to be lost behind enemy lines, no special effort was put forth to find or rescue them. Their fates were tied to those of their units. They would return to friendly lines the next day after their terrible odyssey. Most of the Vietnamese Marines would be lost in the effort.

The weather also precluded Captain Icke or any of the other FACs from helping in a drama that was unfolding at the fire support bases just south of the DMZ. By late morning of 1 April, all positions were under attack by enemy infantry forces and were in danger of being overrun. Col. Don Metcalf, the senior American adviser to the 3d ARVN Division, had directed that his advisers be evacuated from these forward positions. This was his first priority. Helicopter teams of Hueys and Cobras from F Troop of the 8th Cavalry were in the area to fly the missions, and several were run successfully throughout the morning.[10]

But the situation at one of the fire support bases had become especially critical. A U.S. Marine fire control team from the 1st ANGLICO had been sent to Fire Support Base Alpha-2 to control naval gunfire from the ships offshore. As the enemy troops surrounded the advanced position, the team leader, 1st Lt. David Bruggeman, requested an emergency evacuation for himself and his four Marines. A rescue mission was flown by UH-1s and Cobra gunships from F Troop of the 8th Cavalry. But one man, Cpl. James Worth, was left behind. Additionally, Lieutenant Bruggeman was wounded and died en route to Da Nang.

By the end of the day, Fire Support Bases Nui Ba Ho, Sarge, and Holcomb had been overrun, and all strong points along the northern line had been evacuated. For the most part, the evacuations were orderly and were carried out according to plan. Engineers were attached to the 2d and 57th regiments to wire and, if necessary, blow the bridges over the Mieu Giang–Cam Lo River at Cam Lo and Dong Ha. But some mistakes were made. Artillery batteries were not evacuated at Alpha-2 or Charlie-1, and, as a result, six 105mm and six 155mm howitzers were captured by the NVA. By the end of the day, eleven major fire support bases had been lost. The last two remaining fire support bases, at Camp Carroll and Mai Loc, were under very heavy artillery and probing ground attacks.

Seventh Air Force was beginning to react to the tactical situation along the DMZ. Late that evening, they notified the 3d ARVN Division command post at Ai Tu that they would be receiving twenty-five Skyspots and seven B-52 strikes on a daily basis.[11] Responding to the lack of FAC coverage over the growing battle, planners at Seventh Air Force began to reassign American FACs to work with the 3d ARVN Division and attached units. The 20th TASS was directed to begin flying forty-two FAC flight hours daily in the 3d ARVN Division area of operation. Also, by 10 April the U.S. Marine artillery observers would be physically transferred to Da Nang to fly in these aircraft.[12] Starting on 7 April, some of the 20th TASS FACs would fly to the airfield at Hue/Phu Bai to pick up the Marine observers there. The Vietnamese FACs would not be shoved aside. They would still fly and, when possible, direct VNAF airstrikes. But their limitations were recognized and, it was hoped, rectified due to clear operational need. Meanwhile, Seventh Air Force began to receive reinforcements. Headquarters, Pacific Air Forces directed the 35th Tactical Fighter Squadron to deploy from Kunsan, Korea, to Udorn Air Base, Thailand. It arrived on 3 April.[13]

To stem the enemy's advance, the South Vietnamese Joint General Staff directed that a defensive line be established and held at Dong Ha. Consequently, at 6:00 P.M. on 1 April, Brigadier General Giai ordered the reorganization of his defensive positions. In order to take advantage of the natural obstacles presented the enemy by the Mieu Giang–Cam Lo River, all divisional forces north of the river were ordered south. Attached Regional and Popular Forces would defend in the east, from the coast to approximately five kilometers inland. The 57th Regiment would hold the line from there to Dong Ha. The city and its immediate vicinity would be defended by the 1st Armor Brigade, a powerful force with mechanized and armor units, which was being attached to the 3d Division. Its main element, the 20th Armor Regiment (with just one battalion) was equipped with M-48 tanks and was just completing its spin-up training at Camp Evans, near Hue.

To the left of the 1st Armor Brigade, the 2d Regiment held the line over to Cam Lo, reinforced with an armored cavalry squadron. To its left, the 56th Regiment, also reinforced with an armored cavalry squadron, was ordered to hold Camp Carroll and all of its artillery. To its south and facing west, the Vietnamese Marine Brigades and battalions held the line as far south as Fire Base Pedro and provided security for the Quang Tri Combat Base at Ai Tu, which was now being used as a forward command post, since the 3d Division headquarters had been relocated to Quang Tri Citadel earlier that day.[14]

In the forward command post, the remaining advisers felt the gravity of the situation. Lieutenant Colonel Turley noted: "The Cam Lo [Mieu Giang]–Cua Viet River was the last natural obstacle for the ARVN to use as a defensive line. If they failed to hold along the river, the North Vietnamese could break the back of the 3rd ARVN Division and move into Quang Tri City."[15]

That evening, the Vietnamese commanders and staff and the American advisers had a meeting in the Ai Tu command bunker. After reviewing the tactical situation, Lieutenant Colonel Turley turned to the Vietnamese commander and assured him that he and the other American advisers were not leaving. They intended to stay at their side and, as a team, defeat the enemy offensive. The South Vietnamese, fighting for their lives below the DMZ, would not be abandoned by the Americans on the ground. Thus Lieutenant Colonel Turley's status changed from that of just a visitor to that of a participant. Now it was his fight, too.[16]

As the sun came up on 2 April, Easter Sunday, the 3d Division's defense appeared to be relatively well organized. With the exception of some stragglers and rear-guard forces, all major units had been withdrawn south of the river line.[17] But appearances were deceptive, for a series of events was about to occur that would radically alter the form of the battle. This day would be fateful for many on the ground and in the air.

The bad weather continued. Low clouds (one-thousand-foot ceiling) and poor visibility kept the fighters from visually attacking the enemy. Less accurate B-52 Arc Lights and fighter Skyspot strikes were used as they became available, and they were obviously having an effect on the enemy.[18] But the number of requests coming in from the units was skyrocketing. Major Brookbank and his team were becoming overwhelmed.

One battalion of the 57th Regiment along the main road, QL-1, and elements of the 2d Regiment farther west were still north of the river. They were the rear guards for the retreat. But they were becoming enveloped by enemy units and were in danger of being cut off.[19] At about 9:00 A.M., soldiers from the 57th Regiment reported seeing enemy tanks along QL-1 near the recently evacuated Fire Support Base Charlie-2. Response was swift. Naval gunfire from the U.S. Navy destroyers off the coast was quickly brought to bear on the columns, and coordination was begun to divert airstrikes on them. But the weather still grounded most strike aircraft.[20]

As Major Brookbank tried to orchestrate an air response to this serious turn of events, his Vietnamese counterpart, the Vietnamese ALO to the 3d ARVN Division and his entire tactical air control party, packed up their gear and left the forward command post. Brookbank questioned their actions. The Vietnamese captain responded with "What's the use?" and departed. By default, Dave Brookbank, former B-52 pilot, just three weeks in Vietnam, was now the ALO to the 3d ARVN Division as it faced the onslaught.[21]

With the commitment of the tanks, the ARVN commanders could begin to see the NVA's plan. A major thrust was developing, apparently aimed directly down QL-1 and directed to seize Dong Ha and Quang Tri. The rear-guard battalion from the 57th Regiment began to pull back. In Dong Ha, the 3d Vietnamese Marine Battalion was attached to the 20th Armor Regiment, under the control of the 1st Armor Brigade. Their mission was to defend Dong Ha and hold the critical railroad and vehicular bridges there. The commander of the 20th Armor considered moving his tanks north of the river to engage the enemy tanks. But this could not be properly coordinated and the idea was abandoned.[22] Instead, they would fight it out along the river.

To the west, the last stragglers of the 2d Regiment were crossing the river over the Cam Lo bridge. But they did not destroy it, because NVA units were literally on their tail. This was ominous, because this was the only bridge on the river that would support heavy armor, other than the Dong Ha bridges.[23] However, the bridge was covered by the artillery of the 56th Regiment, located just southwest at Camp Carroll. But Carroll was coming under increasing NVA artillery and ground attack. The incessant artillery pounding was especially intimidating to the ARVN artillerymen. Their responses to fire requests were becoming more infrequent, and they were not returning fire against the NVA artillery.[24] These events naturally had a negative impact on the morale of the soldiers on the line.

Just to the south, the fire support base at Mai Loc was receiving the same treatment. Artillery fire was mixed with probing ground assaults and 57mm recoilless fire directed at specific bunkers. The fighting at both bases was becoming so heavy that resupply helicopters could not get into either location.

Concurrently with the struggle on the ground, a battle was raging in the skies above. As cover for the invading troops, the air-defense regiments were deployed forward and looking for targets. They claimed their first victim at about 2:30 P.M., when a FAC O-2 from the 20th TASS, call sign Mike 81, was hit by antiaircraft fire near the DMZ.[25] The fire so damaged the aircraft that it went into a spin. The pilot, 1st Lt. Richard Abbot, had to climb out of a side window to bail out. In the process he broke an arm, but fortunately, he was out over the Gulf of Tonkin when he jumped.

Captain Icke, Bilk 11, was standing in the operations section at the 20th TASS when the word came in concerning Mike 81. He was directed to get airborne and begin a rescue operation for the downed American. He was off the ground in twenty minutes.[26] Right behind him, two HH-53 Jolly Green Giant rescue helicopters, Jolly Green 65 and 67, also launched out of Da Nang for the pickup. They were escorted by two A-1s, Sandy 07 and 08.[27]

Fortunately, Mike 81 had been able to get several miles out to sea before he had abandoned his stricken aircraft. Before the SAR forces could arrive, he was picked up by the USS *Hamner*.[28] When the orbiting HC-130 King aircraft heard that Mike 81 had been recovered, the rescue effort was canceled. Bilk 11 was directed to take Mike 81's place along the DMZ, and the SAR forces were directed to orbit south of Quang Tri, pending an operation to extract some of the Team 155 American advisers out of Ai Tu.

To relieve the enemy pressure on Carroll, Skyspot airstrikes were planned around it. But as the weather broke up a little, a FAC was requested for the besieged fire support base. Bilk 07, an O-2, arrived on station at about 2:00 P.M.[29] But the weather was still too bad for visual airstrikes, so he concentrated his efforts on trying to locate the harassing artillery. Throughout the morning, Carroll had been under continuous artillery attack. The enemy also made numerous probes against the outer defenses, leaving some bodies in the wire. They were testing the defenses of this key position.

But that afternoon, the regimental commander, Lt. Col. Pham Van Dinh, for reasons still unexplained, decided to surrender his unit and the base to the invading NVA. In doing so, he surrendered eighteen hundred soldiers and twenty-two artillery pieces to the enemy. The impact was devastating to the 3d ARVN Division. In one strike, a large hole was blown in their defensive line, and the key bridge at Cam Lo—fully operational—was left unprotected.[30]

The two U.S. Army advisers, Lt. Col. Bill Camper and Maj. Joe Brown, and a few ARVN troops escaped through the wire and were rescued by a U.S. Army CH-47 escorted by AH-1 gunships from F Troop of the 8th Cavalry.[31] As soon as he could get to a radio, Lieutenant Colonel Camper requested that the lost base be struck by B-52s. Maj. Dave Brookbank acknowledged the call and forwarded the request. The next day he heard through South Vietnamese intelligence that most of the captured soldiers had been marched to a karst formation called the Rockpile and executed.[32]

Throughout the day the Marines at Mai Loc had been taking the same pounding as had Camp Carroll. But the loss of Carroll and the 56th Regiment made the defense of the Mai Loc fire support base untenable. Accordingly, the commander of the 147th Marine Brigade asked for permission to evacuate his unit to the east. He was instructed to move his unit to Quang Tri, where it would be replaced by the 369th Marine Brigade and allowed to regroup and refit.[33] Before leaving the fire support base, his Marines fired off all of their artillery rounds and spiked their guns.[34]

Almost simultaneously, events were coming to a head at Dong Ha. The ARVN troops from the 57th Regiment retreated across the Dong Ha bridge with the NVA armor on their heels. The bridge had been partly wired with explosives for destruction but was not blown by the ARVN engineers. At about 1:30 P.M., the north end of the vehicular bridge was struck with a Skyspot airstrike and partly destroyed.[35] Maj. Jim Smock, senior adviser to the 20th Armor, reported this to the 3d Division command post and also stated that the bridge was still passable.[36] Tanks from the 20th Armor attempted to shoot out the bridge supports and struts with their main guns, but the bridge was too strong. While the ARVN tanks and Vietnamese Marines dueled with their opposites across the river, the adviser to the 3d Vietnamese Marine Battalion, Capt. John Ripley, and Major Smock emplaced additional charges under the south end of the bridge. The detonations dropped the southern spans of the bridge and set it on fire. It was now impassable. For the time being, the NVA drive had been stopped.[37]

As the smoke cleared from the explosion, the clouds began to break up somewhat. A Vietnamese FAC from the 3d Division was overhead in an O-1. He spotted the tanks bottled up north of the bridges, calling for air support. VNAF A-1s took off from Da Nang Air Base and flew to Dong Ha. Their arrival overhead was a tonic for the hard-pressed troops.[38] For over an hour, six different flights of VNAF A-1s attacked the tanks, armored personnel carriers, and troops of their enemy. The results were devastating. They claimed a total of twenty-nine tanks destroyed.[39]

But as the last flight was finishing, the enemy struck back. Captain Ripley watched as troops on the north shore launched a heat-seeking SA-7 antiaircraft missile against the lead aircraft. The missile scored a direct hit on the machine, destroying its engine and forcing it down. The pilot attempted to turn south before bailing out. Directly over the river, he ejected. His parachute blossomed normally, but the winds were from the south, and they carried him back into enemy hands. The Marines watched helplessly as the pilot was captured.[40]

The destruction of the Dong Ha bridges brought the NVA drive down QL-1 to a complete halt. The only other crossing point was the bridge at Cam Lo, which had not yet been destroyed.[41] Later that evening, Captain Ripley heard the remaining NVA tanks start their engines and begin moving to the west toward Cam Lo. He did not know about Camp Carroll and the 56th Regiment. But with several U.S. Navy ships offshore, he immediately called for naval gunfire and destroyed numerous tanks before they moved west, beyond the range of the guns.[42]

Now the bridge at Cam Lo was the big worry. With the fall of the 56th Regiment, it had to be destroyed. The 20th Armor extended their lines to the west to cover the Cam Lo bridge until the 2d Regiment could consolidate itself and fill the gap left by the surrender of the 56th Regiment.[43] They reported that the bridge would support sixty tons and that the retreating ARVN units had refused to blow it, citing enemy pressure and the loss of necessary equipment. Perhaps with the slow but steady clearing away of the low clouds, it could be taken out by an airstrike. Maj. Dave Brookbank was optimistic that it could be done, because they had just been able, on short notice, to divert a B-52 mission to destroy the abandoned artillery at Carroll.[44]

3

★

Beeper, beeper, come up voice.
Bilk 34

The Shootdown

EVEN THOUGH THE WEATHER was breaking up near the ground, there were several layers of clouds topping out at fifteen thousand feet. Other than the A-1s, the only strike missions going in were either fighters on Skyspot strikes or B-52s performing radar bombing. As these events were unfolding on the ground, an Arc Light cell of three B-52s (call sign Copper) was approaching the area to strike a target a few kilometers northwest of Camp Carroll, along a major axis of approach for the NVA ground forces. This area was becoming infested with electronically guided surface-to-air missiles (SAMs), a key part of the North Vietnamese air defenses.

The B-52s were equipped with onboard jamming

transmitters that could be used to deceive or fool the radar signals of the SAMs. But because of the increased SAM threat, the B-52s were escorted by two EB-66s, call signs Bat 21 and Bat 22, flown by the 42d Tactical Electronic Warfare Squadron (TEWS) at Korat Air Base, Thailand. Bat 22 was an EB-66E. It had special equipment on board that also could jam the missile-guidance radars of the SAM sites and hence augment the B-52s during their bombing run. Its crew consisted of a pilot, a navigator, and an electronic-warfare officer (EWO).

Bat 21 was an EB-66C. It had special antennae on board that could be used to locate the enemy SAM sites. If necessary, these antennae could also be used to jam the sites for self-protection. But Bat 21 was tagging along with the others to take advantage of their protective capabilities, so that its crew could concentrate on locating the dangerous SAMs that were sprouting up all over the area and hampering air operations. Its crew consisted of a pilot, a navigator, and four EWOs.

Originally the B-52s had been scheduled to make the bomb run by themselves. But because of the threat, Seventh Air Force planners decided that they needed "Tinny Tim," or EB-66 support. So the Souis, as the EB-66s were affectionately called by the crews, were added on short notice. Consequently, the 42d TEWS had to scramble to get the aircraft ready and find two crews. The senior navigator in the squadron was Lt. Col. Iceal Hambleton, who scheduled the navigators for flights. Due to the increased recent flying, though, he was shorthanded. So he scheduled himself to fly as the navigator on Bat 21.[1]

The mission was put together and briefed to the crews fairly rapidly. Maj. Ed Anderson, one of the squadron

EWOs scheduled for the mission, recalled that no mention was made of the ground invasion or any unusual enemy activity, other than the increased activity of the SAM sites in southern North Vietnam. Their mission was to increase the level of protection for the B-52s as they came within possible range of those sites. But they were given no indications of any SAM sites actually in South Vietnam.[2]

Approaching the target area, the B-52s and EB-66s were joined by two fighters (call signs Cain 1 and 2), for air-to-air protection from possible enemy MiGs, and two F-105Gs (call signs Coy 1 and 2). The F-105Gs were carrying special missiles that, when launched, would home on and destroy SAM sites that might try to track the formation and launch surface-to-air missiles at it. Coy flight's missiles could also be launched against radars being used to direct antiaircraft guns.[3]

During the run to the target at about 4:50 P.M., Copper cell and their supporting aircraft began receiving indications that enemy radars had discovered their approach and were tracking them. Just south of the target area, two SA-2 Fan song radars, located to the west near Khe Sanh, locked on to the flight with their guidance radars and launched four missiles. The EWOs on the B-52s initiated onboard jamming. Bat 22 was situated between the sites and Copper cell. Because of his own onboard jamming, Major Anderson did not hear the Fan Song radars with his audio equipment, but he picked up the tones of the distinct missile-guidance signal loud and clear. That meant that a missile was in the air and coming at them. He called a warning to his pilot, Maj. Bob Chappelle, and navigator, Lt. Col. Jim Ely, to take evasive action. Chappelle violently turned the aircraft down and into the missiles and began dropping chaff. The missiles detonated between Bat 22 and the B-52s in a box pattern.[4] Anderson also switched on his ultra-high-frequency (UHF) radio transmitter to the emergency frequency and transmitted, "SAM uplink, vicinity of DMZ, Bat 22," as a warning to other aircraft.

Then Chappelle pulled up out of his maneuver to keep from losing too much altitude. The EB-66 was an old aircraft that had not been designed for this kind of flying. It was underpowered for such tactical maneuvers and would lose energy quickly. Altitude was a form of energy that had to be saved. But as he began to climb back up, Jim Ely told him that this was strange, because intelligence had not briefed him that there were any SAM sites this far south, and he had none marked on his map. Chappelle invited his navigator and EWO to look for themselves, the four airbursts being clearly visible out the window. Anderson took a quick look. They were definitely there. He keyed his radio again and called a second warning, "SAM visual, vicinity of DMZ, Bat 22."[5]

Almost simultaneously another set of sites to the east began tracking the force. Six more missiles were launched. Below the B-52s, Bilk 11, Captain Icke, saw the missiles. He could not believe what he was seeing and felt naked in his little O-2, because lousy weather, little airplanes, and big, fast missiles were a bad combination.[6]

Once again, all of the B-52s began onboard jamming against the missile-tracking radars. Additionally, Copper 01 aborted his bomb run and broke to the right. Copper 02 and 03 released their bombs before taking evasive action. The missiles went off around the flight, but no one was damaged. They were accompanied by radar-controlled 100mm antiaircraft fire, which burst above the flight. The two F-105Gs turned and launched their suppression missiles against the radars that were directing the 100mm antiaircraft guns.

The pilot on Bat 22 saw the second salvo of missiles. He screamed, "Oh shit," and reinitiated his breaking evasive maneuver. But this time he was not so quick to pull out of his dive. As the flight continued its right turn to depart the target area, another site began tracking the aircraft. It was located northwest, just above the DMZ. Bat 21 was between the site and the bombers, and was level at twenty-nine thousand feet. The site launched three missiles at the formation. One of the EWOs on Bat 21 electronically observed the site as it began tracking his aircraft, and he detected the SAM missile launches. He called a warning to the flight. For self-protection, the crew of Bat 21 began electronic jamming, and the pilot initiated a right jink turn into the missile. The EWO then called, "No, no, move left, move left!" and the pilot tried to reverse his turn. It was too late. The missile smashed into the middle underside of the aircraft, and the resulting explosion enveloped it in a massive ball of fire.[7] The other aircraft escaped the barrage of missiles.

Lt. Col. Iceal Hambleton, the navigator of Bat 21, was seated just behind the pilot—the EB-66 did not have a position for a copilot.[8] The missile hit right below Hambleton's seat and knocked out the intercom system. As the aircraft began to drop out of control, the pilot gave Hambleton a hand signal to eject. Hambleton squeezed the ejection handles and rocketed away from the aircraft. As he rose in his ejection seat, he looked down and saw the pilot looking up at him. A few seconds later, he heard another loud explosion. It occurred to him later that either the aircraft had exploded or it had been hit by a second missile.[9]

There were some witnesses to this event. Maj. Jimmy Kempton of the 390th Tactical Fighter Squadron, Da Nang Air Base, was leading a flight of four F-4s on a Skyspot drop just south of the DMZ, when he began to receive SAM warnings on his radar homing and warning gear. This made him nervous enough to loosen up the four-ship formation, because the broken cloud cover prevented visual sightings of the missiles until almost too late. He then heard a SAM launch warning on his emergency "Guard" radio receiver and saw three missiles pop out of the clouds approximately two miles ahead of his formation. He realized that they were not guiding on him or his flight and initially thought that they were ballistic. But he followed the missiles and saw one hit an unknown aircraft at a higher altitude. He immediately switched his radio to the emergency frequency and began calling King, the airborne rescue command-and-control aircraft in orbit along the coast, to report the downing. Kempton also used his long-range radio to report the incident to the Tactical Air Control Center (Bluechip) in Saigon.[10]

King 22, the orbiting rescue HC-130, responded to the call. But the crew was already aware of the situation. When Mike 81 had been shot down, they had moved north and were orbiting south of Quang Tri. Maj. Bruce Driscoll, the mission commander on board, had actually seen the explosion of Bat 21, although he had not at the time realized that the downed aircraft had been hit by a missile. He and his crew began taking the preliminary steps to start a search-and-rescue operation. They contacted the Joint Search and Rescue Center in Saigon and briefed them on the developing situation. But King 22 had a problem. They had been on station all day and were down to their last hour's fuel. Normally King aircraft did not orbit at night, so no relief was scheduled. However, a King aircraft and crew were kept on alert for just such contingencies. So King 22 called their home station at Korat and told them to launch the alert aircraft.

Just before Bat 21 went down, 1st Lt. Bill Jankowski (Bilk 34) was almost directly below the EB-66, at about five thousand feet. He was flying an O-2 and had Capt. Lyle Wilson in his right seat. They were attempting to find and target the attacking NVA forces. But it was very difficult because of the weather and the almost solid cloud layer below three thousand feet. Bill also heard the SAM call and took what evasive action he could in the slow O-2. He also saw the SAMs as they passed through the cloud layers. He watched them streak upward and observed one explosion. By the size of the fireball, he knew that it had hit someone. He then spotted the aircraft and watched the wreckage spiral down and disappear into the solid clouds below him.[11]

Then Jankowski heard the piercing beeper and what he thought was a Mayday call from Bat 21 Alpha. Following ingrained standard procedure, he radioed, "Beeper, beeper, come up voice!"[12] In response he got a call from Bat 21 Bravo on the Guard emergency frequency, stating that he had Jankowski in sight. To confirm this, Jankowski rocked his wings, and the survivor acknowledged the wing rock. Jankowski commented to Wilson that Bat 21 Bravo must have great eyes, because he could not see anything through the clouds below.

The survivor then called again and stated that he had Jankowski in an orbit below him. Jankowski rolled his wings, looked up, and sure enough, there was the survivor in his parachute a few thousand feet above him.[13]

Bat 22 was just pulling out of its evasive dive when they heard the calls between Jankowski and Hambleton. They were horrified that their wingman had been shot down. It occurred to Major Anderson that things had happened so quickly that the survivor, whoever he was, had not even had time to reach the ground yet. Since their mission with the B-52s was complete, they requested permission to stay on to support the blossoming SAR effort. They were directed by King to proceed to a refueling tanker to top off their tanks, so that they could return to the Dong Ha area.[14]

Meanwhile, Bat 21 Bravo descended with pieces of the aircraft falling around him. Jankowski continued to orbit just above Hambleton, as he reported to King 22 the disposition and general situation of the survivor. King passed that information to headquarters in Saigon. Watching him dangle in the parachute, Jankowski actually considered slowing down and attempting to snag him and pull him into the aircraft, but he and Wilson rejected this as impractical.[15]

As Hambleton broke out below the clouds, he could see fighting and troops over the entire area. Fortunately, he was only visible below the clouds for a few seconds before he landed and collapsed his parachute. He had landed in a rice paddy. He quickly got over next to a small rise that gave him some protection. Later, when it was fully dark, he moved into a clump of trees.[16]

Jankowski had continued to descend with Hambleton. They entered the clouds at about three thousand feet and broke out at about nine hundred feet above the ground. They quickly spotted his parachute on the ground and plotted his position north of the river and east of the village of Cam Lo. Bill reported this position to King.[17]

Hambleton had landed within one mile of the bridge at Cam Lo. He was literally in the middle of one pincer of the invasion force coming from the north and west. Jankowski was shocked by what he saw. There were tanks, troops, and vehicles of all kinds jamming the roads. And they all began shooting at him—or so it seemed. As he attempted to orbit Hambleton's position, he popped up into the clouds frequently to try to throw off the gunners. It did not help much, for each time he reemerged, the antiaircraft fire resumed. It was "all kinds from everywhere."[18]

The operations center at Korat Air Base in Thailand had received King 22's directive to launch the alert King aircraft. Maj. Dennis Constant was the mission commander on the alert bird. In the last month of his tour, he spent most of his time training others and rarely sat alert anymore. He had spent his career in rescue, and, as the chief of aircrew standardization and training, he was probably the most experienced pilot in the squadron. Responding to the Klaxon, he and his crew of King 27 were out the door and airborne in minutes.

En route to Quang Tri, Major Constant got an update from Saigon. Little information was available other than the fact that there was reportedly just one survivor of a multi-crew aircraft. But apparently he was down in a generally friendly area with little reported enemy activity. Nothing whatsoever was said about a major NVA invasion with infantry, tanks, artillery, and heavy air defenses. It occurred to Major Constant that perhaps the most dangerous part of this mission would be crossing the Ho Chi Minh Trail.[19]

Back at Cam Lo, 1st Lt. Bill Jankowski was now the on-scene commander for the blossoming rescue effort for the downed American. Bill's perseverance had paid off. He was able to provide the critical initial data necessary to begin the process of marshaling and dispatching rescue forces to recover the survivor. Fortuitously, some of those forces were not far away.[20]

4

The numerous helicopters operated in South Vietnam
by the U.S. Army and Marines provide an immediate
capability for aircrew recovery.

1968 Seventh Air Force manual

[It] was just a natural thing that when anyone had
trouble, if you were in the area, and you had the
capability, you just responded. It was SOP.
There were no questions asked.

Capt. Mike Rosebeary, Blueghost 28

I have never known the Army [helicopters]
to turn us down.

Capt. Fred Boli, Sandy 01

Cavalry to the Rescue

TIME WAS OF the essence, and it was short. Bill Jankowski knew that sometimes the best plan was to get
whatever helicopters and fighters that were available in
the area to come in to try an immediate recovery, before
the enemy could respond to a downed crew. The pilots

called it a "quick snatch." So he came up on the emergency frequency and called for any support available to rendezvous with him for the SAR effort.

Sandy 07 and 08, two A-1s led by Capt. Don Morse, responded to the call. They were in the area, having been launched earlier for two missions. They were scrambled to support the two HH-53 Jolly Greens that had launched to pick up Mike 81. After his successful pickup by the Navy, they had been told to orbit and to be ready too support the helicopter evacuation of some of the Team 155 personnel from the Ai Tu combat base. This evacuation was also canceled when most personnel were moved out by truck.

The two A-1s were still escorting Jolly Greens 65 and 67 and were just east of Quang Tri. Responding to the emergency call, Sandy 07 instructed the Jolly Greens to hold south of Quang Tri, and turned the two A-1s north to find Bilk 34. Captain Morse thought that since the aircraft had gone down in South Vietnam, the SAR effort should be fairly easy.

Jankowski told them to proceed to Cam Lo. Not being familiar with the area, they wandered too far west, out by the lost fire support base at Mai Loc, and began to take quite a bit of ground fire, including some kind of unguided rocket that almost hit Sandy 07, Captain Morse. The weather was overcast at about fifteen hundred feet, with light rain lowering the visibility. They found Jankowski right over Cam Lo. Ground fire—mostly of the barrage type—was extremely heavy from the north and east. The FAC directed them north of the river and showed them the survivor's location. He was in a clump of trees just north of a small village. On the ground, Hambleton was amazed that they had responded so fast. He had not realized that they were already in the area.

Sandy 07 took over as the on-scene commander, and Bilk 34 flew south looking for more support.[1] Sandy 07, Captain Morse, was shocked at the ground situation. He had never seen so many guns, not even up in Mu Gia Pass, the hottest place in Laos. Intelligence had not briefed him that anything of this magnitude was occurring. Prior to launch, he and his wingman had received the standard daily briefing, without any indications that anything unusual was happening. It appeared as though the whole NVA had come south. Captain Morse quickly rethought his estimate of the situation. This was going to be one tough SAR.[2]

Bilk 34's call for emergency support was monitored by a U.S. Army helicopter flying near Hue, call sign Blueghost 39. It was a UH-1H Huey from F Troop of the 8th Cavalry. Normally based near Da Nang at Marble Mountain Airfield, it was one of several unit aircraft that had been assigned missions in the Hue–Quang Tri area that day.

On board as passengers were Capt. Thomas White, the troop operations officer, and Stu Kellerman, a reporter for United Press International. Earlier in the day, Blueghost 39 had taken Kellerman on an aerial tour of the Dong Ha area to get a firsthand view of the unfolding battle. While returning, they were instructed to swing by Hue/Phu Bai and pick up Captain White for the return home to Marble Mountain. At Hue/Phu Bai the copilot, WO Guy Laughlin, changed aircraft with WO John Frink, the copilot on another unit Huey, Blueghost 30. They swapped because Frink had already spent several days up at Hue/Phu Bai and was scheduled to return to home base for a few days off. Blueghost 39 was his ride back.[3]

The emergency call changed all that. Captain White briefly considered having the helicopter turn north and immediately proceed to Cam Lo. But the emergency call specified that there were possibly six survivors. Captain White knew that six added to the six already on board would overload the Huey. Besides, he could not risk the life of the reporter. So he directed the crew to drop him and Kellerman off back at the Hue/Phu Bai tactical operations center. There, using command radios, Captain White could monitor the events. While unloading, he directed the helicopter crew to proceed to the Hue/Phu Bai Airfield, refuel, and be ready for immediate tasking.

In the refueling pits, they were joined by two F Troop AH-1 Cobra gunships, call signs Blueghost 28 and 24. Earlier in the day the two had been working out of the Quang Tri Airfield a few miles east, when it had come under heavy NVA artillery fire. They scrambled off, literally to save themselves and their aircraft and proceeded to Hue/Phu Bai for safety.

Their other unit Huey was also there. Its call sign was Blueghost 30, and it was flown by WO Ben Nielsen, the one who had made the rescue up at Fire Support Base Alpha-2 the day before. Nielsen had no specific tasking but was on call for whatever might develop.

Based on what little he knew about the shot-down aircraft and the developing land battle, Captain White directed Blueghost 28, Capt. Mike Rosebeary, to immediately lift off with the other gunship, Blueghost 24, WO George Ezell, and one of the Hueys, Blueghost 39. Their mission was to respond to the emergency call. Rosebeary acknowledged the call and took off with his three helicopters. White then called him in the air and stated that it appeared that six crewmembers from an Air Force aircraft were down north of Cam Lo. He instructed Rosebeary to contact an Air Force FAC, call sign Bilk 34, on the emergency Guard frequency to coordinate the rescue. He also informed him that the enemy forces were plentiful and well armed, and he directed him not to take his flight north of the Cam Lo River without fighter support.

Five minutes later Captain White decided to augment the flight with the other Huey and directed Blueghost 30 to take off and join the others in the effort. Nielsen had been monitoring the radio calls and was becoming concerned. He knew the area well and began calling on the radio for Blueghost 39 not to cross the river. However, his calls were not acknowledged.[4]

Captain White called Rosebeary and informed him that the second Huey was being launched. Rosebeary made a critical decision. Not realizing what he was heading for, he directed his second Cobra, Blueghost 24, piloted by Warrant Officer Ezell, to drop back and join up with the second Huey, actually just a few minutes behind. By doing so he reduced by 50 percent the firepower that he and Blueghost 39 would have when they reached the river.

Flying north, Rosebeary and his team checked in with Bilk 34. Jankowski gave them a cursory situation briefing and instructed them to proceed up to Dong Ha, cross the river, and proceed west to the one survivor who was located near where the river made a big bend back to the east. Rosebeary acknowledged the information but further queried the FAC on the threat. Jankowski told them that there were many guns in the area and possibly SAMs, but that A-1s and F-4s were already hitting them. Satisfied, Rosebeary committed his two lead helicopters to the attempt.

Blueghosts 28 and 39 entered the area at low altitude, with the Huey leading at fifty feet above the ground. Blueghost 28 was at three hundred feet, about three thousand feet behind, in proper position to deliver rocket and machine-gun fire against anything that might shoot at the vulnerable Huey. But as they passed Dong Ha and crossed to the north side of the river, both helicopters began to take heavy ground fire. Blueghost 28 responded with rockets and 40mm fire against the guns. But the ground fire was coming from everywhere and immediately began scoring against both helicopters. Captain Rosebeary was thrown off balance. He could hear and feel the rounds slamming into his aircraft. Some shattered his canopy; others ripped at the vital components of his machine. Critical systems began to fail, and all types of warning lights began to illuminate in the cockpit. Rosebeary's trusty Cobra was being rapidly converted into a piece of torn wreckage.

He could also see that Blueghost 39 was taking hits. Rosebeary called for the two of them to turn and leave the area. Blueghost 39 did not respond verbally, but Rosebeary could see that he was beginning to turn. Then the Huey began to smoke from the engine area, and Rosebeary watched as it crossed behind a tree line and set down in a controlled landing about fifteen hundred meters north of the river.[5]

The crew of Blueghost 39, consisting of pilots 1st Lt. Byron Kulland and WO John Frink, crewchief Sp5c. Ronald Paschall, and gunner Sp5c. Jose Astorga, was down behind enemy lines and in serious trouble. During the run in, they had also seen all of the muzzle flashes of the challenging enemy guns. The pilot, First Lieutenant Kulland, had begun a descent to try to use the terrain and trees for protective cover. The gunner, Specialist Five Astorga, had called out "Ground fire!" to him and begun returning fire against the overwhelming force.

But his gun jammed and he was hit in the leg and chest. He momentarily passed out, but came to when the helicopter lurched to a stop on the ground. Astorga quickly unstrapped and crawled to the cockpit to check on the other three. One pilot and Paschall were conscious. Somebody threw Astorga a survival vest, and he began to crawl away from the chopper. But, realizing that he was alone, he decided to turn back to make an effort to pull out the rest of the crew. Then someone yelled "VC!" and he could see enemy troops closing in. They were firing their weapons at the helicopter, which exploded in a violent fireball with the other three crewmembers still on board. The wave of heat from the explosion swept over Astorga, and he renewed his efforts to crawl away. Immediately he was set upon by NVA troops and captured. He began his long journey north to Hanoi. He never saw his two pilots or crewchief again.[6]

Captain Rosebeary did not know any of this as he struggled to keep his ripped and shattered helicopter in the air. Fortunately, his main radio still worked. So as he fled south, he called a warning to the other two choppers not to cross the river. He also made his own Mayday call, announcing that he was badly damaged and heading southeast to escape. Jolly Green 67, one of the HH-53s that had launched for Mike 81, was still in the area. He acknowledged the call and proceeded to rendezvous with Blueghost 28. Rosebeary put his wrecked helicopter on the beach. The Jolly Green picked them up.[7]

Back over Hambleton's position, Sandy 07 and 08 continued to strike enemy targets. Hambleton was acting as a ground FAC, calling out targets and giving them corrections. The Sandys were impressed with the survivor: given the situation that he was in, he was maintaining his composure. Indeed, he was becoming a major player in this fight.

But several things concerned Morse. First, the weather was worsening. This was making it more and more difficult to put in airstrikes. Second, it was getting dark. He called Bilk 34 to determine the progress of the Army helicopters; only then did he discover that they were involved in their own SAR and would be of little use to him. Given these two factors and the withering ground fire, he chose not to commit the two waiting Jolly Greens. The area was just too hot. Too much work had to be done to prepare the area for a pickup attempt. The quick snatch had not worked. So he turned over on-scene command to another FAC and pointed the two noticeably damaged A-1s toward Da Nang. Jankowski, Bilk 34, was not far behind.[8]

As Bilk 34 and the Sandys were heading for Da Nang, Jolly Green 67 landed at Hue/Phu Bai to drop off Captain Rosebeary and his gunner, Warrant Officer Gorski. Captain White was there to meet them. Just a few moments earlier, he had gotten a call from First Regional Assistance Command headquarters notifying him that two of his helicopters were down up north. The caller did not specify which two. When White heard that the

Jolly Green was inbound, he could only hope that it had his men.

Rosebeary and Gorski climbed out and told him what happened. Even though it was now almost completely dark, White immediately decided to mount a search for his downed crew. He had another flight of two AH-1s in the rearm-refuel pit. It consisted of Blueghost Red, Capt. Tim Sprouse, and 1st Lt. Chuck LaCelle, Blueghost 26. This ubiquitous tag team seemed to be everywhere in the battle. They were the same ones who had covered the rescue at Fire Base Alpha-2 the day before, as well as the one at Camp Carroll earlier today. White directed Sprouse to take Blueghost 30 and the other gunship to search the Dong Ha area for any sign of the lost crew.

The three crews launched off in the dark to look for their missing mates. But low clouds had moved in over Dong Ha. Every time they tried to drop down below them to search the area, NVA gunners opened up on them, and Sprouse was unnerved by the "big red tennis balls" that were being fired at them. Several times they heard an emergency beeper, but nobody ever responded to their calls to "come up voice." At one point Sprouse also observed somebody firing what appeared to be small "pengun" signaling flares that were carried by all crewmembers. But without voice contact, he was hesitant to commit one of his helicopters for a pickup or even a closer look. It could easily have been a trap.[9]

Captain Morse and his wingman landed at Da Nang. Both aircraft were so badly damaged that they would require several days of repair work before being flyable again. They debriefed the intelligence officers on the dramatic events unfolding up north. Then Morse got on the phone and called back to his squadron commander at Nakhon Phanom. Morse told him of the situation and stated that they needed more A-1s at Da Nang. It was going to require an extensive effort to fish this guy out of the middle of the NVA. His commander replied that several A-1s would be dispatched that night to augment the effort.

Then Morse tried to get some sleep. He knew that tomorrow was going to be a very busy day. The effort was going to be difficult, but there was no doubt that they would go back in to get him. That was what the rescue forces did; that was why they were there. Just as for any other downed airman, all efforts would be made to get him out as long as he was still alive and free.

But Morse could not doze off. The thought of the guns haunted him—there were so many. Instead, he paced or shook all night long. It was, he said, "the worst night of my life."[10]

5

That others may live.
Motto of the Air Rescue and Recovery Service

Decisions in Saigon

As noted at the beginning, recovery of downed crew-members was important to the morale of air-crews. By March 1972, the American war in Southeast Asia was an air war, run for the most part by the commander, Seventh Air Force. He was responsible for the search and rescue of downed aircrews throughout the theater of operations.[1]

But at this critical juncture, the command of Seventh Air Force was in some disarray. In late March the commander, Gen. John D. Lavelle, had been recalled to Washington and subsequently relieved of his duties by the chief of staff of the Air Force, Gen. John D. Ryan.[2] Apparently it was thought that he had been condoning illegal airstrikes against North Vietnam, as well as efforts to falsely report them. Until a new commander could be appointed and sent out, the commander of Thirteenth Air Force, Lt. Gen. Marvin McNickle, was directed to serve as acting commander. He would shuttle between his headquarters at Clark Air Base and Saigon. Maj. Gen. Winton W. Marshall, the vice commander of Seventh, would run the day-to-day affairs.[3]

The headquarters for Seventh Air Force was located at Tan Son Nhut Air Base, just outside of Saigon. In the same massive complex was the Joint Search and Rescue Center (JSARC, call sign Joker), under the direction of the director of aerospace rescue (DAR). As the DAR, this individual, Col. Cecil Muirhead, could call upon any unit in the theater for SAR support. He could also take any procedural actions necessary to restrict specific airspace strictly for the use of SAR forces. This was routinely done in SARs throughout the war so that the rescue forces could operate unhampered.[4]

Colonel Muirhead was also the commander of the 3d Aerospace Rescue and Recovery Group (ARRG). In this role he commanded all dedicated assets, such as regional Recovery Coordination Centers, the HC-130 King aircraft, and the rescue helicopters themselves. Colonel Muirhead was working in his office when the duty controller at Joker, M.Sgt. Daryl Tincher, informed him that they had received simultaneous notification from Bluechip, King 22, and the Rescue Coordination Center at Da Nang (call sign Queen) that an EB-66 had been downed near the DMZ with one good parachute and contact with the one survivor. The survivor's call sign was Bat 21 Bravo. Rescue assets were in the area, but initial enemy resistance appeared to be heavy.

Based upon the situation around Dong Ha, and the intensity of enemy resistance to the initial efforts to get Bat 21 Bravo out, the DAR decided to forego any more rescue attempts until the area could be properly prepared for another attempt. Consequently he directed that Bat 21 Bravo be given twenty-four-hour FAC coverage and that the FACs begin striking hostile positions to soften the antiaircraft fire enough for a Jolly Green (HH-53) rescue helicopter to pick up the survivor.[5] Colonel Muirhead and the controllers in Joker were generally aware that the NVA were active along the DMZ. That explained the intensity of the enemy resistance to the first rescue attempt. But MACV had not told them of the nature or intensity of the land battle that was taking place near Dong Ha. And no mention was made of Blueghost 39.

Master Sergeant Tincher was the noncommissioned officer in charge of Joker and on duty when the word came in about Bat 21 Bravo. He had been in Southeast Asia for seven months and had worked numerous SARs. Reacting instinctively, he began scrambling to get more helicopters and A-1s ready for the effort if needed. He also directed the 8th Tactical Fighter Wing at Ubon to begin loading special area-denial mines on some of its F-4s to drop around Hambleton. With so many enemy troops in the area, he had to be protected. Sergeant Tincher plotted Hambleton's position on the map. He knew that ARVN troops were active in the area. To preclude any interference between their operations and the now blossoming effort to rescue Bat 21 Bravo, he considered establishing a no-fire zone around the survivor's position.

No-fire zones were routinely used during the war by

both American and South Vietnamese forces to deconflict often overlapping operations. They were especially
common along the Ho Chi Minh Trail and in Cambodia, where special intelligence teams would slip in to
monitor enemy operations. Generally such zones were
several kilometers in diameter. This served two purposes:
first, it gave the forces operating in the mission room to
maneuver, unhampered by other forces. Second, it did
not reveal the location of the team, element, or survivor.
Such areas were not always circular; they could be irreg-
ular in shape and defined by grid lines or geographic
references such as rivers, ridgelines, or roads. Additionally, their size varied.

Several factors were considered besides the protected
operation itself. The planners also had to weigh ongoing
activities in the area. In this case, Sergeant Tincher knew
that the ARVN was active. He also knew that the antiaircraft fire was heavy and that enemy troops were moving
about. He did not know that a major invasion was under
way. Consequently his concerns were parochial: he had a
SAR to run. Normally he would be assisted in this by the
Army artillery officer assigned as the MACV liaison to
JSARC. But that individual had recently gone home and
had not been replaced. So to give the growing air armada plenty of room to maneuver free of ground interference and to preclude endangering the ARVN units
with the SAR effort, Sergeant Tincher established a no-
fire zone around the survivor that would be large
enough to address all of these needs: it would be twenty-
seven kilometers in radius. The necessary messages were
sent out through command channels.[6]

Sergeant Tincher's actions were routine, and Colonel
Muirhead did not intercede when his senior controller

directed that the standard no-fire zone be placed over Bat 21 Bravo's position near the Cam Lo bridge. No airstrikes, artillery, or naval gunfire would be allowed in the area of Bat 21 Bravo without Seventh Air Force approval.[7] As the messages were flowing out, the colonel briefed Maj. Gen. Alton V. Slay, the director of operations, and Maj. Gen. Winton W. Marshall, the vice commander of Seventh Air Force, on the details of the SAR for Bat 21 Bravo.

In turn, Major General Marshall briefed Maj. Gen. John Carley, the operations officer for MACV, on the developing operation. General Carley had received clear verbal instructions from General Abrams that no expense was to be spared in attempting to recapture American prisoners or rescue downed aircrews. This was to have top priority over all other missions. He also knew that the 3d ARRG was a well-functioning organization with years of experience. Direction from MACV would just slow them down. Consequently he did not intercede, but directed that his staff be updated on developments.[8]

As evening stretched over the area, Trail 34, an O-2 from the 20th TASS at Da Nang, was on station over Bat 21 Bravo.[9] King 27, commanded by Maj. Dennis Constant, had come on station to relieve King 22 and was orbiting just south of Dong Ha. Constant was in contact with the FACs and the survivor. The story that they were telling him about the ground troops and antiaircraft guns and SAM firings just did not square with the intelligence he was getting from Saigon. He specifically asked for the frequency and call sign of someone with the friendly ground forces whom he could contact and was told that was not necessary.

But Constant was still uneasy. Because they were so close to North Vietnam, he requested that F-4s armed for air-to-air combat be dispatched for protection from North Vietnamese MiGs. The reports of SAM activity also concerned him. The HC-130 had no electronic gear on board to warn of SAM activity or launches, so he requested an EB-66 for early warning and jamming support against the reported SAM sites. Anticipating this, Bat 22 had been repeatedly refueling from a KC-135 tanker. Full of fuel, it was sent back to the Dong Ha area to rejoin the expanding SAR. Constant also began the process of diverting strike flights and FACs to provide continuous coverage over the survivor.[10]

At about 9:00 P.M., the 3d Division command post received a message stating that because of a SAR for a downed American airman, a no-fire zone had been imposed by Seventh Air Force for twenty-seven kilometers around a point seven hundred meters northwest of the Cam Lo bridge, and that any fire into this area would have to be approved by Seventh Air Force.[11] This approval would have to be obtained through the First Direct Air Support Center in Da Nang, over eighty kilometers away, with whom the division had tenuous communication at best. As the message arrived at the division command post, it was given to Major Brookbank, now the de facto division ALO. He read the message carefully but could not believe what he was being told. This restricted zone encompassed the entire area of operations of the division and all attached units.

In the middle of a pitched battle against advancing enemy armor, while they were locked in mortal combat with an uncompromising foe, Brookbank was being told that a headquarters several hundred miles from the battle was restricting the use of their own artillery and supporting naval gunfire and even airstrikes. The directive, if complied with, would have a devastating impact on the operations of the struggling ARVN. He reported the matter to Col. Donald Metcalf, who was the senior adviser to the division commander and located with him at Quang Tri. The colonel directed that the matter be referred back to the First Regional Assistance Command for relief.[12]

Queries to that headquarters were met with a stock response: "Hey, there is an American pilot [sic] down and everything possible has to be done to rescue him."[13]

Lt. Col. D'Wayne Gray, commander of Sub Unit One of the 1st ANGLICO, had come up north to check on some of his detachments and happened to be in the command center as the messages and calls were flying back and forth. He could not believe what he was hearing. A twenty-seven-kilometer radius zone was too big even for peacetime operations; in the current tactical situation, it was obscene. Even though he had no operational role to play in this headquarters, he attempted to intercede. He went into a rage that sent him absolutely "up the wall." He tried to convince an Air Force colonel that all of this was ridiculous, given the serious tactical situation. The colonel responded that Saigon had told him to handle a SAR that way, and he was going to do it that way. Neither the colonel nor his Army seniors would intercede. That Vietnamese and other American lives were being put at risk for this one individual carried no weight whatsoever at that time.[14] Lieutenant Colonel Gray noticed an Air Force brigadier general who was also visiting, and he took the matter up with him. Somehow the general had the idea that there were two survivors. As Gray recalls it, the general told him, "I would rather lose two ARVN divisions than those two U.S. Air Force crewmen."[15] Gray says that he could not get anyone to do anything.

Approximately one half hour after receiving this directive, the division command post was notified by one of the forward units that they had sighted twenty enemy tanks and many infantry north of the river but were not engaging them due to the restriction. It was also noted that the communication link with First Regional Assistance Command was down, so a clearance to fire could not even be requested. It took thirty crucial minutes for the clearances to be obtained and the targets engaged. Almost immediately, the command post received another report of another twenty enemy tanks moving into the area.[16]

6

Sleep did not come, as I lay awake
shaking from fear most of the night.
Capt. Don Morse, Sandy 07

Everybody is busting ass to get these guys.
1st Lt. Tim Brady,
1st Special Operations Squadron recorder, log

Heavy Action

AT ABOUT THE SAME time, Nail 59, a Pave Nail
modified OV-10 from the 23d TASS out of Nakhon
Phanom Air Base, Thailand, came on station to take over
as the on-scene commander for Bat 21 Bravo. The pilot
was Capt. Gary Ferentchak. As noted earlier, the Pave
Nails, with the LORAN navigational capability and laser
designator, had become an integral part of SAR opera-

tions. They were used just about anywhere that a SAR was going on, even in the area of operations of another TASS.

Ferentchak had launched out of Nakhon Phanom to work a standard mission along the Ho Chi Minh Trail in Laos. But from there he could hear all of the emergency calls being made. Curious as to what was going on, he asked the orbiting control airplane for an update. They gave him a cursory brief and then diverted him to King to work in the effort. Arriving in the area, Ferentchak relieved Trail 34 as the on-scene commander. He and his backseater maintained radio contact with Bat 21 Bravo and revalidated his position with the laser designator.[1]

Orbiting above, the crew on King 27 was doing the coordination necessary to flow strike fighters into the area to support the SAR. But most flights had to deliver by Skyspot radar or LORAN because of the weather. By now Major Constant was convinced that something big was going on. Bat 21 Bravo kept talking about vehicles moving on the roads and enemy troops moving all over the area. The FACs who had been able to get below the clouds were reporting the same thing. Therefore, Constant had the survivor ringed with CDU-14 "gravel" so that he could not be captured. Gravel was a specific type of weapon designed for use along the Ho Chi Minh Trail. It consisted of hundreds of little bomblets that would fall to the ground but not explode. Each bomblet would only go off when someone stepped on it. In effect, they were creating a minefield around Hambleton.

While King 27 and Nail 59 were on station, the Vietnamese commanders finally decided that the bridge at Cam Lo had to be taken out and directed that it be bombed. The arrival of Nail 59 overhead at that precise time was fortuitous: a laser-guided bomb was the perfect instrument to cut the bridge. But unfortunately, Nail 59 was in the area to support the SAR. He, like King 27, did not have contact with the 3d ARVN even though his (and King 27's) radios were fully compatible with those in the division command post. In fact (like King 27) he did not know about the ferocious battle that was being waged below. Since he had launched out of Nakhon Phanom to fly a mission in Laos, he had not been given any intelligence on the ground battle developing around Cam Lo.[2]

Nail 59 orbited over the survivor for several hours and attempted to get below the ragged clouds to begin plotting targets. But the weather was getting worse. Below the clouds, increasing rain was diminishing the visibility and making the laser unusable. When his fuel was exhausted, King 27 directed him to proceed to Da Nang, rearm and refuel, and return to the area to continue to cover the survivor.

Ferentchak had never been into Da Nang, but the radar traffic controllers brought him in through the terrible weather. The transient maintenance crew met his aircraft and had him ready to go with full fuel and rockets in thirty minutes. He was not able to get an intelligence briefing in that time, but dutifully, he relaunched and resumed his station over Bat 21 Bravo. He and his backseater had just arrived back overhead when they began to hear warnings of SAM launches along the DMZ just to the north. Fortunately, the sky was clear above the clouds, and they could see the missiles in flight. Ferentchak watched in amazement as some missiles headed toward the orbiting King HC-130 aircraft, which had moved its orbit just a little too far north.

Maj. Dennis Constant had slowed his HC-130 to 140 knots so that he could keep the aircraft on station as long as possible. Bat 22, his supporting EB-66, was still in the area and reported that the SAM sites were up and active. But Constant was having a little trouble hearing Bat 21 Bravo's radio, so he had decided to adjust his orbit just a little farther to the north. His adjustment caught the attention of the NVA missileers.

While on the northbound leg of his orbit, Maj. Ed Anderson, the EWO on Bat 22, called that one of the sites had gone into the launch mode and was salvoing missiles. Major Constant looked out and saw what appeared to be five headlights just above the clouds. It took him a few seconds to realize that they were moving; it took him just a few more to realize that the headlights were actually missiles guiding on his aircraft.

Major Constant called a quick warning to his crew and then wrenched the lumbering HC-130 into a violent turning dive. The missiles detonated with thunderous explosions just above the aircraft, peppering it with shrapnel. Constant pulled out of his dive and made a run to the southeast. The fire warning lights for the number four engine came on, and the crew shut the engine down. Warning lights also came on indicating damage to the aircraft pneumatic system. The crew worked quickly to isolate and limit the damage, but it was obvious that the aircraft would have to leave orbit. Major Constant quickly began coordinating for a replacement as he prepared his aircraft and crew to divert to Da Nang. King 27 was lucky: they had almost joined the growing list of aircraft being bagged by the air defenses of the advancing NVA. From then on the King birds would orbit farther to the south, out of harm's way.[3]

Capt. Gary Ferentchak and his backseater were amazed at what they were seeing. They had not realized that airplanes that big could manage such drastic maneuvers. But they had little time to watch the show, for as Major Constant was diving for his life, the crew of Nail 59 saw three missiles approaching them. Likewise, Ferentchak began to take evasive action. But before turning, he hit the Present Position Hold button on his LORAN to record his exact location at that moment. He then quickly noted the direction from which the missiles were approaching them. This information could be used later to locate the SAM sites, which would have to be eliminated as part of the SAR effort. He then began a hard descending turn to evade the approaching missiles. The sequential explosions of the missiles lit up the cockpit with a stroboscopic effect. The evasive turn was successful, but the aircraft lost a lot of airspeed in the effort.

Then Ferentchak saw two more missiles from another SAM site. He knew that missiles were usually launched in threes, so he asked his backseater if he saw another missile. The latter replied that the third was approaching from right in front of the aircraft. To his horror, the pilot then saw the streaking projectile. As a last-ditch maneuver, he jettisoned his external fuel tanks and rocket and flare pods to lighten the aircraft, rolled upside down, and pulled the aircraft down into a straight vertical dive. The missile exploded right above them.

Almost immediately they entered the thick clouds. Ferentchak had to quickly transition from visual to instrument flying and regain control of the aircraft. When he felt that they were clear of the missile threat, he pulled the aircraft out of its dive and climbed back above the clouds, noting his altitude at the bottom of the maneuver.

At the end of their station time, the crew of Nail 59 flew back to Nakhon Phanom. They had logged almost eleven hours of flying time. Back at intelligence, Ferentchak debriefed what they had encountered. He checked the map to see if the position he had noted with his LORAN and the bearing that he had taken on the SAM sites could be used to pinpoint their locations. He also noticed the height of the terrain where he had made his dive to escape the missiles. By his calculations, he had pulled out just 250 feet above the jungle-covered hills. If he had gone in, nobody would have ever found them or perhaps even known what had happened.[4]

While on station, Nail 59 did not put in any airstrikes or talk to anybody on the ground except Hambleton. Ferentchak's ability to direct laser-guided bombs would have been precisely the right instrument at the right time to destroy either the tanks or the bridge at Cam Lo. But Ferentchak was unaware of any of those possibilities. Unfortunately, the separate command-and-control arrangements being used for the ground battle and the SAR, complicated by the worsening weather, precluded him from doing either.

3 April

Throughout the night the advisers at the 3d ARVN Division command post continued to press for a reduction of the no-fire zone for the SAR. At 1:30 A.M. they were notified that the restriction was modified, to allow fire east of the twenty-three grid line and south of the fifty-three grid line. The main area of interest around Cam

Lo was still restricted. However, some exceptions were being allowed. A FAC continued to cover the withdrawal of the 147th Marine Brigade from Mai Loc. Additionally, an AC-119 Stinger gunship entered the area, but it could not work because of the weather.[5]

At 3:55 A.M., as the 2d Regiment was feverishly working to establish its defensive lines (it had temporarily been put under the operational control of the 1st Armor Brigade), the 20th Armor to its right spotted ten enemy tanks crossing the Cam Lo bridge. They were engaged by direct fire. Finally, at 4:45 A.M. the bridge was bombed. A subsequent bomb-damage assessment report indicated that it was impassable for vehicles but could be used by foot traffic.[6]

Hambleton heard and felt the strike on the bridge. All night long he had listened to enemy troops and vehicles passing his position. He was constantly passing targets up to the FACs. But he had to be very careful, because enemy troops were all around him. At one point, he later said, an enemy patrol paused just twenty-five feet from his position.[7]

Over at Nakhon Phanom, Thailand, other Pave Nail crewmembers were getting briefed for missions in support of the SAR. The first was Nail 25, Capt. Rocky Smith and Capt. Rick Atchison. They were due on station at first light. Smith and Atchison normally flew together and had in fact worked a number of SARs since the Pave Nail program had been inaugurated. They would be replaced by Nail 38, Capt. Bill Henderson and 1st Lt. Mark Clark. Nail 25 would refuel at Da Nang and then fly a second mission on station over Bat 21 Bravo prior to returning to Nakhon Phanom. Nail 38 would return directly to Nakhon Phanom for other duties.[8]

Both crews were briefed for the SAR mission by intelligence personnel, who became intimately involved in the details of every rescue. They characteristically exerted extra efforts to gather anything useful to the undertaking. But their information on the evolving ground battle was sorely lacking. They neither knew of nor briefed the aircrews about the extent of the battle that was developing in Military Region 1. However, they were aware of the increased anti-aircraft threat moving with the NVA—especially the SAM threat—and they passed that information along to the aircrews.[9]

After arriving on station, the crew of Nail 25 descended down below the clouds to get a look at the area. They were amazed at what they saw: there were vehicles everywhere. They thought that perhaps they were too far south and were looking at rear-area ARVN units. Then they began taking ground fire from all directions. Looking more closely, they noticed the red stars on the trucks and tanks below. Common sense prevailed, and they rapidly climbed out of the area. As they did so, it occurred to Rocky Smith that they had not been briefed on all of this. This was much worse than anything he had seen on the Ho Chi Minh Trail. And down there somewhere, there were friendly troops and a survivor.[10]

That first morning, Nail 25 stayed on station for over four hours and worked airstrikes against targets as the weather allowed. They were also able to "zot" the location of the survivor with their laser designator to determine his exact position in LORAN coordinates (accurate to within ten meters), so that precise all-weather drops could be accomplished.[11] They then directed several

LORAN drops of special area-denial ordnance to protect Bat 21 Bravo from capture.[12] Colonel Muirhead at Joker had authorized the use of any ordnance needed to seal Hambleton's position from intruders. This specifically included CBU-30 tear gas and BLU-52 incapacitant dust. Either would make exposed personnel incapable of controlled body movement for a few hours but would have no lasting effect.

Meanwhile, over Hambleton, a shift change was taking place. At the conclusion of their first mission, Nail 25 was relieved on station by Nail 38. Henderson and Clark continued the efforts to soften up the area and identify targets to support the SAR effort. Smith and Atchison then proceeded to Da Nang, where they ate, refueled, and got an intelligence update. Four hours later they were scheduled to relaunch and replace Nail 38.[13]

To support the SAR, the 3d ARRG deployed extra HH-53s and A-1s from Nakhon Phanom to Da Nang Air Base. These HH-53s from the 40th ARRS (Aerospace Rescue and Recovery Squadron) were specially modified with night-rescue devices that would give the rescue forces another pickup option. The Jolly Greens were flown by Maj. Gary Gamble and Capt. Mark Schibler.[14] While Nail 25 was working overhead, the 3d ARRG decided to launch a SAR task force. During the morning, two A-1s—Sandys 07 and 08—and two HH-53s from the 37th ARRS at Da Nang, Jolly Greens 65 and 67, launched for the effort. Jolly Green 65 was commanded by Lt. Cdr. Jay Crowe, a U.S. Coast Guard officer on an exchange tour assigned to the squadron at Da Nang. He had been flying helicopters for more than seven years and had a wealth of experience in rescue operations of all types.

Lieutenant Commander Crowe was a valuable addition to the unit. By this late stage of the war, most career Air Force helicopter pilots were on their second or third tours. To protect this important resource, the Air Force had begun augmenting them with flyers cross-trained from other types of aircraft, such as cargo, bombers, and fighters. But even though they were experienced pilots, as helicopter pilots they were rookies. Consequently, exchange officers like Crowe raised the experience level of the whole squadron.

On the morning of 3 April, it was his turn to fly. When Crowe first heard about the mission, he was both relieved and concerned. He was relieved because the area of the pickup was well known to the squadron—they frequently used it as a training area for practice pickups and low-level navigation missions. And things had been so relatively quiet for the last several months that most of their flying had been for training. But he was also concerned, because the area had little vegetation. They were used to making their pickups over heavy jungle foliage. This afforded them visual protection from gunners as they hovered. Around Dong Ha, there was little foliage. This could be a problem.[15] Crowe had heard some rumors about a big enemy push up north, but the intelligence briefing for the mission was routine. The briefer did not indicate any significant increase in enemy activity, but some of the Sandy pilots who had flown the day before had said that the ground fire had been extremely heavy.

When all was ready, the task force departed Da Nang. Arriving in the area, the Sandys proceeded to the survivor's area and the Jolly Greens held out over the ocean. Sandy 07, Capt. Don Morse, was the Sandy Lead. There he was joined by four more A-1s—Sandys 05 and 06, who had launched out of Ubon Air Base, and Sandys 03 and 04, who had launched out of Nakhon Phanom, Thailand. First Lt. Glen Priebe was Sandy 05, and Capt. Robert Burke was Sandy 03. Their intelligence briefings that morning had not included any specific mention of the developing situation south of the DMZ.[16]

Morse checked in with the on-scene commander, Nail 25. The weather was unworkable for visual strikes. Nail 25 was putting in fighters using LORAN deliveries through the clouds. The NVA air defenses were especially active: numerous SAM calls were heard. Sandy 07 called the orbiting King aircraft to ensure that "Iron Hand" SAM suppression aircraft were on station. They were, but the constant SAM launches kept forcing the aircraft to take evasive action.[17] Morse determined that the situation did not warrant a rescue attempt, so he directed Sandys 03 and 04 to proceed to Da Nang to refuel and rearm. But before they left, he showed them Hambleton's location.

Sandys 07 and 08 worked the area of the survivor as best they could under the weather. But when their weapons were expended, they had to return to Da Nang to rearm and refuel. Prior to departing, however, Sandy 07 briefed Sandys 05 and 06 on the situation. Sandy 07, Captain Morse, had now flown two missions in the area and was very familiar with the battle. He advised them that the best approach to the area would be from the south or southeast, that the whole area was very hot, and that at all costs they should avoid the area to the north and west and along the river to the east. Sandy 05 acknowledged it all and checked in with Nail 38, who had replaced Nail 25.

The weather was beginning to lift and break up a bit. Sandy 05 and Nail 38 concurred that the numerous air-strikes during the morning seemed to have suppressed the ground fire enough that an attempt could be made. Sandy 05, First Lieutenant Priebe, was now the onscene commander. He decided to commit Jolly Green 65 for the pickup. Sandys 05 and 06 rendezvoused with him and Nail 38 at the holding point. Sandy 05 briefed how he wanted the run in and the pickup to go. Nail 38 had stored the survivor's location in his LORAN computer and would lead the force down through the clouds directly to Hambleton's position. Once below the clouds, the two Sandys would cover Jolly for the run in and hover. Jolly Green 67 would trail the flight and stay above the clouds. Everybody acknowledged the plan; to Lieutenant Commander Crowe, it seemed like a good plan. Other than more radio chatter than usual for a SAR, it seemed fairly normal.

When everyone was ready, Nail 38 led the gaggle through the weather.[18] Breaking out below the clouds, he peeled off of the formation, and Sandy 05 began leading the Jolly Green to the survivor. They were going as fast as the helicopter could go. Immediately the pararescuemen on board Jolly Green 65 began spotting and shooting at enemy targets with the side-mounted miniguns. They were amazed at what they saw: there were trucks and tanks and soldiers and guns everywhere, and they all began shooting back. The helicopter began taking hits. The dashboard in front of the pilots began to disintegrate as rounds smashed through the instruments. The gyro system was shot out and all navigational and flight instruments failed. Emergency warning lights all over the cockpit came on indicating that the electrical, hydraulic, and flight-control systems were going out.

Crowe and his copilot fought to control the aircraft. Crowe radioed that they were hit badly and had to get out of the area. Sandy 05 told him to turn south. Since his flight and navigational instruments were no longer working, Crowe had to rely on his situational awareness to make this critical turn. He could also feel that the flight controls were becoming very heavy. He initiated a climb back up into the clouds, but as his speed bled off, he could feel the flight controls having less effect. So to maintain control, he leveled off in the clouds to reestablish his speed. But without flight instruments, he could not long maintain controlled flight in the weather. So he reinitiated the climb and popped out above the clouds. There, he rendezvoused with Jolly Green 67 and the Sandys.

The intercom system had also been shot out, but by shouting above the wind noise, Crowe was able to ascertain that his crew was okay. Now he had to decide what to do with this badly damaged helicopter. It took the coordinated movements of both pilots to control it. Fortunately, the engines and transmission had not been damaged. Crowe slowed the craft to determine its controllability at landing speeds. Below 120 knots, it became very unstable; maximum speed for lowering the landing gear was 105 knots. He considered having the pararescuemen bail out, since they were the only crewmembers with parachutes. But unsure of his height above the ground, he ruled that out. They were going to have to ride the helicopter down. He would have to make a high-speed approach and attempt to fight the aircraft to the ground. The question was where to put it.

Since they were heading south, Sandy 05 called the tower at Hue/Phu Bai Airfield for landing instructions. Hue Airfield did not want them to land there. They were conducting heavy combat operations and were under rocket attack. After several exchanges of especially colorful language, Sandy 05 convinced the tower controller that they had no other choice, and the controller directed them to land on the taxiway.

Crowe lined up the aircraft for his approach. He slowed it as much as he could while still maintaining control. They touched down at about 105 knots. Since the hydraulic system had been shot out, the aircraft had no brakes. So Crowe shut off both engines to let it coast to a stop. But there was a large crater in the taxiway, recently caused by an exploding rocket. Crowe saw it just in time: he was able to get just enough lift out of the still-rotating blades to hop the helicopter over the hole. Major Kennedy and several other pilots of F Troop watched the show being put on by the damaged helicopter. They were impressed.

As Crowe finally brought his craft to a stop, a small fire started in the back of the craft. He ordered the crew to abandon the machine. As they exited the hulk, they could hear the sounds of rockets impacting on the airfield. An Army vehicle picked them up and took them into combat operations. There Crowe and his crew met with U.S. Army intelligence officers, who briefed them on the unfolding ground battle. Crowe was flabbergasted. He had not been told any of this by Air Force intelligence at Da Nang that morning, but now the comments of the Sandys made sense. That survivor was in the middle of a full-scale invasion.

After the rocket attack ended, Jolly Green 67 landed,

picked up Crowe and his crew, and took them back to Da Nang. There Crowe went directly into intelligence and briefed them on what had happened and what he had seen. It was totally at variance with what they were getting from Seventh Air Force. Crowe hung around for a while, noting that nobody made any effort to forward his information to Saigon or brief other crews going out on missions. They were getting the same innocuous briefing that he had gotten that morning.[19]

After Jolly Green 65 landed at Hue/Phu Bai, Sandys 05 and 06 returned to the survivor's location. Queen, the rescue center at Da Nang, informed them that two more helicopters, Jolly Greens 66 and 60, had launched and were proceeding to the holding point. Sandys 05 and 06 joined them there. A few minutes later, Sandys 03 and 04 launched and joined the force. Sandy 03, the flight lead, was Capt. Robert Burke. He took his two A-1s into the target area and began coordinating with Nail 38, who was still in the area. Nail 38 briefed him on the failed attempt of Jolly 65 and then had to depart to refuel. In the interim he was replaced by Nail 22, another Pave Nail from Nakhon Phanom. But in the action and confusion of the morning, Captain Henderson, the pilot of Nail 38, had let his fuel get too low to return to Nakhon Phanom. Instead he decided to go to Da Nang for gas and then return to his base in Thailand.[20]

Sandy 03 took over as on-scene commander. Again he began trolling the area for enemy response. There was little ground fire, and the weather was improving. With two fresh Jolly Greens on station, he decided on another attempt. He briefed the plan. Once again the Nail FAC would lead in Jolly Green 66, escorted by Sandys 05 and 06. Sandys 03 and 04 would be overhead to cap the pickup, and Jolly Green 60 would hold back in a high orbit. Everybody acknowledged his call.

Jolly Green 66 was being flown by Lt. Col. Bill Harris, the commander of the 37th ARRS at Da Nang. Like most of the pilots in the squadron, he was not a helicopter pilot by trade. He had flown both fighters and bombers in a career that reached back to B-24s in the last stages of World War II. He had volunteered for rescue duty while assigned as a flight test pilot at Edwards Air Force Base, California. Lieutenant Colonel Harris had been in command of the unit since the previous September. Regardless of his myriad other duties, he directed that he be included in the normal rotation of pilots and fly his share of all missions. Today it was his turn to fly one of the hot ones, but Harris felt that this was necessary for unit morale. He could not ask his guys to do something he would not do himself.[21]

When all the participants were ready, Sandy 03 told them to execute. Dutifully, Nail 22 announced on the radio that he was departing the holding point with the Jolly Green and escort A-1s in tow. But to his horror, Sandy 03 saw that instead of approaching from the southeast, they were approaching from the east—north of Dong Ha. And the NVA gunners knew it, for even though the force had not yet penetrated the clouds, Harris began calling that they were taking heavy fire. He could see "orange balls of fire" passing close by. Burke considered aborting the mission, but he felt that the survivor's location was relatively quiet and that a quick pickup offered the best chance for the survivor. He had them continue.

Sandys 05 and 06 arrived over Hambleton's position slightly ahead of the Jolly Green. Burke quickly told them where he wanted their bombs and rockets. They began delivering their weapons. But as Harris brought his craft down through a hole in the clouds, he began taking hits. His pararescuemen manning the miniguns began calling out and engaging targets on all sides. Harris noticed that they were approaching the survivor along a small dirt road. He observed ten tanks as they pulled off their camouflage netting and began firing at the slowing helicopter. Harris spotted Hambleton's position and began his final approach for the pickup, approaching to within one hundred meters of the survivor. Sandy 03 asked him where the fire was coming from. Lieutenant Colonel Harris could not give him a specific direction because his crew indicated that it was coming from everywhere. So Burke told them to discontinue and exit the area. Jolly Green 66 aborted his run, turned south, and began to climb.[22]

Jolly Green 60 rejoined him and told Harris that his craft was riddled with holes. So like his predecessor that morning, Harris made an emergency landing at Hue/ Phu Bai and parked next to Jolly Green 65. There he inspected his aircraft and discovered that among other things, the main spar on one of the rotor blades had been heavily damaged. If it had come off in flight, they would have crashed. Harris and his crew had pushed their luck to the limit.[23]

The four Sandys continued to work the area until their ordnance was expended. Then Sandys 05 and 06 departed for Da Nang to join the growing SAR force there. No FAC was overhead, so Sandy 03 asked King for strike flights that he would direct. A flight of two F-4s arrived with MK-82 500-pound bombs. He directed them against the bridge at Cam Lo, but they missed it. A flight of two VNAF A-37s checked in with Sandy, carrying MK-81 250-pound bombs. They hit the bridge with several bombs, but the lighter projectiles were not powerful enough to drop it.

Back at Da Nang, Lieutenant Commander Crowe continued to monitor the radios and the progress of the ongoing missions. As he listened to Jolly 66 get shot off and compared it to his own experience that morning, he was convinced that they were not receiving accurate data on the situation through Air Force channels. Being a Coast Guard Officer, he maintained personal liaisons with numerous other military organizations in the Da Nang area. He went to see some of them. They helped him get a briefing from Vietnamese intelligence. He could not believe what he was being told. This was a full-scale invasion of main-force NVA units, fully intent on overrunning and defeating the South. It included infantry, artillery, tanks, engineers—all conventional forces, and all being coordinated with local VC units. Once again he went back to wing intelligence and reported what he had been told. The briefers there would not accept his information. They said that they could only brief what had been sent down to them through Air Force channels.[24]

As the momentous battle was being fought in the air over Dong Ha, other more mundane events continued to take place. One in particular would lead four unsuspecting Americans into the ongoing maelstrom. This event has never been fully explained. At approximately 8:30 A.M., a UH-1H helicopter assigned to the 37th Signal Battalion (call sign Cavalier 70) departed its home station at Marble Mountain Airfield, just east of the air base at Da Nang. It was on a routine resupply to signal sites in the Quang Tri area. By 10:00 A.M. it had not arrived at its ultimate destination near Quang Tri. The battalion operations officer began to conduct a search. None of the sites where it was supposed to land reported seeing it. Then he contacted the airfield at Hue/Phu Bai; the helicopter had not landed there to refuel. Most of the morning the weather had been terrible, with visibility about two to three miles and almost solid clouds from three hundred feet to three thousand feet above the ground.

The operations officer then checked with the other aircraft from the unit that were also flying in the area. One crew reported hearing Cavalier 70 relay a call from another helicopter to the radar controllers at Hue/Phu Bai. He then called the radar controllers. One of the on-duty controllers told him that he had indeed received a call from Cavalier 70 at about 9:39 A.M., stating that he was in the clear above the weather at four thousand feet but was lost. The pilot had told the controller that he thought they were somewhere in the vicinity of Quang Tri, but he needed a radar verification of their actual location and vectors to Hue/Phu Bai. The controller had talked with the pilot for approximately twenty minutes, but he had not been able to pick up the helicopter on his radar. At 10:10 A.M. he had lost contact with the aircraft, and it had not responded to subsequent radio calls. Cavalier 70 had disappeared, with its crew of WO Larry Zich, pilot; WO Douglas O'Neill, copilot; Sp5c. Allen Christensen, crewchief; and Sp4c. Edward Williams, door gunner.

At the time of fuel starvation, the operations officer reported the loss to higher headquarters and contacted the 37th ARRS for assistance. However, they were consumed with the Bat 21 operation and could not be of much help. At the time, their plate was completely full.

During the morning, helicopters from the 37th Signal Battalion searched for Cavalier 70. But they did not proceed north of Quang Tri, due to the threat. No traces of the helicopter were found. A subsequent board of investigation determined that the crew had probably been forced down by enemy antiaircraft fire or perhaps even a SAM. Level at four thousand feet and just above the clouds without any way of knowing that they were in a known SAM area or in fact being tracked by hostile radar, they would have been sitting ducks for a radar-guided missile. It had probably been another kill for the NVA SAM batteries that had been causing such problems for the air units. Those four hapless soldiers probably never knew what hit them.[25]

Like Crowe, Lieutenant Colonel Harris was concerned about the situation. He was convinced that the NVA knew that a downed American airman was hidden in the immediate area. He felt that they were perfectly content to either leave him alone, thus holding American attention while the invaders moved elsewhere, or use him as bait to draw in more vulnerable SAR forces. Either way, Harris thought that the whole area was just too well defended for any kind of helicopter rescue attempt.

Harris's fears and suspicions were well placed, for by this stage of the war, the NVA was well aware of how the United States used its helicopters for general troop transport, commando insertion, and rescue. The enemy had carefully studied U.S. tactics and knew that any helicopter was a threat. Consequently, they had issued instructions to their personnel on how to shoot them down. The field instruction stated in part: "In attacking aircraft of this type [helicopters], we must aim right at the cockpit compartment where the pilot sits in the nose of the helicopter—and open fire. It contains the controls for the mechanical systems and a fuel tank. [Another] is the hump on the back of the aircraft under the main rotor. That area also contains very complex machinery."[26]

If the helicopter was observed to be inserting commandos, NVA soldiers were admonished to attempt to shoot it down on its approach. If the commandos were deposited, they were instructed to form a loose perimeter around the enemy troops and observe them. When the opportunity presented itself, they were to attack by surprise to demoralize and destroy them.[27]

Instructions concerning how to deal with downed pilots were more detailed. Soldiers were taught about the types of ordnance, such as smoke bombs, tear gas, and different types of CBUs (cluster bomb units), that could be used. They studied the makeup of the SAR task force, including the number of helicopters and A-1s that they could expect to see. And they received detailed instructions on how to build a trap to lure in the helicopters so that they could be ambushed. One article from a soldier's magazine was explicit:

To capture pilots, we must disperse from our position in many directions and quickly and tightly encircle them. This movement must be organized and include tight, 360-degree inner and outer perimeters. After capturing pilots, they must be stripped of radio transmitters, weapons, and documents and immediately taken from the area under guard. When conditions are right, the pilot's radio transmitter and signal flares can

be used to lure enemy aircraft into the ambush sites.
The element on the outer perimeter fires at the A-1s.
The one on the inner perimeter must conceal itself and
suddenly open fire when the [helicopter] hovers and
drops its rope ladder to rescue the pilot![28]

Consequently, any helicopter that flew over the enemy
forces in that area, for whatever reason, would be opposed. It was an extremely dangerous situation. Harris
sensed that and called Colonel Muirhead at 3d ARRG to
discuss it with him. Muirhead responded that he knew it
was hot but felt that with enough preparation, another
attempt could be made.[29]

As the A-37s were finishing their strike around the
Cam Lo bridge, two more A-1s, Sandys 01 and 02, arrived. Sandy 01, Capt. Fred Boli, was the flight lead.
Sandy 03, Captain Burke, gave him a situation briefing,
turned over on-scene command to him, and headed for
Da Nang.[30] King then advised Sandy 01 that no rescue
helicopters were available for any more attempts that
day. They were directed to expend their ordnance and
also return to Da Nang.[31] Dutifully, Captain Boli and
his wingman went to work.

As the A-1s were about to leave the area, Nail 38
checked in. While on the ground at Da Nang, the pilot,
Captain Henderson, had called back to the operations
center at Nakhon Phanom and been told that since they
were there, he and Clark were to relaunch and fly another mission in the rescue prior to returning to Nakhon
Phanom. It looked as though the weather was beginning
to lift somewhat. Since Henderson and Clark were familiar with the operation, they could continue to attack
NVA targets or lead in another attempt if any helicopters

became available. Henderson acknowledged and flew back to Cam Lo, ready to do another stint over the survivor. Sandy 01 directed Nail 38 to reenter the SAR area. Henderson and Clark descended down to about two thousand feet to get below the clouds. But as the two arrived back over Cam Lo, they received a warning of a SAM launch in the DMZ area. Henderson was not too concerned, because he figured that they were below the minimum effective altitude for the SAM radars to find and track aircraft. But even though neither he nor Clark saw any missiles coming at them, he took evasive action.

His action was prescient but ineffective. Unobserved by the crew, one of the missiles hit their aircraft in the tail, and the explosion violently ripped the machine. Clark had been searching the ground with his binoculars, but the explosion knocked them to the floor. As he bent down to get them, he felt a blast of extremely hot air. He attempted to call Henderson. The intercom was dead. Henderson also felt the overpressure of the blast. The canopy on all sides disintegrated; the aircraft pitched nose up and rapidly lost airspeed. It was immediately obvious to Clark that it could no longer fly, so he ejected. Henderson followed his backseater.[32]

Both crewmembers cleanly cleared the aircraft with good chutes. Clark spotted his frontseater. Henderson, Nail 38 Alpha, was coming down north of the Mieu Giang River and north of the main eastwest road, which was covered with refugees. As he descended he could hear people shooting at him. He landed in a large field and initially hid in a pile of rocks. He watched as an old man came up and rolled up his parachute and walked away with it. He then moved to a thin clump of bamboo. He got out his survival radio and told the covering aircraft that he was okay.[33]

Clark, Nail 38 Bravo, was farther south. He attempted to steer his chute toward Henderson, but when he discovered that his efforts were going to put him actually in the Mieu Giang River, he made a quick right turn and landed five meters from the water on the south bank. He also came up on his radio and said that he was in one piece. Both crewmembers had landed within two kilometers of Bat 21 Bravo.[34]

Like his predecessor the day before, Sandy 01 decided to attempt a quick pickup with whatever helicopters he could find. He made another emergency call on the Guard frequency. His call was answered almost immediately by Blueghosts Red and 26, the Cobra tag team of Sprouse and LaCelle. They were in the area with WO Ben Nielsen in Blueghost 30—a Huey—scouting for NVA units trailing the Vietnamese remnants that were fleeing Mai Loc, and, once again, willing to help.

Sandy 01 directed them to rendezvous with him south of Dong Ha. En route to the survivors' location, Sprouse heard somebody call "SAM, SAM, vicinity of Khe Sanh!" He usually ignored such calls because he normally flew below the effective altitude of the large missiles. Then Sandy 01 shouted, "Here it comes guys—hit the deck!" Sprouse slammed the control stick full forward as the missiles screamed overhead. He went into a vertical dive so steep that he almost could not recover before hitting the trees. He climbed back to altitude only to have to repeat the maneuver again, when a second volley of missiles was fired. That was not supposed to happen to helicopters, he thought. Once again badly shaken, he continued to lead his team toward the survivors.[35]

Sandy 01 quickly devised a plan. He and Sandy 02 and the Cobras would escort the Huey for a pickup of Clark, then Henderson and Hambleton, too, if they could get him. He briefly discussed it with the others. They had no objections, so Sandy 01 fired several marking rockets to direct Blueghost 30 in to the survivors. But about one kilometer south of Clark's position, Blueghost 30, in spite of the suppression fire being laid down by the two A-1s and two Cobras, began to take extremely heavy enemy fire. The pilot, Warrant Officer Nielsen, could hear small-arms rounds hitting the aircraft. Then "something really big," according to Nielsen, opened up on them. He could hear the whomp of the shells as they passed by. The right side of the windshield disintegrated, showering them with pieces of glass. Then the right cargo door was blown cleanly off of the aircraft. It was too much. For the sake of personal survival, he and the covering Cobras had to turn back.

The three helicopters flew to Quang Tri Airfield. Amazingly, none of the crew on any of the helicopters was injured. But the helicopters were total losses, further charges against the mounting bill for Bat 21 Bravo.[36]

Unaware of what was happening to the helicopters, Sandy 01 contacted the survivors and told them to get ready for a quick pickup. But Clark and Henderson watched as Blueghost 30 and the gunships were driven away by the ground fire.[37] Clark then realized that he was probably going to be spending some time there. He found a line of concertina wire that had been overgrown with weeds and crawled in. Under the wire he was perfectly covered, but he had an excellent field of view across the river to the north.

Henderson also knew that he would not be picked up that day. So he covered himself as best he could in the bamboo. After dark, a squad of NVA troops entered the field where he had landed and began digging a pit for an antiaircraft gun. It was no more than twenty feet from him. But when they were finished digging, instead of setting up the weapon, they left. Henderson decided that later that night, he would sneak down to the river and float downstream. But he was concerned about crossing the road, so he decided instead to wait until early morning to move.

But about an hour later, the NVA squad returned. One soldier grabbed a machete and came over and began cutting bamboo literally right over Henderson. In a near panic, he considered shooting the unknowing troop, but that would have drawn the other soldiers. Searching quickly, Henderson realized that he had no immediate avenue of escape. Then the issue became moot when the soldier spotted him and ran away yelling. Other soldiers responded and began firing into the bushes. With no other options, the trapped pilot stepped out and raised his hands.

The soldiers immediately frisked him. They took his cigarettes and then offered him one of theirs. Then they loosely bound him. The team had a medic, who gave Henderson some first aid for the injuries he had sustained in the ejection. His face was burned, and he had been hit with shrapnel in the chest. Without realizing it, he had lost quite a bit of blood. The medic treated his wounds with sulfa drugs and bandaged his chest.

They began to move him north. The first village that

they passed through had been hit with BLU-52 riot-control dust. It still persisted. The soldiers put on their gas masks, but Henderson did not have one and got sick from the chemical.[38]

Forward elements of the 3d ARVN Division watched Nail 38 get shot down. Nail 38 Bravo landed not more than a few kilometers from friendly lines. The battle lines were being reformed: the 2d Regiment had been removed from the 1st Armor Brigade and returned to division control. A new unit, the 11th Cavalry Regiment, with two squadrons of infantry in M-113s and some M-41 light tanks, was positioned between the 2d and the 20th Armor, under the control of the 1st Armor Brigade. Upon assuming its position on the line, its troops were immediately in contact with enemy forces attempting to cross the river.[39] The 2d Regiment was asked if it could move a team forward and recover the survivor south of the river—Clark. It refused, stating that they "will not move out of Cam Lo because they are afraid of the VC."[40]

As another night settled over the area, Bilk 11 was back on station to baby-sit the survivors. He continued the process of hourly check-ins and directed more airstrikes against targets in the area. Later that evening, though, he lost contact with Nail 38 Alpha.[41] Henderson had begun his journey north. On his way, he saw troops and equipment everywhere. He could not believe the number of SAMs. He also noticed that the aid stations were filled to overflowing with wounded soldiers.[42] He was taken to a series of headquarters until he reached a holding camp, which he estimates was just north of the DMZ. There he joined a group of South Vietnamese artillerymen who had also been captured. He also had a chance encounter with Sp5c. Jose Astorga, the door gunner of Blueghost 39, the Army UH-1H that had been shot down on 2 April when it had participated in the first attempt to get to Hambleton. The two prisoners quickly exchanged names before their captors separated them.[43]

4 April

The next day was generally quiet along the lines, as the NVA appeared to pull back somewhat and regroup. During the day, the 3d ARVN began to receive reinforcements from the 1st, 4th, and 5th Ranger Groups flown in from down south. They went on the line south of the 2d Regiment, facing to the west.[44] Yet all units reported contacts of some sort, and the 20th Armor and the 11th Cavalry both reported repelling several enemy attempts to cross the river. Some American FACs launched and attempted to work with ARVN units outside the restricted area. But because of the weather, about the best that they could do was to spot targets for LORAN or Skyspot drops.

The low ceilings and visibility precluded any attempts to rescue the two survivors. Instead, the rescue forces received a comprehensive briefing on the enemy forces in the area; they were shocked. They knew that they were meeting stiff competition, but they had no idea that they were up against a total invasion force consisting of more than two divisions of infantry, tanks, and artillery, protected by hundreds of antiaircraft guns and SAMs.[45]

About noon the weather began to lift, and four A-1 Sandys were launched to check out the area and put in airstrikes. Upon arriving in the area, they found Bilk 11 on station. He had been in the area since morning and had already had a good scare. One of the F-4s that he had been directing against an NVA target had taken a hit in the wing and had just about been lost. Fortunately the damage was actually to the wing-mounted drop tank. The pilot had been able to jettison it and recover at Da Nang.[46]

Shortly the A-1s were joined by another SAR task force of six more A-1s and two HH-53s, launched for a possible pickup. As the full force rendezvoused over the area, Bilk 11 passed on-scene command to Sandy lead. He briefed his task force on the basic plan and sent the A-1s to work to continue to try to soften the area enough for the helicopters to get in. The force was greeted with intense antiaircraft gunfire, eight observed SAM launches, and even artillery fire. Once again the Sandys began their deadly duel with the guns on the ground. But the valiant air warriors could not prevail; the defenses were just too strong. They could not commit the helicopters for an attempt. Instead, the Sandy force was mauled badly. One aircraft was hit in the engine, and it began running roughly, so the pilot declared an emergency and headed back to Da Nang. The landing was uneventful.

Lieutenant Commander Crowe went out to inspect the damaged craft. The bottom of the engine had been hit: inspection revealed the remnants of some type of missile. Explosive-ordnance personnel removed the pieces, and Commander Crowe and some of the Sandy pilots took them to wing intelligence. There the briefers still denied the existence of any heat-seeking SA-7 missiles in the area. Crowe and his team proceeded to the wing commander's office. He looked at it and concurred with the pilots. He had the pieces strapped into the backseat of an F-4 and flown to Saigon. That night Seventh Air Force began to update the intelligence briefings for the invasion to reflect the heightened threat.[47]

But the worst damage was suffered by Capt. Don Morse. The aircraft that he was flying was hit by several 37mm shells in the right wing, just inboard of the wing-mounted gun. A fire broke out immediately. He dumped hydraulic pressure and jettisoned all of his ordnance; he then turned his crippled craft southeast and called out his predicament on the radio. He had two immediate concerns: first, to get out of the Dong Ha area, since he did not want to eject into the inferno below. Second, the A-1 had folding wings. He feared that the lock mechanism would be damaged by the spreading fire and the wing would fold on him, causing the aircraft to rapidly fall out of control. So as he turned to leave the area, several of the other Sandys and the helicopters trailed him on his way toward Da Nang.[48]

But as he proceeded down the coast, the fire continued to burn, setting off some of the 20mm gun ammunition in the gun mount in the wing. At times, flames trailed forty feet behind the aircraft. Inside the cockpit Morse leaned over to the left side, because the right side was physically too hot to touch. Pieces began to fall off of the wing, and aircraft control became more and more difficult. Because a portion of the actual lifting surface of the wing was being destroyed, the aircraft wanted to turn to the right. He had to fight to keep it heading straight, and it took almost full left aileron and rudder to do so. Anticipating that the gear would not extend, Captain Morse requested that the runway be foamed. Da

Nang tower complied with his request, but he had to orbit while the trucks spread the foam. By the time the runway was ready, Captain Morse ended up making a nighttime, gear-up, blacked-out, marginally controllable zero-instruments landing.[49]

But Morse was not yet home safe. He landed his aircraft in the fire-suppressing foam. As it skidded to a stop, he quickly unstrapped and got out of the aircraft. But the foam was extremely slippery. As he stepped off of the wing, he slipped in the slimy material. Struggling to get his footing and move away from the burning aircraft, he noticed to his horror that one of the fire trucks was heading directly for him. The driver finally saw him and hit his brakes, which were only marginally effective in the suppressant foam. The huge vehicle slid through the white slop, stopping just short of the appalled Morse. One of its enormous tires came to rest within inches of his head. The flight surgeon helped him up and handed Morse a beer. It was the best beer of his life.[50]

Of the ten A-1s launched that day, eight received battle damage. Of these eight, two received major damage and one (Morse's) would never fly again.[51] Toward sunset the poor weather returned. The rescue forces at Da Nang had a big meeting, reviewing the events to that point. Crowe had spent some more time with Vietnamese intelligence, who had convinced him that the whole area was a trap. They had told him that the NVA knew the survivors were there, but that they were along a boundary between the major NVA attacking units, and nobody wanted to bother picking them up. The invaders were aware that the survivors were calling targets to the FACs. But apparently the survivors were the focus of American attention in the area; therefore the NVA were more than happy to let the stranded American fliers tie up U.S. efforts in that critical sector. They fully intended to just keep the Americans pinned down and extract whatever price they could for them.

Lieutenant Commander Crowe and Lieutenant Colonel Harris considered other courses of action. Perhaps they should just wait for the battle to move south. Hopefully the antiaircraft artillery (AAA) would go with the main units and thus make the survivors more accessible, or maybe some kind of ground team could be inserted to snatch them. There was an outfit down in Saigon that did those kinds of things. A small subunit of MACV, it occasionally ran missions to recover Americans or Vietnamese being held prisoner or evading capture. Such missions were called Bright Light operations.[52]

5 April

The bad weather persisted throughout the next day. Most airstrikes were LORAN deliveries or Skyspots; the SAR restrictions were still in effect. At 8:30 A.M. Vietnamese Marine forward observers spotted NVA tanks approximately two kilometers north of the Cam Lo bridge. An immediate airstrike was requested, but clearance had to be obtained from Seventh Air Force. After a ninety-minute delay, clearance was obtained and the target struck by Skyspot. Two of the tanks were destroyed, but several others escaped. Additionally, some VNAF 0-1s and A-1s were able to come up and work under the weather on a selective basis and work targets such as tanks and artillery outside the restricted zone.[53]

The rescue forces used the day to develop alternative

plans and repair their badly shot-up fleet of machines.[54] The Sandys, Jolly Greens, and FACs were now fully aware of what they were up against. The situation was unprecedented in the history of rescue attempts: never before had a SAR force attempted to extract a survivor from the middle of two attacking enemy divisions. Capt. Mark Schibler flew a maintenance crew up to Phu Bai to recover the damaged HH-53s that had gone in there two days earlier. They worked feverishly to repair the wounded birds, because they needed every aircraft they could get. They also developed extensive lists of targets to be struck prior to any more rescue attempts. These included SAM sites, antiaircraft guns, vehicles, major roads, and known enemy concentrations.

But a few visual airstrikes were put in. One was flown by 1st Lt. Mike Carlin, an F-4 pilot with the 13th Tactical Fighter Squadron (TFS) out of Udorn Air Base, Thailand. He was number two in a flight of two Phantoms that delivered four canisters each of CBU-42 WAAPMs (wide-area antipersonnel munitions) around Bat 21 Bravo's position. These weapons would release hundreds of little bomblets that, upon hitting the ground, would not explode, but instead would extend trip wires that when snagged by a person would explode. It helped to fortify a minefield created around Hambleton's position.[55]

Carlin had a difficult time getting into the target area because of the weather. He followed his leader as they descended down to eight hundred feet out over the water and were then vectored into the target by an orbiting FAC. The low ceiling forced them to fly level deliveries and exposed them to unbelievable ground fire from everywhere. Carlin had been briefed that the mission was in support of a SAR. But he did not know that the survivors were surrounded by such a large enemy force. As he delivered his ordnance, he was amazed at how large the billowing white smoke from the FAC's marking rocket was. It was not until later that he figured why it appeared so big: never before had he delivered ordnance so low or been so close to an exploding rocket.[56]

At about the same time, General Abrams, concerned by the intensity of the unremitting attacks now spreading across Vietnam, made an urgent request for more deployments of tactical airpower. The Joint Chiefs of Staff (JCS) in Washington responded immediately. That day they ordered the deployment of an F-105G electronic countermeasures squadron from McConnell Air Force Base, Kansas, to Korat Air Base, Thailand. Additionally, they directed the Air Force to immediately deploy two United States–based F-4 squadrons, also to Thailand. This operation, called Constant Guard I, was completed by the 11 April, with all units in theater and ready for employment. Concurrently, although separately, eight EB-66s deployed to replace lost and damaged aircraft and were also in place by the eleventh.[57]

The JCS also ordered the commander in chief, Pacific, to deploy two U.S. Marine F-4 squadrons from Iwakuni Marine Corps Air Station, Japan. They arrived at Da Nang Air Base, Vietnam, by 8 April and formed Marine Air Group 15. A third squadron of F-4s was ordered to deploy to Da Nang from Kaneohe Marine Corps Air Station, Hawaii. They arrived on 13 April.[58]

The U.S. Navy also responded. On the third of April, the aircraft carrier *Kitty Hawk* joined the *Hancock* and *Coral Sea*. On the eighth, they were joined by the *Constellation*. Each ship added about sixty aircraft to the rapidly growing armada joining the fight against the enemy offensive.

General Abrams also asked for more B-52s. Again the JCS concurred and ordered the Strategic Air Command to begin deploying more of the giant bombers to the theater. Within a week, fifty-four B-52D and G models would arrive at Andersen Air Force Base, Guam. These deployments went extremely well: in some cases the B-52s were flying combat missions less than seventy-two hours after receiving the deployment alert at their stateside bases.[59]

As evening was stretching over the land, American intelligence monitored a North Vietnamese radio message in clear language, announcing the downing of a B-52 on the afternoon of 2 April, by home-guard units in the Vinh Linh area just north of the DMZ. In the message, they explained that in spite of the fact that the

> Fliers used every trick to confuse ground detection . . . they could not cheat the radar observers of Unit 62 . . . the men quickly fixed the enemy on their screens. . . . The whole battleground shook in the deafening burst of the missiles streaking up into the clouds in their glowing trajectories. One of the B-52s was hit, burst into flames and exploded. Its debris were scattered over a wide area. The rest of the eight-engine craft together with their escort jet fighters fled in disorder.[60]

That "B-52" was Bat 21.

7

★

Jolly Green, Jolly Green
It's all painted brown and green.
Well, the prettiest bird that
I've ever seen is that Jolly Green.
"Jolly Green" song, courtesy of Charles Rouhier, 37th ARRS

Turn south Jolly, turn right!
Everybody

Flight of the Jolly Green

THE NEXT MORNING, 6 April, dawned bright, with only scattered clouds at fifteen thousand feet and unrestricted visibility. The SAR task force sat on ground alert as fifty-two different sets of fighters and four B-52 strikes hit all of the targets previously identified by the Sandys. First Lt. Mark Clark watched some of the strikes from his hiding place just south of the river. He marveled at their destructive power and at the devastation they inflicted on the enemy and civilians caught up in the battle. But what really got his attention was a volley of artillery fire that landed very close to his position. Some rounds came so close that they blew some of the concealment from his hiding place.[1] Not knowing or caring why the rounds had been fired, he quickly got on his radio and directed the orbiting FAC to get it stopped. It took a few minutes to do so.

The VNAF also took advantage of the weather: O-1 FACs took off and began spotting targets for the ground commanders. They were concerned about the enemy buildup in the Cam Lo area and the apparent movement of more NVA from the west along the south side of the river. Accustomed to the cover provided by bad weather, on this day the NVA were caught in the open. VNAF A-1s responded to the FAC spottings and delivered devastating strikes on enemy formations south and east of the restricted area.[2]

At approximately 3:15 P.M., Capt. Fred Boli as Sandy 01 took off from Da Nang with three other A-11s—Sandys 02, 05, and 06—and two rescue helicopters, Jolly Greens 67 and 60.[3] The two Jolly Green helicopters from the 40th ARRS also launched as backups.[4] Lieutenant Commander Crowe, from the 37th ARRS, briefed the mission; it had several objectives. Hambleton had now been on the ground four days and needed resupply. Therefore one A-1 (Boli's) would be rigged to drop him a Madden resupply kit full of goodies such as food, water, ammunition, and extra radios. A pickup could be attempted if Sandy lead felt that the situation warranted it; it would be his call. But as the force headed out, Crowe did not expect them to make an attempt. He felt that it was just too hot.[5]

Lieutenant Colonel Harris was concerned about the mission. He intended to fly the lead Jolly Green, but his squadron mates insisted that he stand down. They felt that he had done his share on 3 April and that now it was someone else's turn. He reluctantly stood aside as Capt. Peter Chapman stepped forward and vigorously insisted that he be allowed to fly the mission. He was given the job. Harris was deeply impressed: Chapman did not have to do this. He was not next in the rotation, and, in fact, had orders back to the United States to fly with the presidential air unit at Andrews Air Force Base, Maryland. But his actions were typical of those of any man in his squadron, who so easily accepted danger and were ready to risk their lives to save others. He was paired up with 1st Lt. John Call III, copilot; T.Sgt. Roy Prater, mechanic; Sgt. William Pearson, pararescueman; T.Sgt. Allen Avery, pararescueman; and Sgt. James Alley, photographer.[6]

The gaggle of airplanes proceeded to a holding point southeast of Quang Tri, where Jolly Greens 67 and 60 and Sandys 05 and 06 orbited while Sandys 01 and 02 entered the battle area to assess the threat for an attempted pickup. There they took over from Bilk 11 and Nail 59, who had been working the area jointly and finishing up the preparatory airstrikes.[7] The two Jolly Greens from the 40th held east of Hue, just off the coast.[8]

Captain Bolı noticed a friendly tank position approximately six kilometers south of the survivors. He decided to make the final holding point for the helicopters right over them. He was especially concerned about the five

NVA battalions that Army intelligence had told him were located between the friendlies and the survivors. (This was the force that the ARVN had observed moving in from the west on the south side of the Mieu Giang River.) He spent the next thirty minutes trolling the planned ingress route for the helicopters using his pod-mounted 7.62mm minigun to strafe anything that looked suspicious. Neither he nor Sandy 02 observed any appreciable enemy reaction. However, they did receive some SAM calls on the radio.[9]

The ARVN ground units observed the air armada as it entered the area. Forward units reported that approximately forty aircraft were working to rescue the downed fliers.[10] At approximately 4:15 P.M., Captain Boli directed the two FACs to terminate the airstrikes so that he could overfly the survivors' immediate area and troll there for enemy reaction. He got Nail 59, Bilk 11, Sandy 02, and both survivors on the same radio frequency and had all of them watch him while he flew low around their positions. While doing so, he also attempted to drop the Madden supply kit to Bat 21 Bravo. But the arming wire on the device failed, and it did not release from the aircraft. Boli did not know that until he landed back at Da Nang.[11]

He also shot 20mm strafe into suspected NVA locations and had Sandy 02 drop CBU on others—widening his area of search as he did so. Several areas concerned him, so he directed the FACs to hit them with more airstrikes. While this was being carried out, he ordered Jolly Green 60 to hold southeast of Quang Tri as the high helicopter, with Jolly Green 67 and Sandys 05 and 06 proceeding to the final holding point.

As the aircraft were repositioning, Captain Boli began

his final briefing for all the participants. Bat 21 Bravo would be picked up first. As the situation developed, Nail 38 Bravo would follow, picked up by either Jolly Green 67 or one of the others. But the briefing was rudely interrupted by a SAM call that forced all aircraft to dive for the deck to avoid the missiles. Boli noted that the SAM launches were not accompanied by any antiaircraft guns.

At 5:10 P.M., Sandy 03 joined the force with a full load of white phosphorus smoke that could be used to lay a smoke screen. Boli finished briefing the plan—Sandy 02 would lead Jolly Green 67 in with a series of smoke rockets to pick up Bat 21 Bravo and then Nail 38 Bravo if the area was quiet. He would then join with Sandys 05 and 06 in a "daisy chain" around the Jolly Green to provide suppressive fire. Sandy 03 would lay a series of well-placed smoke screens and then join the daisy chain. Sandy 01 would orbit above to direct the operation and call ground fire.

A few minutes later, Sandy 01 determined that all requested targets had been struck to his satisfaction. He had the FACs and remaining strikes hold high and dry while he reentered the survivors' immediate area to brief them and take one last look. He reviewed the plan and situation in his mind. He knew that it could be a trap, but the preparation had been so thorough, the trolling and probing so intense. And the enemy response had been so slack. It was time to go.[12]

But just as he was ready to give the word, Boli noticed an airstrike going in just south of the Cam Lo bridge. It was a set of VNAF A-37s. He checked with his FACs; none of them was working it. It took several minutes for Nail 59 to go through the various radio frequencies and find the VNAF FAC controlling them. He got them to terminate and move out of the area.[13] Finally, everything was ready. Boli directed the task force to execute the pickup. Immediately Sandy 02 laid down his marks for the ingress to Bat 21 Bravo. The route took him directly over Clark. Sandy 03 put down his smoke screen, and Sandys 02, 05, and 06 began the daisy chain to protect the vulnerable helicopter. They also began expending CBU-25 and 20mm strafe on anything that looked in any way threatening. A slight wind shift caused some of the smoke screen to partly obscure Bat 21 Bravo's position, but the confusion was quickly resolved and the force pressed on.[14] Overhead, in the swirling mass of airplanes, Nail 59, Capt. Gary Ferentchak, took out his personal camera and began to take pictures. He wanted to record what he thought was going to be a historic rescue.

As Jolly Green 67 crossed the river, the naked helicopter began to take ground fire from just about all quarters. Seconds later as it approached to within one hundred meters of Bat 21 Bravo, Boli called for the survivor to pop his red smoke so that the Jolly Green crew themselves could find his location. Almost simultaneously someone on Jolly Green 67 called, "I'm hit!" It was later determined that he also added, "They got a fuel line." Bat 21 Bravo heard all of this on his survival radio, and, realizing the gravity of the situation, did not pop his smoke, thus not revealing his position.

As the enemy rounds slammed into the lumbering helicopter, the crew of Jolly Green 67 fought to control their damaged aircraft. Boli had briefed them that if they began taking ground fire, they were to immediately exit the area on a heading of southeast. Realizing the desperate situation that they were in, the crew began to turn their craft to the egress heading and depart the cauldron of withering fire.[15]

Boli ordered the other Sandys to cover the wounded Jolly Green, and he began strafing in front of the stricken helicopter as it tried to gain speed. But instead of turning southeast as briefed, the crew began heading due east toward the enemy concentrations north of the river. Apparently one of the crewmembers on the Jolly Green was holding down his microphone-transmit button, because numerous calls to him to "Turn south Jolly! Turn right!" were blocked. The crew finally turned south about one kilometer east of the planned route after Boli warned them not to cross over a village. As the Jolly Green crew made their turn, Boli flew up behind them and strafed the village.[16]

But the harried and endangered Jolly Green pilots overshot their turn and took up a heading to the southwest. Boli ordered them to turn back to the left. Someone else came on the radio and told them to turn right. Boli tells the story from there:

Jolly hesitated, and again I ordered, "No! Turn left, Jolly, turn south." He initiated the turn and I was about to order him to climb when, as I passed on a strafe pass, I observed a fire suddenly break out between the middle of the left engine and the main rotor. Immediately pieces flew off of the tail rotor and struck the main rotor, causing it to disintegrate. Jolly Green 67 continued to roll left and crashed on his left side about one and a half kilometers south of Nail 38 Bravo's position. Fire immediately spread throughout

the aircraft. No beepers were ever heard . . . The time
was [5:40 P.M.].[17]

On the tactical frequency, Boli began calling; "Jolly's
down, Jolly's down!" His call was answered with ob-
scenities. Jolly Green 67 and its crew had been transformed into a heap of burning, smoking wreckage. The
fire would continue for several days, interrupted only by
the exploding ordnance on board. It would become so
hot that some of the metal would melt into the ground.
By that time the flesh was long gone. There were no
survivors and there would be no SAR. Instead, six more
names were added to the mounting bill for Hambleton.
They were also another mark on the mounting scorecard
for the NVA air-defense meat grinder. The smoke was a
lingering pyre for the brave crewmembers who had paid
the full price of war.[18]

Boli conducted a roll call of his task force: all others
were present. Capt. Mark Schibler, leading the two
backup helicopters, monitored all of this. He immediately began to move his two aircraft to the holding
point, meeting the rest of the force as they were egres-
sing. The two masses of aircraft quickly joined into an
orbiting gaggle and tried to sort out the disaster. Everybody had an opinion. But they all agreed that it was just
too hot, and since Jolly Green 67 apparently had no
survivors, another attempt did not appear justified at this
time.[19]

Captain Boli listened to it all. As the task-force leader,
it was his call to make. He concurred: it was just too hot.
They would abort. So Captain Boli turned on-scene
command over to Bilk 11 with another list of targets to

be struck, told the survivors to remain hidden, and took his shaken force back to Da Nang.[20]

Back at the air base, Lieutenant Commander Crowe was shocked. He had not expected them to attempt a pickup. And Lieutenant Colonel Harris was very upset. The loss of the Jolly Green vindicated his earlier fears: this area was just too dangerous for helicopters. The cost was too high for two men. Once again he called Colonel Muirhead at 3d ARRG. He told him they had to find another way.[21] Colonel Muirhead concurred with Boli's decision and Harris's recommendations to terminate the attempts. As required, he notified Major General Marshall that "all reasonable actions have been accomplished," and the area was too dangerous for a helicopter pickup.[22]

There were many witnesses on the ground. Observers with the 20th Armor reported the shootdown. They also pinpointed the ground fire from the village, and shortly thereafter they were given authority to fire on any village north of the river.[23] Nail 38 Bravo also watched it all. There was so much firing going on that he could not distinguish who was firing at whom. But as the Jolly Green passed over him heading south, he could tell that it was not gaining altitude, and then he heard it crash. Clark was devastated. His immediate thought was, "I really cocked this up. Six more guys dying because I fucked up and didn't . . . Was there a gun pit out there that I should have called in?" And then the realization set in that he was not going to be picked up that day. A few minutes later, he observed the ARVN artillery fire as it slammed into the villages. The civilians attempted to flee west along the river.[24]

Bat 21 Bravo watched it too. He cried for the death of

the six brave men—lives given up in sacrifice for his. Although he was tired, hungry, and demoralized, the fifty-three-year-old navigator resolved then and there: "Hell, I'm going to get out of this, regardless."[25]

As the SAR task force departed the area, the VNAF FACs continued to take advantage of the good weather. There were targets everywhere, and their calls for support were answered with both A-1s and A-37s out of Da Nang. They were able to destroy more tanks, supplies, and enemy troops as the larger battle for Military Region I went on unabated.[26]

8

This is Red Crown on Guard. SAM, SAM, DMZ.

More Bad News

RED CROWN WAS A GODSEND. It was Big Brother and Eye in the Sky rolled into one. To the embattled aircrews nervously patrolling the skies over the DMZ, it was a timely voice of warning on the radio. But in reality, it was a U.S. Navy ship on patrol in the Gulf of Tonkin that acted as a fusion center for much of the electronic intelligence being instantaneously collected on North Vietnam. Its various sensors could detect the activation of SAM radars and missile launches. It could also detect the takeoff and flight path of MiG fighters. Such information would be broadcast to aircrews in blanket warnings for specific geographical areas. In early April, Red Crown was very busy.

On 7 April, no SAR forces launched. Instead, meetings were held at Da Nang and Saigon to reevaluate the situation in light of the tragic incidents of the previous few days. Serious thought was given to another course of action. Would it be possible to rescue them with some kind of ground action, or perhaps by inserting a small ground team along the river?[1]

Bilk 11 and other FACs were back on station, both to baby-sit Bat 21 Bravo and Nail 38 Bravo and to take the war to the invaders. The weather was workable for airstrikes along the coast, but it was undercast farther inland. Most airstrikes were VNAF A-1s. American fighters were limited, because strikes were now being flown against North Vietnam.[2]

The ARVN was concerned about the buildup of enemy forces around the Cam Lo area in particular, and along the western front in general. NVA artillery attacks were steadily increasing. Additionally, enemy units continued to infiltrate across the Mieu Giang River and probe 1st Armor Brigade positions.[3] One group of approximately three hundred soldiers was spotted crossing the river near Mark Clark's position, and artillery fire was directed against it.[4] Mark was shaken by the blasts: he got right on the radio and asked that they be stopped. He was not aware of the enemy movement.

At about 10:30 A.M., 1st Lt. Bruce Walker of the 20th TASS, call sign Covey 282, took off from Da Nang in an OV-10. He was scheduled to fly in the area of the DMZ to interdict enemy supplies heading down to the front lines around Dong Ha and Cam Lo. But today he would also have an artillery observer with him. He landed at Hue/Phu Bai and picked up U.S. Marine first lieutenant

Larry Potts, a member of the naval gunfire liaison team assigned to coordinate the fire from the ships offshore.

Immediately after getting airborne, they checked in on the artillery control frequency. Marine first lieutenant Joel Eisenstein, the naval gunfire liaison officer working with the 3d ARVN Division at Ai Tu, directed them to visually reconnoiter around the abandoned fire support base at Charlie-1, about six kilometers north of Dong Ha on Route QL-1.[5] Many vehicles were reported to be moving through the area.

At about the same time, Nail 21, a Pave Nail OV-10, entered the area specifically to work around the survivors. The crew was Capt. Tuck Ernst and 1st Lt. Dave Talley. Dave and Mark Clark were very good friends. They had both previously flown RF-4s and had transferred to OV-10s together. As the Pave Nail arrived overhead, the crew checked in with both survivors on the ground and began setting up to put in more airstrikes in the area. But the enemy air-defense units were making the work difficult. The gunners were constantly hosing them, and the SAM sites were particularly active.[6]

At approximately 11:15 A.M., one of the SAM missiles scored a direct hit on Covey 282, and both crewmembers ejected.[7] Ernst and Talley heard Walker's Mayday call. The crew of the orbiting King HC-130 also heard it. They called Nail 21 and directed that he move over and assume duties as the on-scene commander for yet another SAR in the DMZ area. He complied immediately.

Nail 21 had not observed the shootdown, so as they moved into Covey 282's area, they began a search pattern for the survivors. The pilot, First Lieutenant

Walker, Covey 282 Alpha, immediately came up on his radio. He was on the ground unhurt and was moving away from his parachute. He did not know the status of his backseater, First Lieutenant Potts, Covey 282 Bravo. The crew of Nail 21 reported this through the chain of command. Now there were three and possibly four downed airmen to worry about in the DMZ area.[8]

When the missile hit Covey 282's aircraft, Potts had been talking with First Lieutenant Eisenstein at Ai Tu on the artillery command-and-control frequency to begin coordinating naval artillery fire. He also called, "Mayday! Mayday!" on his radio. Eisenstein was startled by the call. He immediately asked Potts to confirm that he had been hit. When Potts did not respond, he directed another observer, flying in the backseat of a VNAF O-1, to begin a search for the possibly downed aircraft. But that aircraft itself was shortly thereafter hit by an SA-7 missile and crash-landed at Quang Tri Airfield.[9]

At approximately 11:30 A.M., U.S. Navy lieutenant David Throop, the senior observer assigned to the gunfire liaison team, departed Phu Bai in the backseat of another VNAF O-1 to search for the crew of the downed OV-10. They searched along the river between Dong Ha and Cam Lo, taking plenty of ground fire but spotting nothing except the still-burning wreckage of Jolly Green 67. They then flew along QL-1 as far north as the DMZ with the same results. Eisenstein then ordered him to direct naval gunfire against the SAM sites that were active in the area of the old Charlie-2 fire support base. After thirty minutes, they terminated the fire mission and searched along the shore line as far north as the DMZ before returning to base. They never spotted the OV-10 or made contact with either crewmember.[10]

In an attempt to avoid the SAMs and to conduct a more effective search, Captain Ernst took his OV-10 down to about fifteen hundred feet. From that altitude, they easily spotted Walker's parachute. He was down about six kilometers northeast of Bat 21 Bravo. First Lieutenant Talley was able to zot the location and pass it to King.[11] But since Walker had moved some distance away from it, the position was not exact.

Potts did not come up on his radio. The FACs continued to call him, but with no response. As they were searching, they observed quite a bit of ground fire. Walker was constantly calling warnings to them. Then they observed a contrail pass by the left side of the aircraft and explode above them. That was enough: they decided to move out over the water. There they rendezvoused with Nail 25, Capt. Rocky Smith and Capt. Rick Atchison, who were also flying in the area. Rocky and Rick visually inspected Nail 21's OV-10: it had no apparent battle damage. So Rocky and Rick returned to their duties while Nail 21 continued to work with Walker and search for Potts.

Nail 21 stayed on station for about another hour and began to put in airstrikes around Covey 282 Alpha's general position. They were never able to locate Walker's exact position or make contact with Potts before they were replaced as on-scene commander by Nail 25. As they made their way back to Nakhon Phanom, they had another SA-2 fired at them in Laos.[12]

Nail 25 had been launched into the area for interdiction against NVA forces. They were scheduled for two sorties of four hours each, specifically to use the laser and LORAN gear to get accurate plots of various fords, road intersections, and choke points for targeting during periods of bad weather. But once again they were diverted for SAR duties. Taking over from Nail 21, they confirmed Walker's general location and status. As they attempted to pinpoint his location, they began to receive SAM warnings for the DMZ area. Rocky pointed the OV-10 out over the water.

But they were not quick enough. As they crossed over the beach, they heard a SAM launch call. Rick described it: "We had a SAM call, and I couldn't see it, and when you can't see it, boy you are naked in that airplane. Rocky just happened to jink, broke to the right, and that son of a gun was coming from the tail . . . Rocky took the aircraft and just put it into damn near ninety degrees, and that damned thing went off in full view of the canopy. . . . It shook us up so badly, we had to go out over the water and take about a two-minute water break."[13]

Rick counted ten missiles launched against them; they were later told by the folks at Red Crown that eighty-three SAMs were fired in that area that day.[14] It was now obvious to the planners at Seventh Air Force that the SAMs and guns had to be dealt with. The NVA air-defense meat grinder was seriously affecting air operations in the DMZ area. They had credibly challenged American air superiority over the battlefield; consequently, flights were directed to hit the SAM and radar sites. That afternoon crews from the various squadrons of the 366th Tactical Fighter Wing at Da Nang were sent after the sites. They realized the importance of these strikes.

Lt. Col. John O'Gorman, commander of the 421st TFS, pointed out that the air defenses had to be eliminated before the invasion through the DMZ could be effectively challenged by the air units. He stated in a

New York Times article that "Our first approach has to be counter-air. If they have SAMs, we have to go after the SAMs. . . . Our main effort has to be against their air defense before we can start interdicting." His counterpart in the 390th TFS, Lt. Col. Walt Bjorneby, stated that it was "vitally important that we take care of the SAMs because they have begun to menace South Vietnamese airspace."[15]

The best tactic for hitting the SAM sites was a very low and fast attack. Such a run in would put the aircraft below the radar coverage and speed gave them some protection against the guns. The sites were surrounded by hundreds of guns of all calibers. "Every truck was towing one," said Lieutenant Colonel O'Gorman. He explained this method of attack. "We evaded their radar and came in across the coast very fast. We got in so fast they weren't even able to cock their guns."[16]

The FACs in their much slower O-1s, O-2s, and OV-10s did not have that option. And they were not there to attack the sites but to find the enemy units and direct the fighter bombers against them. The SAMs were hindering their work. Capt. Harold Icke pointed this out in another *Times* article: "When you are dodging a SAM, you're not doing your mission." First Lt. Bill Jankowski added that the SAMs had been in the back of his mind all of the time. Neither the U.S. FAC airplanes nor any of the VNAF aircraft had SAM radar-warning receivers. That afternoon, as the Da Nang F-4s went after the SAM sites, a VNAF O-1 and A-1 were blown out of the sky by SAMs north of Dong Ha. There were no parachutes and no SARs.[17]

First Lt. Bruce Walker was moot testimony to the danger of the NVA air defenses. Once again Seventh Air

Force imposed a massive no-fire zone around this latest survivor. However, sanity prevailed this time, and the restricted area was rapidly reduced to a two-kilometer square around Covey 282 Alpha.[18] But before the restriction was reduced, U.S. advisers on the bridge at Dong Ha saw enemy tanks move through the restricted area. The restriction precluded them from firing artillery, and before this could be sorted out, the tanks had completely passed through the area and gone into hiding.[19]

But coordination problems did not hamper just those on the ground. Nail 25, while trying to work the SAR for Covey 282 Alpha, had to constantly dodge the naval artillery being fired by the ships offshore against targets north of Dong Ha. This was the fire mission being directed by Lieutenant Throop against the SAM site near the old ARVN fire support base at Charlie-2. He was directly below them in the VNAF O-1. But Rocky and Rick were never able to establish satisfactory communications with him or with the 3d ARVN Division at Ai Tu to effectively coordinate the fire.[20]

Bat 21 Bravo and Nail 38 Bravo also heard that Covey 282 was down. It was another blow to their already rock-bottom morale.[21] Meanwhile, the commanders at Seventh Air Force were becoming concerned about the lack of success and rising cost of the rescue efforts for Bat 21 Bravo, Nail 38 Bravo, and now Covey 282 Alpha. Obviously a conventional helicopter pickup was not going to work for these SARs. Perhaps sensing this, General Abrams decreed that there would be no further attempts to pick up the survivors by helicopter.[22]

Late in the afternoon, General Marshall got a call from Lt. Col. Andy Anderson, USMC. He was the commander of the Joint Personnel Recovery Center in Saigon and had been monitoring the rescue efforts. He had some ideas about another method of pickup that he wanted to discuss with the general, and they arranged a meeting for the next day. General Marshall then had to brief these events to the new commander of Seventh Air Force.

That afternoon, Gen. John Vogt arrived to replace General Lavelle and the interim Lieutenant General McNickle. He was well versed in the war, having previously served as the director for plans and operations at Pacific Air Force headquarters in Hawaii and as director of the Joint Staff in Washington. But it would take him a few weeks to learn the intimate details of the day-to-day operations in Southeast Asia.[23]

Bat 21 Bravo was unaware of any of this. He was consumed with his own personal misery. As the sun went down that evening, he was notified that he would not have a baby-sitter that evening, since the number of FAC sorties was being reduced. Later that night several B-52 strikes and Skyspots went in not too far away. Hambleton, for the first time, felt alone and wondered if he was being left behind by the war.[24]

9

★

General, I think that I can get a ground team in there.
Lt. Col. Andy Anderson, USMC

Bright Light

Lᴛ. Cᴏʟ. Aɴᴅʏ Aɴᴅᴇʀsᴏɴ's organization, the Joint Personnel Recovery Center (JPRC) was attached to the J-2 Intelligence Division of MACV as of 15 March 1972. It acted as the staff agency and joint coordinating authority within MACV for post-SAR personnel-recovery operations.[1] In this capacity, Lieutenant Colonel Anderson and his people had been closely watching the developments at Cam Lo. His organization was also involved in the rescue business and, until March, had been the cover organization for the Recovery Studies Division (MACSOG-80) of the Military Assistance Command Studies and Observations Group (MACSOG).

The commander of MACSOG reported directly to the commander of MACV, General Abrams, and exercised operational command over the U.S. forces assigned or attached to MACSOG. His forces were active throughout the theater in a variety of air, sea, and land operations. Teams searched enemy base areas, monitored traffic along the Ho Chi Minh Trail, and occasionally snatched prisoners or hunted down Viet Cong leaders. The teams could also be used to recover captured or downed friendly personnel. The operative element for these missions was the Recovery Studies Division, which ran numerous programs to locate and recover lost personnel. It constantly monitored intelligence for any information on friendly sightings. It ran an active reward program and dropped millions of leaflets all over Southeast Asia soliciting such data on lost friendlies. It also published a list of escape-and-evasion code letters for aircrews to use if they were shot down and evading enemy capture. If downed and unable to communicate by radio, the crewmembers would craft the evasion letter so that it could be clearly seen from the air. SAR forces would then respond. The letters would be changed monthly or as necessary to prevent being compromised by the enemy.[2]

When warranted, the Recovery Studies Division could order team operations to search for and recover downed or lost personnel. But they were not meant as a competitor for the Air Force's rescue forces. They were designed to be used if the more conventional means failed. When MACSOG-80 teams operated, the missions were codenamed Bright Light. During the war, MACSOG ran numerous such missions. One narrative in particular illustrates the kind of effort put forth and, unfortunately, the frustrations felt in these operations:

On 24 March 1971, 1st Lt. Jack Butcher of the 20th TASS, call sign Covey 231, took off in an OV-10 from Da Nang. While searching for trucks along the Ho Chi Minh Trail, he was shot down by a 37mm antiaircraft gun. Wounded in the ejection, he was treated by a North Vietnamese medical team in preparation for movement to North Vietnam.[3] When he was strong enough, two guards were assigned to begin taking him north. Butcher watched the guards closely. A week later he saw an opportunity and escaped. All he had was the hat, pajamas, and tennis shoes that he was wearing.

A few days later the JPRC received intelligence that First Lieutenant Butcher had escaped and was loose near Tchepone in central Laos. They immediately ordered photo and visual reconnaissance of the area. Butcher tried to move away from people, but the trail area was heavily populated. Moving to higher ground, he found a machete and a canteen. He used the blade to cut enough bushes to fashion a large letter N, which was the correct escape-and-evasion code letter for the previous month.

But it took a few days for the bushes to discolor enough to be noticed. After a three-day wait, Butcher was weak from lack of food and water. He realized that he had to move. So he left a message with his service number and an arrow to indicate the direction that he was going, and he set off. He was still near Tchepone in central Laos.

Nearing a village, he found a pineapple grove and took five. He ate three immediately and put the other two into a backpack that he had made. Then he attempted to follow a trail to the west. Unfortunately he stumbled into a camouflaged village and was recaptured.[4] On that same day, in an open area on the side of a hill, JPRC spotted the escape-and-evasion code letter. An escape-and-evasion kit was dropped on the site by aircraft but was not picked up. Two Bright Light teams were inserted but could not make contact. Enemy forces quickly detected their presence and began to pursue and attack them, and the teams had to be extracted under heavy fire. Air search was resumed and confirmed that First Lieutenant Butcher had been recaptured. He was eventually moved to Hanoi and released two years later.[5]

The near miss with Butcher was indicative of the frustrations felt by the JPRC troops. Overall during the war, the results for JPRC were a mixed bag. The leaflet drops, reward programs, and intelligence and team operations led to the recovery of 492 Vietnamese prisoners and 101 U.S. remains. But through March 1972, despite the best of efforts, JPRC had not successfully recovered any live Americans. There had not yet been a fully successful Bright Light operation.

By 1972 MACSOG's operations were being curtailed. Units were being withdrawn or deactivated, as the U.S. Congress had directed that no American personnel could be engaged in ground operations in Laos or Cambodia after 8 February 1971, except for the purpose of recovering downed American aircrew members. Therefore, what non-SAR operations were still being run were all within South Vietnam. In fact, MACSOG had been ordered to cease operations on 31 March and deactivate on 30 April 1972. Most remaining personnel were being transferred to Strategic Technical Directorate Advisory Team (STDAT) 158 to work directly with the Vietnamese as they picked up these missions.[6] Indeed, as the survivors waited up north, the remnants of the JPRC were being split. A few under Lieutenant Colonel Anderson remained under MACSOG-80 to wrap up its affairs. The rest, under Maj. Don Lunday, Anderson's deputy, had transferred to J-2 and assumed a more classical role of intelligence collection on Americans still missing in the war.

Yet Anderson and his people still held a sense of mission. He also knew that his organization's time was limited, and he wanted it to know some measure of success before being deactivated. So when Anderson heard about Bat 21, Blueghost 39, Nail 38, Jolly Green 67, and Covey 282, he directed his personnel to begin monitoring the operations in case the individuals were not recovered. Additionally, he directed his operations and intelligence officer, Capt. Bob Covalucci, to begin preliminary intelligence gathering and planning for a possible recovery attempt.[7] Then he made a bold and perhaps dangerous decision: he decided to go completely out of his chain of command and directly call Major General Marshall.

General Marshall gladly took the call. The next morning, 8 April, he held a meeting in his office with Colonel Muirhead and Lieutenant Colonel Anderson. They were given an intelligence update on the land battle and a detailed briefing on the pickup attempts led by Captain Boli. Major General Marshall concurred with Colonel Muirhead that helicopter attempts should be terminated, and he relayed General Abram's guidance on the subject. But he was not ready to write off the survivors. He turned to Anderson for ideas. Anderson reviewed the situation and told the general that he felt that a team of sea commandos could possibly use the Cua Viet or the

Mieu Giang River to ingress and recover all three survivors. The operation would be tricky and require carefully planned air support, but it was achievable. In fact, Lieutenant Colonel Anderson was so enthusiastic about it that he decided to lead the mission himself. General Marshall told him that he could have everything he needed to directly support him.[8]

Then Major General Marshall personally briefed General Abrams on the status of the SARs. The two generals were old friends and had had several previous assignments together. They had an excellent working relationship. But General Abrams was concerned about the high level of ordnance expenditure for this operation and the diversion of assets required for it—assets that were also needed to fend off the other two developing invasions. Yet, except for the restrictions on helicopters, he did not interfere; in fact, he allowed some B-52 strikes to be used in support of the operation. He also directed that his staff be continuously briefed on the details of the efforts.[9]

That afternoon, Anderson flew to Da Nang in General Marshall's jet. There he was scheduled to meet with numerous Army, Marine, and Air Force personnel who had been working in the ongoing operation. There was lots to discuss. He walked in on a briefing attended by all of the participants, to review the situation to date. Capt. Fred Boli started the meeting by briefing what his forces had and had not been able to do. Then he left the gathering to lead several of his A-1s back to Nakhon Phanom. The next day Boli was flown to Saigon, so that he could brief General Marshall on the attempts.[10]

Lieutenant Commander Crowe from the Jolly Greens briefed their part of the mission. He was impressed with the effort and cooperation being put forth by every one involved. Capt. Rick Atchison from the Nails suggested using a small OH-6 "Loach" helicopter at night to slip in for the pickup, but he was apprised of General Abrams's directive forbidding any more helicopter attempts. Then Col. Al Gray, commander of the U.S. Marine force aboard ships off the coast, entered the room and made an interesting proposal. Rick described the scene: "Then in walked a Marine colonel—I will never forget him. He was a short stocky guy, built like a fire hydrant. Basically, his conversation was, 'I understand you have people you want taken out?' 'Yes sir we do.' 'Well I have a boat load of guys that would love to do something like that.' We showed him where they were."[11]

That sounded promising. But then Anderson stood up and informed them all that he and his small team had been given the mission. Quickly, he laid out the basic plan. He would take his group forward as far as possible through the 3d ARVN's area and attempt to move along the river to pick up Bat 21 Bravo and Nail 38 Bravo. Covey 282 Alpha would also be moved south to the river for rescue. Because of his position farther to the north, he would be last. Each of the survivors would have to be moved to the pickup sites, and Anderson coordinated with the FACs from Da Nang to pass messages to each one to reposition. They were doing most of the SAR work now: Pave Nail sorties to Military Region 1 were being reduced. The Pave Nail fleet, both aircraft and aircrews, were stretched to the limit and were needed for other SARs going on in the theater.[12]

Obviously the survivors could not be told in clear terms on their survival radios how they were to move or where. So the commanders of their parent units were contacted and asked to prepare a message based on each survivor's background that would clearly tell him to move to a specific location but would be understood only by him. Since Mark Clark was right by the river, his movement would be the easiest. He was told, "When the moon goes over the mountains, become Esther Williams and get in the Snake and go from Boise to Twin Falls." Clark had to have the message repeated several times before he understood, and then he could not remember whether Boise was east or west of Twin Falls. So they told him to "go to Eglin" (Air Force Base in Florida). That made sense. Mark had already decided that if he was not rescued after ten days, he was going to get in the river and take his chances on floating out.[13]

Bilk 11 relayed the message to Hambleton. He told him that they were going to take him down to the Suwannee, and that when he got there, he was to make like Esther Williams and Charlie the Tuna. Hambleton was flabbergasted. He called Bilk 11 back and asked him what he had been smoking. It was the "damnedest thing that I had ever heard!" Bilk 11 repeated the message and told him to think about it. Hambleton asked him, "Why Charlie the Tuna?" Bilk replied, "Because nobody ever catches Charlie the Tuna!" Then Hambleton figured it out.[14] But Hambleton's movement was going to be more difficult than Clark's. He was over one kilometer from the river and had to move either through or around villages and enemy positions. Yet in checking with his squadron back at Korat, the planners at 3d ARRG discovered that Hambleton was an avid golfer with a precise memory of golf courses. So they coordinated with his squadron mates to move him to the river using a series of specific golf-course holes—each representing a specific heading and distance.[15]

Needless to say, this made for some very strange radio calls from Bilk 11 to the survivors that evening. He had to repeat them several times, but finally Bat 21 Bravo and Nail 38 Bravo understood. Bat 21 Bravo began moving to the river. Over the next two days, he would "play" a total of nine "holes" and move through several fields and a village to reach the river.[16]

Covey 282 Alpha's situation was more complicated. He was literally surrounded by constantly moving enemy units. The planners hoped to be able to move him to the Mieu Giang River to be picked up by the team. Of the three, he was the youngest and in excellent physical condition. Hopefully he could best stand the ordeal.[17]

In the command centers at Seventh Air Force in Saigon and all of the other rescue headquarters, the various staff personnel and controllers monitored this amazing drama with fascination. The three survivors were becoming celebrities, especially the fifty-three-year-old navigator. Everybody followed every detail with intense interest. They knew that a dramatic story was unfolding in front of them, and they did not want to miss any of it. The survivors had their own cheering sections in Saigon, Da Nang, and Nakhon Phanom.

At Da Nang Anderson began to plan his small team. It would consist of five Vietnamese commandos and perhaps one other American. He paid a visit to the Naval Advisory Detachment (NAD) there at Da Nang. NAD was another cover for MACSOG. In reality it was the Maritime Studies Group (MACSOG-37), responsible for covert maritime operations conducted now almost exclusively by the South Vietnamese Coastal Security

Service. Through the South Vietnamese, Anderson co-ordinated for the team of sea commandos. They would be commanded by Lieutenant Tho, a "superb, hard charging guy."[18]

From there, Anderson called down to Saigon to STDAT 158 and talked to Lt. Cdr. Craig Dorman about an American to accompany the team. Dorman was in a tough spot. He was in the process of shutting down the NAD up at Da Nang and could not spare his only American still assigned up there. Additionally, all of his operators assigned in Saigon were scheduled to return to the United States in three days. But sitting in his office at that exact moment was a young Navy SEAL, Lt. Tom Norris. Norris was currently assigned to STDAT 158 and was involved in training the Vietnamese in sea-commando operations. Previously, Tom had been on a tour in South Vietnam with SEAL Team Two and spoke some Vietnamese. He had several more months left on his tour.

Norris had grown up in Maryland, where he had wrestled for four years on the varsity team at the University of Maryland. Physically, he was as tough as one man could be and had the reflexes of a cat. He had joined the Navy in 1968 with a desire to be a fighter pilot, but he had been washed out of the flying program at Pensacola. While waiting for reassignment, he had run across a recruiting pamphlet for the SEALs. It sounded challenging and exciting, so he signed up. It was a perfect fit.

All of this training combined with his in-country experience meant that he was the right man for this job. Anderson knew Norris slightly from some missions run in the Mekong Delta. He and Dorman sensed the match and made their decision. Norris was on the next plane to Da Nang.[19]

That evening the team gathered. Lieutenant Colonel Anderson had spent the day coordinating the mission through MACV, Seventh Air Force, First Regional Assistance Command, and the Vietnamese I Corps. He briefed the team on the mission, carefully covering the enemy threat and the extent of their advance into South Vietnam. As Norris listened, he felt that the mission had a good chance of success. The NVA were so preoccupied with achieving their objectives, he thought, that they would not give much importance to a few downed fliers. They were more concerned with beating the ARVN, and a small ground team would have a reasonable chance of slipping in and out.[20]

Because of the intensity of the ongoing ground battle, Anderson stated that they would proceed to the northwesternmost friendly position along the Mieu Giang River, set up an observation position, and wait for Bat 21 Bravo and Nail 38 Bravo to float down to them. Under no circumstances would they move more than one kilometer into enemy-controlled territory.[21]

Until that moment, Lieutenant Norris had never directly worked with Lieutenant Colonel Anderson, and he only knew two of the Vietnamese. He listened to the briefing very carefully and chafed at the concept of the operation. It was obvious to him that Anderson was not familiar with small-team water operations. To Norris, the plan was much too restrictive: he liked to work independently. The SEALs were accustomed to being given a mission and maximum rein to carry it out. He felt that the mission would be very difficult, but that they would get it done. Afterward, Lieutenant Tho cornered him and asked him what he thought of the plan. Norris told him not to worry, that once they got out on their own, they would do what they needed to do to accomplish the mission and tell Anderson what he wanted to hear. Norris had a stubborn streak, and it was beginning to show.[22]

10

★

This phase of the rescue says volumes
about the nobility and ingenuity of man
when the chips are really down.
Lt. Cdr. Jay Crowe

Battles—Large and Small

ON 9 APRIL, activity picked up on the ground. The
NVA force that had been building up in the Cam
Lo area attacked to the east along Route QL-9. They
were met by the 20th Armor and 5th Ranger Group,
both under the operational control of the 1st Armor
Brigade, about six kilometers west of Dong Ha. In a
battle that lasted several hours, the friendly units used
naval gunfire, airstrikes, and the direct fire of their main
tank guns to stop the attack before it could gain any
ground.[1]

The ground commanders in the area declared a tactical
emergency, meaning that they needed immediate help.
Captain Icke, Bilk 11, was scrambled from Da Nang in

his intrepid O-2 to support the ARVN. But before he could arrive overhead, the ground situation stabilized and he was diverted to work in support of the SAR operations. As he orbited and talked to the survivors, he watched and dodged more SAM launches. One of the missiles hit a B-52; the aircraft was seriously damaged but landed at Da Nang.[2]

At almost the same time, the NVA also launched an attack against Fire Base Pedro, to the south. The day before, the 6th Vietnamese Marine Battalion had taken over defense of the position from a Ranger battalion. Upon arriving, they were advised that an attack was imminent. They were ready: the battalion commander, Major Tung, had learned from watching the NVA. He moved the majority of his battalion off of the fixed fire support base and dispersed it along a battle line. Then he devised a combined-arms plan, including the use of land mines, artillery, tanks, and airstrikes, to stop the enemy force.

The battle for Pedro started at about sunrise. NVA tanks charged right into the bunkers of the base and methodically began destroying them. The Marines counterattacked, but the enemy seemed to be gaining the momentum. Then the low clouds partly broke, and two VNAF A-1s were able to get in and destroy four enemy tanks. The NVA had moved in antiaircraft guns with the attacking units, and they shot down one of the VNAF planes. The pilot was killed.

Some NVA tanks attempted to bypass Pedro and became entangled in the minefield. Simultaneously, a counterattack force of mounted infantry and tanks from Ai Tu struck them. Using well-coordinated artillery, airstrikes, and direct fire, they routed the NVA force and blunted the enemy's effort to drive deep into the ARVN rear.[3]

These two ARVN actions were significant. For the first time since the beginning of the offensive, ARVN units had stopped and defeated major NVA units. And both had been almost exclusively Vietnamese actions. In the Route 9 action, 653 enemy soldiers were reported killed and twenty-four tanks destroyed or captured. At Pedro, twenty-two more tanks were destroyed or captured, eighty-five crew-served weapons were seized, and 424 enemy soldiers were killed.[4] In both battles, friendly losses were minimal.

Significant actions were also taking place in the air. Rockly Smith and Rick Atchison were back flying yet another mission in the continuing effort for the three survivors. While orbiting over them, they observed a large column of tanks coming down QL-1 toward Dong Ha. They immediately reported this through secure voice radio, and a few minutes later, six B-52s were diverted to catch the NVA in the open. Long strings of bombs devastated the enemy column.[5] Later, the province chief for that area reported that three artillery pieces and twenty-seven tanks had been destroyed. He had also seen large explosions for thirty minutes.[6] Thus, on this one day the enemy lost seventy-three tanks. The defense was stiffening.

While these battles were raging, Anderson and his team were helilifted to 3d ARVN Division headquarters. There he briefed the commander, Brigadier General Giai, on the operation. The general was very pessimistic about the operation and made it clear that he could not guarantee their safety. Norris also noted that, given the size of the battle in which he was engaged, he was not too concerned about three downed airmen. But the general did agree to provide them transportation to his forwardmost unit. This was a platoon of Rangers supported by three M-48 tanks from the 20th Armor, positioned along QL-9 to keep an eye on the Cam Lo bridge.[7]

From there they traveled to the headquarters of the 1st Armor Brigade near Dong Ha. They met with the commander and his senior U.S. adviser, Lt. Col. Louis Wagner, who gave them a comprehensive briefing on their situation. They exchanged a set of frequencies and codes and decided how best to proceed with the "ball game." The next morning they moved by armored personnel carrier (APC) to the forward location. Anderson did not like what he found: the platoon consisted of about twenty soldiers under the command of a young and obviously scared second lieutenant. The position itself was strong. It consisted of an old French bunker on top of a small hill overlooking Cam Lo and the river. The tanks were dug in, covering QL-9, but each only had three rounds of main-gun ammunition. Out from the position about 150 yards were the hulks of three burned-out T-54 tanks, remnants of the previous day's battles.

The Vietnamese troops were tired and hungry. Wisely, Anderson had brought extra rations for just this contingency: he needed to establish a quick rapport with these troops. But when he explained his mission to the Vietnamese lieutenant, the latter wanted no part of it. Anderson, who could speak Vietnamese, stated that he had immediate access to airstrikes if any sizable threat developed. He then threatened to shoot anyone who deserted the position. As the Vietnamese troops were digesting all of that, Anderson got on the radio to his covering FAC and had him tell Bat 21 Bravo and Nail 38 Bravo to plan on a pickup that night.

By nightfall they were ready to begin the operation. Anderson contacted the survivors to make sure that they were moving. Hambleton was getting weak; Nail 38 Bravo was the closest to the team and would be first. He was instructed to be ready to get in the water and let the current carry him down. Lieutenant Norris took his team and began moving to the river. But the area was heavily patrolled by NVA troops, so the going was very slow. Anderson and his team of Rangers positioned themselves farther downstream to catch Clark if he got by Norris.[8]

Movement had to be very precise, because Anderson had pre-planned both airstrikes and artillery to disrupt enemy forces in the area. Both teams had to pause several times during their movement because of enemy patrols. Norris initially moved his team to the river to test the water for temperature and current. He decided that it was too strong for the Vietnamese to swim against and that they would have to move overland. He also decided that they would go beyond the one-kilometer restriction that Anderson had given them. But as he began to move through the fields, he became concerned when he saw a column of NVA tanks, trucks, and support vehicles move down across the Cam Lo bridge and turn east along QL-9. As the column approached, he debated calling in an airstrike on it. But approximately five hundred meters west of his position, the vehicles turned off on a side road and proceeded south.[9]

Norris and his team had to skirt numerous NVA patrols and positions as they moved generally parallel to the river. The enemy security was uncharacteristically lax, and the soldiers were easy to see even in the dark. But the team still had to move slowly and carefully, because they could not afford to give up the element of surprise. They traveled about two kilometers before they finally set up an observation point on the river and began to wait for Nail 38 Bravo. The position gave the team good cover while also allowing them excellent visibility of the river. Norris had two of his Vietnamese go down to test the water and wait for the first survivor. He had one of the ships on the gun line occasionally fire an illumination flare into the area for light. Now they had to just sit and wait.

As directed by the FAC overhead, Clark had gotten into the water and begun his journey. He had not gone too far when one side of his life preserver snagged on a branch and inflated. The sudden sound horrified him, but it did not draw any enemy response. Fortuitously, it was just enough to keep his head above water while the rest of his body was hidden. He also wore his mosquito net over his head as camouflage. But while passing through the rapids, he got caught in some debris along the shore. The current forced him underwater and he lost his footing. To keep from drowning, he quickly inflated the other side of the preserver, which brought him back to the surface. It also helped him to decide to get out and walk for about one hundred yards. Then he got back in the water. He figured that the distant flares were for the benefit of the pickup team and that he did not have much farther to go.[10]

Sometime between 2:00 and 3:00 A.M., Norris heard and then saw Clark floating down with the current. The water was cold and the survivor was breathing hard. At the same time, an NVA patrol passed between him and the cold and tired Mark Clark. Norris could not move; he had to let Clark pass by. The patrol consisted of six soldiers. Norris immediately considered killing them, but again, he did not want to make his presence known. So he let them pass off to the west. But after the patrol had cleared, he could no longer see Clark. So he slipped into the water and attempted to swim after him. After a few hundred yards, he could not find his target. He got out of the water and proceeded to patrol along the south bank, back as far as his team. Still he made no contact. He quickly reported the situation to Anderson.[11]

Anderson promptly called Clark and ordered him to the south shore. He then directed Norris to begin patrolling to the east. Additionally, he requested a situation update from Norris. Norris did not feel like explaining the situation, so he acknowledged Anderson's directive, turned off his radio, and moved out with his team. He got back in the water while the commandos searched the shore. This was a meticulous, drawn-out process, since the river had areas of twisting rapids and heavy undergrowth. But as dawn approached, Norris rounded a bend and noticed movement near a sunken sampan. He knew that it was Clark and called him by name.

Clark did not realize who Norris was. Instinctively he moved for cover. Norris tells the story: "He had no idea who I was. I don't even think that he got a good sight of me, he just heard something and went for cover. So I started talking to him. I took off my hat, put my gun behind me, and started telling him who I was. I gave him . . . you know, when a pilot goes down he has a series of codes that he leaves, something only he or his family would know. That's how you identify who you are when you come up on the radio, to show him you are not a bad guy. I used that to talk to him and slowly his head came up from behind the sampan and he realized that I was an American. He stood up and there was relief in his eyes."[12]

Norris rendezvoused with the rest of his team and notified Anderson that Clark had been recovered. He then gave the Air Force navigator a quick course in being an infantryman, since they had to thread their way back through enemy territory to the platoon location. Upon arriving back at the bunker, Clark was given some first aid and food. An APC arrived from the brigade to medevac him to Dong Ha. From there, he was flown by helicopter to Da Nang.[13]

At 10:15 A.M., the 3d ARVN Division Tactical Operations Center (TOC) received the following message: "1Lt MARK N CLARK, USAF . . . 23d TAC air SPT SQK, arrived Tm 155 location accompanied by LTC WAGNER, SA, 1st ARMD Bde. Lt. CLARK, downed Pilot, was recovered by team on night of 10 Apr."[14]

One survivor down, two to go. Anderson thought that the mission had gone fairly smoothly. Norris did not tell him how far west they had gone or the number of enemy patrols or tanks they had observed. He also did not mention that for most of the time he had had his radio turned off. Norris, when given a mission, liked to do things his way, with minimal supervisory interference. When queried about some missed radio calls, he said that he was having some problems with his radio.[15]

Anderson next turned his attention to planning the pickup of Bat 21 Bravo that night. He gave the FACs targets that he wanted struck in preparation. He spotted another tank column crossing at Cam Lo and had it attacked. Three tanks were destroyed, and several trucks were left burning. Meanwhile, Bilk 11 came back on station for yet another sortie in support of the SAR. Anderson had him inform Hambleton that Anderson was now on the radio, and his call sign was Leatherneck. Bilk 11 also told Hambleton to stay by the river with his eyes open and not be surprised at anything he saw coming down the *klong* (river).

As Bilk 11 was overhead, the NVA struck back: NVA artillery began to fall around the position. The first round was well over their heads; several of the ARVN laughed at the inaccuracy. But Norris and the Vietnamese lieutenant began shouting for the troops to take cover. Then the rounds began to impact squarely on the position. These were accompanied by B-40 rockets and mortars. Several soldiers went down with serious wounds. Norris and the lieutenant jumped up and began directing the soldiers into protective positions and ordering them to begin firing back at the enemy infantry, but the ARVN began to panic. Anderson had to threaten again to shoot deserters to keep them in their positions.[16]

Bilk 11 was still orbiting overhead. Anderson called him and told him that he needed an immediate airstrike. Prior to the arrival of the strikers, Captain Icke had directed artillery on the enemy. Then his fighters arrived, and Icke led them in. The airstrike stopped the infantry attack, silenced the mortars, and restored ARVN confidence.[17] But the attack did take a toll on the friendly force. Lieutenant Colonel Anderson, while out trying to rally and calm the ARVN, was himself hit. Additionally, Lieutenant Tho was seriously wounded in the arm, and many of the Rangers and one other sea commando were killed or injured. Lieutenant Norris called for APCs to come and medevac the wounded. All of them were evacuated; a helicopter picked up Anderson and Tho and flew them to Da Nang.[18]

Lt. Col. Andy Anderson was transferred back down to a hospital in Saigon. But he could not keep his mind off of the mission. He knew that Norris was in a tough position. The next day he climbed out of the window of his room and talked General Marshall into using his T-39 to fly him back to Da Nang. From there he intended to return to the site of the operation.

His concern was well placed, for Norris was in dire straits. He only had three commandos, none of whom spoke much English. His covering force was badly beaten up and low on ammunition. His survivor had been out nine days now and was very weak. Norris checked with him: he was making progress to the river, but slowly. He was not going to last much longer.

Throughout the rest of the day, Norris and his team planned and prepared to move out that night and snatch Hambleton. Just before sunset, they watched a column of tanks and trucks move west from near Hambleton's original position across the Cam Lo bridge and proceed east along QL-9 toward their position. Norris was surprised by all of this activity, but the Vietnamese Rangers said that it had been going on every night for a week.

After dark, Norris set out with his team of three. But two of his troops began to balk: they did not want to go through such a concentration of enemy regulars for an American. In fact, one stated that he was no longer going to follow an American just to rescue another American. It was a tense moment. In a firm tone, Norris explained to them that he was going to proceed and that they were safer staying together as a group. They reluctantly stayed with him. Norris led them to a position about three and a half kilometers northwest and set up an outpost to watch for the survivor to move to him.

But Bat 21 Bravo had notified the orbiting FAC that he had reached the river and just could not go any farther. Norris could occasionally hear Hambleton, but his descriptions of his location were confusing. So Norris began a search along the shore back toward the platoon position. But he could not make contact, and as dawn approached, he returned his team to the bunker. There he dropped off the two reluctant commandos and returned with PO Nguyen Van Kiet to the river. They grabbed a sampan and searched for two more hours, until it was too light to continue. Disappointed, they headed back to the bunker.[19]

Later that morning, the members of the 37th ARRS gathered outside the south hangar at Da Nang to hold a memorial service for their six lost comrades. Squadron mates eulogized each of the fallen and sang several hymns in their memory. It was hard not to notice the tears as the brave crewmen and pararescuemen sang, "Lord guard and guide the men who fly."[20]

During the day, Norris and his team rested. He had some extra supplies brought for his troops and some paddles for a sampan. Bilk 11 was back overhead; he plotted Hambleton's new position. The tired and weak survivor had only moved fifty meters the night before. Two Sandy A-1s were also on station over him. While a B-52 strike was going in nearby, Sandy 01 came in and dropped a Madden survival kit to Hambleton, filled with food and other supplies. But it landed fifty meters past him and slightly uphill, and he was too weak to climb up and get it. Instead, he came out on a sandbar in the river and began waving a white handkerchief. Captain Icke could not believe what he was seeing: he told Hambleton to get back under cover. The Sandy pilots also saw him and dropped another kit. But he could not reach that one either. Concerned for his obviously failing condition, Icke and the Sandys considered trying another helicopter pickup with whatever they could get into the area. But once again they all agreed that it was too dangerous. They had to stay with the plan—but they did not have much time left.[21]

Hambleton had to come out soon or he was not going to make it. He simply could not move any farther. Norris sensed this, having monitored the conversations between Hambleton and the aircraft. He knew that he would have to go to Hambleton. His original orders had been to proceed no more than one kilometer beyond the bunker position and wait for the survivor to come to him. He had already gone well beyond that. Norris thought it all over, weighing the risks against the possibility of success. The stubborn, tenacious wrestler from Maryland decided to go for it. There really was no other choice. He talked it over with Petty Officer Kiet, the ranking South Vietnamese sea commando. Kiet would accompany him; the other two would remain behind.[22]

After dark the two of them set out, dressed as Vietnamese fishermen. They threaded their way to a bombed-out village on the river. There they found a sampan that was not damaged, and they jumped in and paddled upstream. Fortunately, it was a dark night. But they had to advance very cautiously, because they could hear enemy troops on both banks of the river. At one point Norris stopped along the bank for a map check.

Not ten meters away, he spotted two enemy soldiers sitting in a bunker—sound asleep.

Overhead, the FACs monitored their progress. As they moved up river, Norris constantly passed them targets along both banks; some of these were very significant. Coming around one bend, they were startled by the sound of many tanks starting up their engines. Apparently they had stumbled into an armor battalion assembly area.

Just beyond the tanks, they encountered a fog bank, which gave them added cover. They cautiously continued west until they began to emerge from the fog. To their horror, they discovered that they were directly under the Cam Lo bridge and could see troops crossing. They quickly did a U-turn and proceeded back downstream.

They slowly paddled back down the river and started a sweep of the shore. And then they found him, sitting in a clump of bushes. Hambleton, awake but partly delirious, recognized Norris as an American. Norris quickly checked him over for injuries. He had some minor cuts but was otherwise okay. He could walk but was very weak. Norris considered spending the day there and traveling the next night, but there was just too much enemy activity. So he and Kiet laid Hambleton in the sampan, covered him with some bamboo, and notified the FAC that they were coming out.[23] They had to get him out quickly, because dawn was approaching. Norris also told the FAC to have lots of airstrikes available, just in case. Once again the FAC overhead was Bilk 11, Capt. Harold Icke. He had been on station since before dawn and had launched while the air base at Da Nang was under rocket attack.

The team slipped back into the water and headed downstream. A few hundred yards down, they encountered a patrol that began to shout and run after them. Kiet noted that they spoke with a North Vietnamese accent; he also noticed the white stars on their belt buckles.[24] Norris was becoming concerned: Hambleton was beginning to babble. An American voice would definitely give them away. Additionally, he could not use his radio, because this would also give away their identity. Fortunately, a bend in the river and heavy foliage along the bank allowed them to separate from the threat. But Norris was worried about the tank park and reported it to Icke. As he approached, though, he could see that the tanks were gone.[25]

A little farther on, a soldier on the north bank opened up on them with a heavy machine gun. There was no way around him, so Norris and Kiet paddled to the south bank, hid the boat in some vegetation, and called Bilk 11 for an airstrike. But the FAC did not have any fighters on station. American airstrikes had been reduced because the main air effort was now against North Vietnam. So Bilk 11 came up on the emergency frequency and called for any fighters available in the immediate area.[26]

The response was instantaneous. Garfish, a flight of five A-4s from the USS *Hancock* and led by Lt. Denny Sapp, answered the call. Bilk 11 directed them to his discrete strike frequency and talked them in to the target area. Once they were overhead, he explained the situation. The target was the guns hidden in houses on the north shore of the river. First he visually talked them on to the target. Then to confirm it, he marked the position with a smoke rocket. The Navy fliers had a solid fix on the guns, so Icke cleared them in hot. Antiaircraft fire was surprisingly minimal, so the fighters set up a low bombing pattern and dropped their bombs from three thousand feet. Having lots of gas, they dropped one bomb per pass and worked over the village with tremendous accuracy until the positions were obliterated. Norris was impressed and very thankful. He then gave the FAC all of the enemy positions that he had noticed along the river and told him to unload on them, too.[27]

The orbiting King rescue aircraft was also monitoring the action. They diverted two U.S. A-1s to Bilk 11, and he also had them strike the north shore. First Lt. Tim Brady was the wingman in this flight. Just new in the squadron, he was not yet checked out as a Sandy. He and his lead had been launched as a normal strike flight. But instead of carrying the normal load of Mk-82 500-pound bombs, they were carrying the "soft" load of ordnance, including napalm, rockets, and M47 smoke bombs. This ordnance was designed for pinpoint accuracy and could be dropped near unprotected friendlies without danger to those being supported. It was the ideal load to give Norris the last bit of support he needed. Under the direction of Bilk 11, they devastated what enemy positions remained on the north shore. The last thing they dropped was their M47 smoke bombs. This created a curtain that Norris could then use for cover. Above, Captain Icke pulled out his camera and snapped a picture of the airstrike.

As the A-1s were finishing, Norris and his crew got back in the boat and made the last dash back to the friendly outpost. But as they beached their boat, they began taking small-arms fire from the north shore. ARVN soldiers returned fire. Hambleton could not walk, so several of the Vietnamese helped him up the hill to the bunker.[28]

Upon reaching the bunker, Norris gave Hambleton some quick first aid and then called for an armored personnel carrier to carry him back to the brigade. While waiting for the APC, Hambleton had a cigarette given to him by one of the Vietnamese soldiers. The arrival of the APC was delayed by another mortar and rocket attack on the position; Bilk 11 used more A-4s and A-1s to beat off the heavy ordnance and the enemy troops on the north shore.

After the enemy fire ended, the personnel carrier arrived and carried Hambleton and Norris and the remnants of his team back to Dong Ha. A waiting helicopter then lifted Hambleton back to Da Nang.[29] There he was accosted by a news team. The weak and dazed survivor was asked by the reporter about all that had been done to rescue him. His answer was terse: "It was a hell of a price to pay for one life," he said. "I'm very sorry."[30] Concurrently, another reporter at Dong Ha found Norris and asked, "It must have been tough out there. I bet you wouldn't do that again!" The SEAL bristled. Then coldly he replied, "An American was down in enemy territory. Of course I'd do it again."[31]

Tom Norris and his team were then driven to Quang Tri. There they met with officers from the 3d ARVN Division and briefed them on all of the enemy positions that they had observed.[32] In the meantime, the third survivor, Covey 282 Alpha, had not been able to move through the enemy units to rendezvous with the team along the river. Consequently, Norris and the remnants of his team returned to Da Nang and began to work up an alternative plan to get 1st Lt. Bruce Walker.

So it was done. After eleven and a half days trapped behind enemy lines, Bat 21 Bravo, Lt. Col. Iceal Hambleton, was returned to friendly control. But the cost was high. Among the soldiers and airmen, ten men were killed working or supporting the SAR; one other, like Hambleton, was rescued; two were captured but later released; and one, First Lieutenant Walker, was still evading. On the ground, several members of the recovery team, including Anderson, were injured. Six more aircraft were shot down, and numerous others were damaged, some so badly they would never fly again. More than eight hundred strike sorties, including B-52s, were flown in direct support of this rescue.[33]

For his part in the operation, Petty Officer Kiet was awarded the U.S. Navy Cross, the only Vietnamese of the war to be so honored.[34] For the rescue of the two fliers, Lt. Tom Norris, the stubborn wrestler from Maryland, would be awarded the Medal of Honor by President Gerald Ford on 3 April 1976.[35]

11

When the smoke had cleared, his body was gone.
1st Lt. Mickey Fain

Bruce Walker

WHILE THE ORIGINAL OBJECTIVE had been accomplished, some loose ends had to be taken care of. On the following day, 14 April, the Cam Lo bridge was bombed; the strike resulted in a twenty-foot cut on the bridge and several gaping craters on the approaches.[1] Most important, Covey 282 Alpha, 1st Lt. Bruce Walker, was still on the ground. Daily the FACs orbited over him for both protection and encouragement. Also on 14 April, A-1s dropped a Madden survival kit to him full of food, water, another weapon, and codes to use to call targets to the FACs above.[2]

The weather was steadily improving, but the NVA were as lethal as ever. Their SAMs had quieted down a bit and their supplies were depleted, from both heavy use and the efforts of the Navy and Air Force strike flights that were hunting them down. But their gunners were still up and active. A few hours after the survival kit was dropped to Walker, a Navy F-4J of fighter squadron 114 from the *Kitty Hawk,* call sign Linfield 203, was downed by antiaircraft guns while attacking NVA forces just a few kilometers south of Bat 21 Bravo's former position. The FAC who was working the mission, Covey 244, saw rounds hit the aircraft. He did not observe either crewmember eject before the aircraft impacted the ground in a huge fireball. As per standard procedure, he contacted King to report still another loss south of the DMZ. But because of the continuing series of events in the area and the fact that neither crewmember had been observed ejecting, SAR forces were not launched, and after a short while, the search effort was terminated. It was another success for the North Vietnamese air defenders.[3]

Upon his return to Da Nang, Lieutenant Norris immersed himself in the planning for Bruce Walker's rescue. Originally he had been told that Walker was to be moved to the west into the foothills for a helicopter pickup. But Norris argued for an effort similar to the one he had just concluded for Hambleton and Clark. When Walker could not move south for the pickup, Norris suggested moving him to the east in segments, under the cover of darkness. Then Norris would go in again along one of the streams or over the beach to recover the pilot.[4]

First Lt. Mickey Fain also became heavily involved in the effort to rescue Walker. Since the shootdown he had flown at least one mission each day to cap him. He had put in an average of four airstrikes a day in support of the effort.[5]

On 16 April Walker was still located approximately six kilometers northeast of Hambleton's original position. He was constantly calling targets to the FACs. But it was obvious that he could not move any farther south: the enemy forces were too heavy. The planners concurred with Norris and decided that his best chance was to move to the northeast to the coast. That afternoon Walker was directed through the FACs to move back near his original position so that another Madden kit could be dropped to him the next day. He complied with the directions. But the next day, the A-1 could not get in for the drop because of the intense enemy ground fire. There were just too many NVA troops in the area. So to preclude revealing Walker's position, the drop was canceled.

That day the planners decided on the plan to get Walker out. He was told to rest where he was that day and the next, 18 April, and to be prepared to move on the evening of the eighteenth. The first leg of his journey would have him crossing route QL-1. Then he would be moved only at night, in increments determined by enemy activity and by his condition, through the sand dunes to the coast.[6] He would have constant FAC cover the whole way. Walker acknowledged the plan and settled in for the night. Since he would not be moving, no FAC would be overhead to baby-sit him that night; he would be contacted at first light. Consequently, it was not until the next morning that the rescue forces discovered that Walker had his own plans.

Late in the evening of 17 April, Walker started moving. He crossed QL-1 and kept going through the sand dunes. Late that night he took a break along a dike and was discovered by an elderly Vietnamese man. Taken by surprise, Walker shook hands with him and tried to befriend the man. His name was Ta Van Can. But he spoke no English, and Walker knew no Vietnamese. Nevertheless, Walker, nervous but in good health, was able to convey the idea that he wanted Can to help him. He showed the Vietnamese man his military identification card and offered him silver coins. Can, who could only communicate through hand signals, refused the money. After a few hours, Walker got up and began moving swiftly to the east. He signaled for Can to come along, but the older man could not quite keep up with the scared American.

Can's wife had also seen Walker. When her husband left with him, she went to the Viet Cong cadre commander in the Lam Xuan hamlet and reported the American evader. He sounded the alarm, and local forces began to pursue the pilot.[7] Walker was in deep trouble, and there was no FAC overhead to help him.

First Lt. Mickey Fain was the first FAC on station at sunrise and heard the panic in Walker's voice as he arrived overhead. But first he had to find him: Walker had moved over seven kilometers to the east. He had to use his mirror to mark his position. Fain was shocked at how far he had moved. Then he saw the enemy soldiers; they were indeed closing in.

On the ground, the Viet Cong were pursuing Walker across a rice paddy. They observed the aircraft arriving overhead and were wary of the potential threat. But they wanted to capture the American: they were under strict orders from higher headquarters to do so whenever possible. Fain concocted a plan to move Walker to the canal approximately three hundred meters to the east in the crazy hope that that would somehow make a difference. Briefly he considered landing his small O-2 on a nearby stretch of road, but rejected this as suicidal.

Fain had a flight of four F-4s overhead, call sign Lacey, and they were carrying Mk-82 500-pound bombs. He tried to use the fighters to ward off the VC troops. But as they closed in on Walker, Mickey had to restrict the use of the high-explosive bombs for fear of injuring the survivor.[8] He called in another FAC in an OV-10, Capt. J. D. Caven, to use his .30-caliber machine guns to strafe in close to Walker. Finally he took his own lightly armed aircraft down to dangerously low altitudes to personally engage the enemy troops himself. He made repeated passes at treetop level, firing his white phosphorus rockets in the process. Enemy soldiers were firing at him with all types of weapons, and Fain's aircraft was damaged by the ground fire. He quickly called King and told him that he was going to need a replacement very soon. King called the rescue center at Da Nang for another FAC.

In spite of the airstrikes, several of the guerrillas were able to move close to Walker. They could see him obviously trying to move toward the river. He was talking on his radio and had his signal mirror in his other hand. They wanted to capture him, but the airstrikes and rockets were holding them at bay. Finally they decided that if he could not be captured, he had to be killed. They began shooting at him, and every time Walker used his radio, Fain could hear the increasing fire directed at the survivor. Walker went to ground and called to Bilk 35, "They are shooting at me, babe, they are shooting at me!" Those were his last words.[9]

As he made his passes, Fain could see Walker lying in

the grass. What he could not see was that in the swirling confusion, one of the guerrillas, Vo Van De, crawled up to within six meters and shot Walker with six rounds from his AK-47.[10] Unaware of Walker's fate, Fain noticed that he was no longer talking on the radio. Repeated calls to him elicited no response. Fain continued to work Lacey flight until their bombs were expended and then fired all of his rockets. The smoke from his rounds drifted over Walker, obscuring him from view. When it cleared, Fain could no longer see him in the grass. With other FACs yelling at him from above and with his fuel at critically low levels, he reluctantly turned the battle over to others and headed for Da Nang.

Capt. Harold Icke was scrambled to replace Fain over Walker. He never made contact with the survivor or saw his body. Yet he continued to orbit and, a few minutes later, heard Vietnamese voices on the emergency frequency. He surmised that the VC had killed or captured Walker and were playing with his survival radio. In fact, Vo Van De had done just that. He had taken the survival radio and mirror and carried them some distance before discarding them. Overhead, Icke put in some airstrikes and covered Walker's last position with BLU-52. When his fuel was depleted, he made the sad journey back to Da Nang.[11]

For the next two days, FACs continued to orbit the area to look and listen for Covey 282 Alpha, but their efforts were in vain. On 20 April the effort for 1st Lt. Bruce Walker was terminated.[12]

With the loss of Walker, Lt. Tom Norris's team was dissolved and he returned to his duties with STDAT 158. Sometime later he was identified to be a member of a residual force being considered for more operations of this type. It would consist of as many as 420 troops organized into three companies designed to search for and recover downed fliers throughout Southeast Asia. But Norris was skeptical. He did not feel that a Navy lieutenant would be given the authority to range throughout the theater, crossing national borders as necessary to rescue downed airmen. His skepticism was well placed, for the force was disapproved by the JCS as part of the American withdrawal from Vietnam.[13]

The SARs were over, but the ground war continued. As Bat 21 Bravo was being recovered, Brigadier General Giai, sensing that the NVA had run out of steam, ordered a counterattack. He wanted to reestablish a stronger position along the western front by recapturing Cam Lo, Camp Carroll, and Mai Loc. This operation, called Quang Trung 729, was to kick off on 14 April. But it was an offensive operation in name only. The troops, long in constant contact, did not have it in them to effectively attack. In spite of massive air support, the ground effort was ineffective: General Giai's command was mentally whipped. Endemic problems of command relationships, logistics, and communications finally began to take their toll. Subordinate commanders failed to carry out their orders to advance, citing all of these factors. They demanded more airstrikes, and it became a battle of attrition. General Giai slowly lost control of the situation.

The following week, the defense began to unravel. The commander of the 1st Armor Brigade, sensing another enemy advance from the west, unilaterally began pulling the 20th Armor back along QL-1 to deal with it. When the ARVN troops saw the tanks moving, they were seized with panic and broke and ran. The 3d ARVN

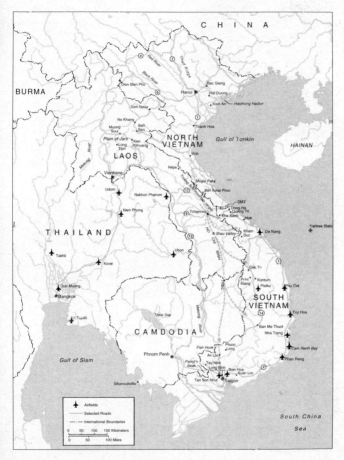

Southeast Asia

Maj. David Brookbank. As the ALO "adviser" to the 3d ARVN Division, he saw and experienced things that airmen rarely see and experience. Courtesy of U.S. Air Force

Bat 21 Bravo Lt. Col. Iceal Hambleton. Courtesy of U.S. Air Force

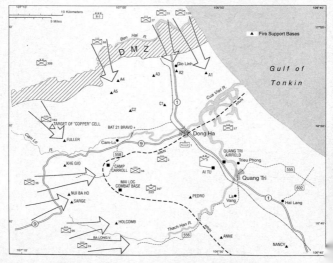

This map shows the situation on 2 April 1972.

A reconnaissance close-up of Bat 21 Bravo's (Lieutenant Colonel Hambleton's) position.
Courtesy of Col. Rick Atchison (Ret.)

The ubiquitous O-2 or Oscar Deuce of the Coveys of the 20th TASS at Da Nang Air Base. Courtesy of Robert F. Dorr

This EB-66C was assigned to the 42d TEWS at Korat Air Base, Thailand. It flew as Bat 21 on April 1972.
Courtesy of Don Logan

1st Lt. Bill Jankowski (Bilk 34) in fatigues, with 1st Lt. Mickey Fain (Bilk 35). Courtesy of Lt. Col. Bill Jankowski

Bilk 11, Capt. Harold Icke at Da Nang Air Base in 1972. Courtesy of Col. Harold Icke

★

The crew of Blueghost 39. Clockwise from top left: Sp5c. Jose Astorga (10A), Sp5c. Ronald Paschall (10B), WO John Frink (10D), 1st Lt. Byron Kulland (10C). Courtesy of families

Captain Mike L. Rosebeary, Blueghost 28. Courtesy of Lt. Col. Mike Rosebeary (Ret.)

The control capsule inside one of the "King" HC-130s. The atmosphere there was characterized by hours of boredom punctuated by periods of absolute panic when someone went down. Courtesy of the author

Nail 25, Capt. Rocky Smith celebrating his last flight as a Nail FAC at NKP Air Base, Thailand. Notice the Pave Nail laser pod under the belly of the aircraft. Courtesy of the author

Capt. Rick Atchison, backseater with Nail 25. Courtesy of Col. Rick Atchison (Ret.)

Capt. Fred Boli, Sandy 01. Courtesy of Col. Fred Boli (Ret.)

This is an A-1 Sandy aircraft. They dueled with the NVA guns.
Courtesy of Robert F. Dorr

Lt. Col. Bill Harris, commander of the 37th ARRS. He flew the second Jolly that attempted to pick up Bat 21 Bravo. Here, he is presenting an award to a young airman from his unit. Courtesy of Col. Bill Harris (Ret.)

Col. Cy Muirhead, commander of the 3d ARRG, making an award presentation to one of his young pararescuemen (PJs) in the summer of 1972. Courtesy of U.S. Air Force

Lt. Cdr. Jay Crowe (right) receiving awards for his Vietnam service. He flew the first Jolly (Jolly Green 65) that attempted to pick up Bat 21 Bravo. Courtesy of Capt. Jay Crowe (Ret.), U.S. Coast Guard

A reconnaissance photo mosaic of the search and rescue area. (1) Bat 21 Bravo. (2) Nail 38 Bravo. (3) Cam Lo Bridge and fording points. Courtesy of Lt. Col. Iceal Hambleton (Ret.)

One of the 37th ARRS Jolly Greens.
Courtesy of Robert F. Dorr

★

Capt. Peter Chapman, air-
craft commander, Jolly
Green 67. Courtesy of
Chapman family

1st Lt. John Call, copilot,
Jolly Green 67. Courtesy of
Call family

T.Sgt. Allen Avery, pararescueman. He was on his 256th
mission! Courtesy of Avery
family

Sgt. William Pearson,
pararescueman.
Courtesy of Pearson family

★

Sgt. James Alley,
photographer.
Courtesy of Alley
family

T.Sgt. Roy Prater, the flight
mechanic on Jolly Green 67.
Courtesy of Prater family

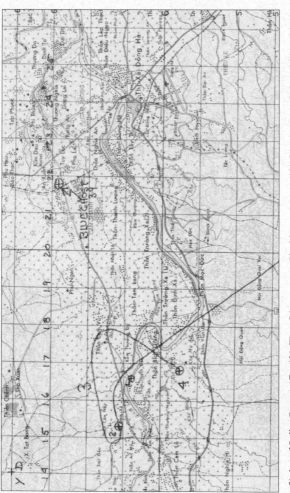

The flight of Jolly Green 67. (1) First Lieutenant Clark's position. (2) Lieutenant Colonel Hambleton's position. (3) "Turn south, Jolly, turn south!" (4) The crash site. The crash site of Blueghost 39 is in the upper right. Various sources

The burning wreckage of Jolly Green 67.
Courtesy of Gary Ferentchak

Lt. Col. "Andy"
Anderson. He led the
rescue team. Courtesy of
author

1st. Lt. Mark Clark (Nail
38 Bravo) upon his return
to NKP. Courtesy of
Mark Clark (Ret.)

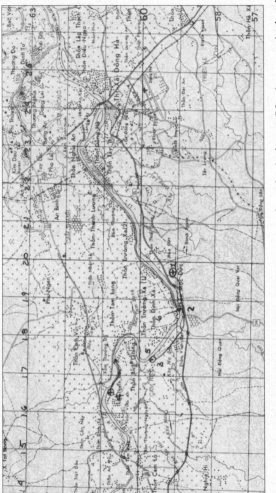

The rescue of 1st Lt. Mark Clark. (1) The ARVN outpost where the Anderson/Norris team waited and planned. (2) Norris spots the NVA tanks heading south. (3) Norris sets up an outpost looking over the river. (4) Clark leaves his position and begins floating down the river. (5) Clark passes Norris. (6) Norris heads back down the river and finds Clark. Various sources

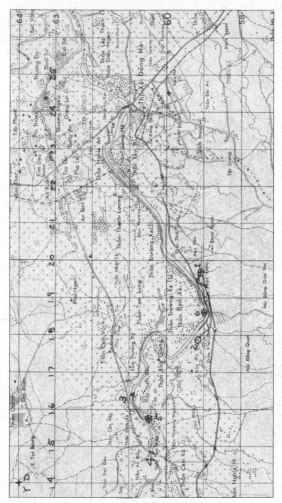

The rescue of Lt. Col. Iceal Hambleton. (1) The ARVN outpost. (2) Norris and Kiet launched upriver in a sampan. (3) They passed by an NVA tank unit, and (4) popped out of a fog bank under the Cam Lo Bridge. (5) Returning downriver, they found Hambleton. (6) They had to call in Garfish and the A-1s to silence the guns on the north bank and cover their dash to safety. Various sources

The A-1 airstrike that covered the escape of Norris, Kiet, and Hambleton. They are in a sampan just under the smoke. Courtesy of Col. Harold Icke

★

1st Lt. Bruce Walker at Da Nang Air Base in 1972. Courtesy of Walker family

U.S. Marine Corps 1st Lt. Larry Potts in 1972. Courtesy of DOD-FOIA

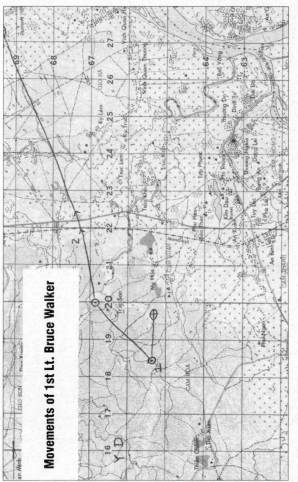

Movements of 1st Lt. Bruce Walker

(1) Initial attempts to move south were blocked by enemy forces. (2) Movement northeast for rescue by sea and the critical road crossing. (3) Run down by the Viet Cong cadre. Various sources

Navy Lt. Tom Norris (far right) receiving the Medal of Honor
from President Gerald Ford in April 1976.
Courtesy of Steve Keibler

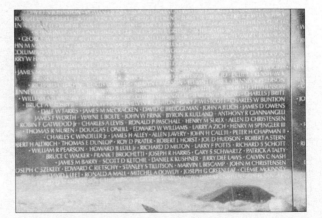

The Wall. This is where you will find them, on panel W-2.
The lost relay team at Firebase A-2, Bat 21, Blueghost 69,
Cavalier 70, Jolly Green 67, Covey 282, Linfield 203. The
names are all interwoven, just like the story.
Courtesy of author

Division was driven back and so badly mauled that it eventually ceased to function as a combat unit, although several of its attached units continued to perform admirably.[14]

But the South Vietnamese formations were driven back until, on 2 May, Quang Tri fell. A rout then ensued along QL-1. But finally, after two more days of intense fighting, the ARVN and Marines were able to dig in along the tiny My Chanh River, just north of Hue, and establish another shaky defensive line. This time the line held, despite ferocious NVA attempts to break it.

Thus the NVA had captured Quang Tri Province. But they would go no farther. In time the ARVN defenses would be reorganized: units would be rebuilt and new ones brought in. New commanders would be called forward to eventually lead a counterattack to recapture Quang Tri, a goal attained only after much heavy fighting and massive American air support. But the North Vietnamese Army would never be completely driven out. The Americans would leave, but NVA presence in South Vietnam was a reality that everyone would eventually have to accept.

The story of Bat 21 Bravo's rescue is a chronicle of his courage and of the heroic efforts of many to save him from the midst of that horrific, swirling ground and air battle. It is one story wrapped in many others, presented against the backdrop of larger desperate events that together made up the mosaic of that last year of the U.S. war in Vietnam.

But there is more to the story than the act of the rescue itself.

12

The real issue was—who was in charge.
Lieutenant Colonel Turley

Controversy

MANY OF THE GROUND participants still maintain that the U.S. Air Force efforts to rescue Bat 21 Bravo and the others in the midst of the raging and critical ground battle interfered with the actions of the South Vietnamese as they fought to fend off the invading forces from the North. Their complaints are threefold:

1. A no-fire zone imposed upon the ARVN by the Seventh Air Force for the operation of rescue forces severely impeded the ARVN's ability to employ airstrikes and artillery for a critical period.

2. Because of this restriction, a critical bridge at Cam

Lo was not destroyed, thus presenting the invading NVA an opportunity to advance across a natural barrier.[1]

3. Some Vietnamese commanders resented the fact that Americans seemed willing to devote more effort to saving one of their own than to supporting the struggling ARVN units in their hour of need.[2] These are serious charges and deserve to be considered singly.

Complaint I: The No-Fire Zone

When the JSARC received word that Bat 21 Bravo was down, they had just concluded a very complicated SAR for an entire AC-130 gunship crew (Spectre 22) that had gone down in southern Laos.[3] In fact, the last several months had been very busy with SARs occurring all over their area of responsibility. The commander and duty officers in Joker had not been briefed on the true impact of the invasion through the DMZ, and they had no feel for the ground battle. Therefore, in response to the shootdown of Bat 21 Bravo, the duty officers reacted automatically as they would to any SAR in the Southeast Asia region and immediately declared a no-fire zone to deconflict operations. This zone was designed to provide space for the rescue forces to work in without their having to worry about interference from other forces in the area—either ground or air—and to protect ground forces from the SAR effort. The SAR effort got first priority on airspace. Maj. Don Lunday from the JPRC, explained their use: "When you had a guy on the ground, you created a sterile zone around him . . . not purely a no-fire zone per se, but only the SAR forces put anything in there that is going to go in."[4]

In other words, it was standard practice to place a no-fire zone around a downed airman. However, later that same night, when the 3d ARVN Division questioned the size of the area, at twenty-seven kilometers in radius, and pointed out that it covered almost the entire area defended by the division, it was reduced. Eventually it was reduced to 5,000 meters, then to 2,700.[5] Lieutenant Colonel Gray at Da Nang continued his efforts to get it removed completely. But no commander in Military Region 1, including Major General Kroesen, the First Regional Assistance Command commander, could override the restriction.

So the advisers at Ai Tu took matters into their own hands. In fact, when they received the message, Lieutenant Colonel Turley remembers telling Brookbank, "Screw it, I am not going to do it!" His logic was straightforward: "I could not shut it [the artillery] down for one man. First of all, we were not the commanders. We were advisers. We did not assume that role. They [the Vietnamese commanders] maneuvered their ground forces, our job was to advise. Sometimes you are only 10 percent effective."

The commander of the Vietnamese Marine Brigade, Col. Ngo Van Dinh, overhead the conversation and asked the advisers for an explanation. When he realized what they were saying—that all of this was for just one man, after the Marines and ARVN had already lost thousands and were fighting for their lives—he held up one finger and, meaning no disrespect, said, "Just one?" The other Vietnamese began to spread the word, and Turley noticed the immediate effect on morale.[6]

Lieutenant Colonel Turley called a meeting of the advisers. Several had immediately contacted the First Direct Air Support Center or First Regional Assistance

Command headquarters. They had not been able to cancel the zone, but they had been able to roughly determine the survivor's location. Armed with that information, Turley drew a three-thousand-meter circle around him. He and the others then agreed that since they knew where the survivor was, they could go ahead and locally "allow" the Vietnamese batteries to fire without endangering Hambleton or, soon thereafter, Clark.[7] But in reality, the ARVN never stopped firing: their guns were in constant use. Against such a rampaging enemy force, it would have been suicide to stop firing. Any aircraft working in that area would have to work through both friendly and enemy artillery; the aircrews just did not know it.

The advisers really had no choice. First of all, as Turley noted, advisers at best had limited effectiveness in their role. Most American officers were junior in rank to the commander to whom they were attached. In most cases they lacked the vast combat experience of their counterparts, especially this late in the war. Very few were able to develop any credibility with the Vietnamese. But they did perform a most vital function. They became, in most cases, the conduits through which the ARVN and Vietnamese Marines could continue to draw upon American resources. They were the catalyst for procuring the American artillery, helicopters, naval gunfire, and airstrikes critical to defeating the NVA. Therefore, at a minimum, they had to be tolerated by the Vietnamese commanders.[8]

Also, the American advisers were reacting to the immediacy of the enemy attacks. They had to keep fighting; it was literally a matter of survival. But there is no indication that they were advised of the progress of the

SAR or that the survivors were moving so that they could adjust their fire. At one point, Mark Clark experienced an artillery barrage very near his position. The strike was targeted against NVA troops crossing the river and was noted in the 3d ARVN Division command log. Obviously, the advisers and commanders on the front lines had a different set of priorities than did Seventh Air Force.

And the timing of the no-fire zone was very critical: it was imposed at absolutely the worst possible moment. Throughout the day on 2 April, the battle had taken a series of dramatic turns: the armor attacks at Dong Ha, the blowing of the Dong Ha bridges, the surrender of Camp Carroll, the rerouting of the NVA armor to Cam Lo. Indeed, the battle was focused there. The action of Seventh Air Force at this exact moment was damaging. Lieutenant Colonel Turley summed up the feeling of those present in the division TOC:

At first glance, this unilateral rear area arrangement of giving the USAF control of all TAC air, naval gunfire, and artillery probably seemed like a rational decision to officers eighty kilometers from the battle lines. However, it was a near tragic decision for the 3rd ARVN Division, which at the time was near collapse from the unrelenting pressure of the North Vietnamese divisions. When viewed in relation to all of the events of the day, a worse decision could not have been made. Of equal significance, the USAF did not coordinate the activation of the "no fire zone" with the 3rd ARVN Division. . . . In essence, this restrictive fire plan would have put the 3rd Division's few remaining artillery batteries in a stand-down posture at a time when the NVA was attacking and winning all across the battlefield.[9]

Maj. Dave Brookbank, the ALO adviser, was more blunt: "With three enemy divisions plus heavy artillery striking the AO [area of operations], the 3rd ARVN was unable to return fire or request TAC air in the area. Some specific targets were struck after considerable delay in obtaining clearance. In my opinion this gave the enemy an opportunity unprecedented in the annals of warfare to advance at will. . . . This operation cost the 3rd ARVN dearly in not being able to fire at known targets of urgent tactical importance. . . . This particular area covered the center of the main NVA offensive thrust from the north at the Cam Lo crossing."[10]

To fight their battle, the commanders and advisers had to violate this restriction. At the very least, they had to expend time and effort at a critical point in the battle to deal with this command and-control problem—even as NVA tanks were bearing down upon them. This debacle caused the advisers to seriously wonder what the priorities were at Seventh Air Force at that critical stage of the war.

The root issue was command and control. At a critical juncture, staff elements many miles away were attempting to interfere in a ferocious tank battle for what appeared to those on the front lines a most specious reason, thereby taking away from a ground commander many of the assets he needed to fight his battle. To Lieutenant Colonel Turley, this was the greatest sin of all.[11] He had no quarrel with attempting a rescue; in fact, he was the one who had made the decision to dispatch the helicopters for the team up at Fire Support Base Alpha-2. But he had not stopped the war to do it. The effort was made in proportion to everything else that was going on at the time.

The actions of Seventh Air Force, in interfering with the local commander's efforts to win his battle, were unconscionable. Perhaps more significantly, the higher American headquarters was directing these restrictions at a lower-level Vietnamese headquarters. There is no record that the restrictions were coordinated in any way with the Vietnamese counterpart to Seventh Air Force: they were imposed arbitrarily. Turley saw the panic and fear of abandonment that this created in the eyes of the South Vietnamese. That was the real danger, the real damage, for it affected the fighting morale of the troops.

Then on 7 April, in response to the Covey 282 shoot-down, Seventh Air Force automatically imposed another large no-fire zone around First Lieutenant Walker and First Lieutenant Potts. Although it was rapidly reduced, the negative suspicions of the advisers and ARVN commanders were reinforced.

As noted, the JSARC also had priority on air assets for SAR missions. As the Bat 21 Bravo situation developed, they began utilizing assets as needed to support the effort. A-1s and HH-53s were moved to Da Nang from Nakhon Phanom, Thailand. Pave Nail OV-10s were brought in to take advantage of their special equipment, even though they would be working in the AO of another FAC squadron. Additionally, as many as ninety airstrikes a day were being diverted to the effort to suppress enemy forces enough for a rescue attempt to be made.[12] Col. Cecil Muirhead, the director of Aerospace Rescue, stated that more than eight hundred strike sorties were eventually used to support this series of SARs.[13]

Obviously, sorties being used to support the SARs could not be used in other places for other missions. The allocation flown in support of the ground units was reduced, and the advisers could see this happening. They needed that air as an integral part of the defense that they were mounting against the NVA.

But in the cases of Bat 21 Bravo, Nail 38 Bravo, and Covey 282 Alpha, the SARs were in the middle of the invading force. Therefore, any strikes flown on their behalf were hitting the same enemy that the 3d ARVN was attempting to fend off. In fact, from an airpower perspective, SAR support operations could be some of the most devastating attacks. Capt. Bill Henderson said that after he was captured, as he was being taken north, he saw wrecked equipment and dead and wounded soldiers everywhere. Capt. Rick Atchison pointed out that while on these SAR missions, the FACs destroyed enemy targets of every sort. In fact, U.S. Army advisers gave them target lists when they were at Da Nang, and while they were on orbit supporting the survivors, they attacked many of those targets.[14]

So in a left-handed way, the 3d ARVN was the beneficiary of this largesse. The shame of it was that the two efforts were not coordinated. No record exists of any attempts to do so. Quite obviously, Seventh Air Force did not stop flying support sorties for the ARVN while the SARs were being run; in fact, the units were still being allocated sorties every day—including B-52 strikes. But there is no record of the priority of missions. "We could possibly have taken advantage of [the SAR effort]," Brookbank said, "if only we had known. We knew that there were survivors, but we did not know the magnitude of the effort that was going on right in front of us."[15]

Lieutenant Colonel Turley was more specific. He acknowledged that the SAR forces hit many targets important to the battle, but the problem was timing. The 3d ARVN and supporting units had to fight the immediate battle; air sorties fragged to them were being used for that purpose. Many of the SAR-support airstrikes were hitting targets of less importance, targets that would not be part of the ground battle for several days and were therefore of less concern to the friendly ground forces. The air and ground efforts against the invaders were not combined and focused.[16]

Unfortunately, for a number of reasons, the Air Force crews were not aware of these developments, at least at this stage of the battle. First of all, they generally were not aware that the attack was imminent. Those few who were occasionally flying over North Vietnam could see the buildup just north of the DMZ. But mostly this was limited to the RF-4 reconnaissance crews and the fighters who escorted them. The vast majority did not initially know that what they were seeing was in fact a major invasion of massed troops. Most, like the FACs (Rocky Smith, Rick Atchison, and Gary Ferentchak) and the Sandys (Fred Boli and Don Morse), initially thought that what they were seeing were ARVN forces moving around. Likewise, the King and Jolly Green crews thought that they were heading out on easy runs over safe territory. Those at the squadron level were clearly taken by surprise by the bold enemy moves. Against them, at least, the NVA air defenses had their intended effect: the effectiveness of air attacks against the invaders was drastically reduced for the first few days.

But Seventh Air Force knew that the offensive was coming. It had received intelligence, both strategic and tactical, showing that something was brewing. Much of that information came from Washington, yet little of it was passed to the tactical units. Major General Marshall himself knew that this was not happening. He stated that they at Seventh Air Force complained about it; when asked to whom they complained, he responded, "To ourselves!" The aircrews paid for that oversight.[17]

Secondly, and more specifically, for the first few days, as the ground battle in Military Region 1 developed, the disparate participants were not given specific, detailed briefings on what was unfolding below them. Air Force intelligence was not geared up at this time to do it. One of the A-1 pilots explained this from the Sandy's perspective. When asked if he had been aware of the SAR's impact on the ground battle, Capt. Don Morse stated that he never got any specific briefings on the ground battle, nor was he ever asked to do anything specifically in support of the ground battle. He recalled: "It never occurred to me to ask about it. . . . Our objective was the guys [survivors] on the ground and that little circle of the battle—of course anything that we did to stop traffic coming down that road would have had some impact, and there was a lot of that, a lot of airstrikes, but no direct support of the friendlies, no. It wasn't discussed. It wasn't talked about. But that was fairly standard. The SAR was our business if you will, and the ground battle was something else. We really didn't cross the line much."[18]

At the same time and place, the 3d ARVN Division

and Seventh Air Force were fighting the same enemy, but for different objectives. During the period of the SARs, this division of effort meant that the invaders were not met with the concentrated power of coordinated and combined air and ground power at the critical place and time.[19] There is no way to calculate the cost in lives of this mistake.

Complaint 2: The Cam Lo Bridge

Once the Dong Ha bridges had been blown, the Cam Lo bridge remained as the only structure that would support heavy vehicles over the lower portions of the Mieu Giang River. The retreating 2d Regiment was assigned engineers to blow it, but in the heat of heavy battle, this was not done. With the concurrent fall of Camp Carroll, the NVA began moving their columns toward the bridge to seize it. By the time the ARVN commanders finally decided to destroy it, events had been overtaken by the Bat 21 Bravo SAR and no-fire zone. Even so, the bridge was bombed early on 3 April, but the airstrike was inconclusive. The flight of F-4s attacked it but missed with their 500-pound bombs. The VNAF A-37s struck it with their 250-pound bombs, but these weapons were not powerful enough to do any serious damage. The approaches were cratered, but the bridge was not dropped, and the enemy continued to use it throughout this period. In fact, one of the missions of the forward-most ARVN units was to watch the bridge, and enemy units were frequently seen crossing. As stated earlier, Lieutenant Norris and Petty Officer Kiet inadvertently slipped under it in the fog bank on the morning of 13 April, just prior to picking up Hambleton, and noted its use by personnel. It was not until the next day, the fourteenth, that the bridge was actually hit and cut.

But how important was the bridge, really? The ARVN commanders obviously thought that it was significant. They had initially scheduled engineers to destroy it during their retreat; apparently, they also ordered the VNAF to do it when the U.S. restrictions were in place. But the A-37s with 250-pound bombs were inadequate for the job. They wanted it dropped, but only the U.S. Air Force and Navy had the resources to do it. Unfortunately, at the time, those resources were going elsewhere.

Yet even with the bridge still intact, many units along the northern line reported enemy troops fording the river, and some also reported that vehicles were doing the same. There can be no doubt that the use of a major bridge across a natural barrier did give the enemy some tactical advantage, but photographs show that there was a ford right next to the bridge. Additionally, Lt. Col. Bill Camper, the adviser to the ill-fated 56th Regiment, reported that there were several other fording points along the river west of Cam Lo.[20]

ARVN commanders watched with dismay as the enemy built up its forces in the Cam Lo area. They also noted that some of these forces were coming from the west—south of the river. But press releases from the North Vietnamese during the offensive talked about the relentless drives eastward against the various fire support bases, and about how the "western gate" had been smashed open.[21] One North Vietnamese press release related their view of the battle for Cam Lo. Intercepted on 3 April, it stated: "Spearheaded by armor, the liberation fighters who had captured a string of enemy bases—Dong Ngo, Dong Toan, Ba Ho, Doi Tron, 'Fuller Base,' Hill 288, Cam Lo, Mai Loc—were rushing eastward with the force of a torrent. U.S. planes swarmed and tried to knock down the Thien Xuan bridge and a bridge spanning the Cam Lo River. But the U.S. pilots harassed by [w]ithering antiaircraft fire from the liberation forces dropped their bombs wantonly on the neighborhood."[22]

The Thien Xuan bridge was west of Camp Carroll on Route 9 and south of the river. It crossed a smaller stream that fed into the main river, and apparently it was of critical importance to the movement of the NVA forces. The target for the Copper cell of B-52s escorted by Bat 21 was just northwest of there. Additionally, a translated North Vietnamese document entitled *Collection of Sketches of Battles: Course Supplement, History of Military Arts,* published by the Republic of Vietnam's Ministry of Defense and released in 1986, indicates that the units that eventually drove back the ARVN along the river line were units that had entered from the west.[23] Perhaps the Cam Lo bridge itself was not that important.

Overall, then, it appears that there was some tactical interference with the ground battle. But how much? Several of the advisers of the Marine units and Major Brookbank cited the rescue operation in their after-action reports. Several claimed that it was a contributing factor to the eventual fall of Quang Tri.[24] However, Lt. Col. Louis Wagner, the senior adviser to the 1st Armor Brigade (the ARVN unit on the battle line nearest to the survivors), in his after-action report for this period, noted the SAR and no-fire zone but did not indicate any impact upon his unit's operations.[25] Col. Donald Metcalf, senior adviser to the 3d ARVN Division, made essentially the same comments in his subsequent writings.[26] Maj. Gen. Frederick Kroesen, the First Regional Assistance Command commander, did not even mention the SARs in his after-action report. Years later, when asked about this, he recalled the incident but stated that his only concern had been that it went on for so long.[27] ARVN general Ngo Quang Truong, the man who took over I Corps after the collapse at Quang Tri, did not mention the SARs in his Indochina monograph, *The Easter Offensive of 1972* (Washington, D.C.: U.S. Army, 1980).

So the results were mixed. Yes, there was interference at the tactical level. However, the SARs brought the 3d ARVN more airpower during the battle than they probably would have received on their own. The shame, of course, is that it was not coordinated with the ground battle. The ARVN commanders could not take advantage of it and in many cases, did not know that it was going on. Nail 59, on station on the night of 2 April in a Pave Nail OV-10, could easily have guided laser bombs to take out the Cam Lo bridge or any number of tanks at exactly the right time—but that was not why he was there.

Consequently, the ground commanders and their advisers felt that they were being cheated by the U.S. Air Force in its desire to protect its own instead of helping them. Turley and Brookbank certainly felt this way, which explains the bitterness of their remarks. One ARVN commander, long accustomed to massive American fire support for his operations, stated, "Where are the American airplanes? Without them, we can't stand up to this! . . . Everything depends on the Americans. If they don't come to our aid, we're lost. But of course, you can't trust the Americans."[28]

So it appears that above this individual battle, the SARs had no larger impact. Indeed, the U.S. airpower is given due credit for helping to stem the NVA attack and, later that summer, for helping the ARVN and Vietnamese Marines to retake Quang Tri. But airpower was the supporting arm: the ARVN soldiers and Marines won the battle. As Major Lunday at the JPRC pointed out, "We [Americans] are quick to criticize the ARVN, and of course, the 3rd ARVN finally collapsed but we were not there on the ground facing what was probably as intense an effort as any American unit had faced in World War II."[29]

Later General Abrams reaffirmed this, when he stated: "This invasion could not have been held at this point without U.S. air support; however, ten times the airpower could not have done the job if the armed forces of South Vietnam had not stood and fought."[30]

Thus in Military Region I, airpower in combination with an ultimately resolute ground defense proved to be the decisive factors in repelling the 1972 NVA offensive. It prevented the NVA from massing their forces in front of Hue for a decisive push to capture that ancient capital. And in the battles that took place throughout South Vietnam that year, the NVA suffered one hundred thousand battlefield casualties and lost over half their tanks and heavy artillery. In fact, the operation was considered to be so disastrous that General Giap was removed as commander of the North Vietnamese Army. He would not lead the Army to ultimate victory in 1975.[31]

Reflecting on the overall results, President Nixon echoed General Abrams when he said: "We can never know whether the South Vietnamese could have won without the assistance of American airpower. But we know for certain that we could not have won with airpower alone. Vietnamization had worked. Our ally had stopped the spring offensive on the ground, and our bombing had crushed it."[32]

One Vietnamese general squared the point neatly: "Saigon's infantry + American firepower > Viet Cong and North Vietnamese Army."[33] That was the strategic equation of the war. In 1972, it held. But the question remains: If the SAR had not interceded, could the combined air and ground efforts have stopped the NVA offensive at a lower cost? We can only speculate.

Complaint 3: The Vietnamese Resentment of the SAR Effort While the Larger Battle Raged

This question—or controversy—is the toughest to address. Was he worth it? Was he or any other American worth all of this, when it had such an impact on our allies?

Part of the legend is that Lt. Col. Hambleton and 1st Lt. Mark Clark were special individuals who warranted extra effort because of what and who they were. Supposedly Clark was the son or grandson of World War II general Mark Clark, commander of the Allied forces that swept through Italy. Such a relationship would have weighed heavily against him if he had been captured. It had already happened to Navy lieutenant John McCain, the son of Navy admiral John McCain, who had been shot down and captured on a raid over North Vietnam early in the war. And supposedly Hambleton could not be allowed to fall into enemy hands because of the highly sensitive information with which he had worked when he had been assigned to the headquarters of the Strategic Air Command—information concerning plans for nuclear war against the Soviet Union.[34]

Both concerns are off the mark. Clark is not in any way related to the general: he comes from a completely separate line of the Clark family.[35] Hambleton, prior to his assignment to the 42d Tactical Electronic Warfare Squadron, had in fact worked in war plans, both at Strategic Air Command headquarters and in the 390th Strategic Missile Wing at Davis-Monthan Air Force Base, Tucson, Arizona. And he had spent much of that time immersed in highly secret and sensitive information. Yet if he was that sensitive, why was he flying to begin with? His previous tours, over ten years in length, had been purely non-flying jobs. He required six months of training at Shaw Air Force Base, South Carolina, to qualify for the assignment to EB-66s. And on this tour he had already flown numerous missions, many of them into high-risk areas where he was exposed to antiaircraft fire, SAMs, and occasionally even enemy fighters. Additionally, as the squadron staff navigator in charge of all of the other navigators, he had scheduled himself for this mission. In fact, it was his sixty-third.[36] If the above line of reasoning as to his sensitivity held true, he should not have been where he was—certainly not flying on this mission, or perhaps even in this assignment.

And how does this claim of special status square with the actions of the Blueghost crews who initially responded to Bilk 34's calls for help, losing one of their own crews in the process and coming dangerously close to losing two others? Capt. Mike Rosebeary explained this: "When we went up there, we didn't have the slightest idea of who we were trying to get. We just knew that there was an American pilot [*sic*] from the Air Force who was on the ground who had been shot down and needed to be extracted. When we got the call, we just responded to the need."[37] Their initial efforts on behalf of Bat 21 Bravo were mirror copies of the unhesitating actions to rescue Lieutenant Colonel Camper and Major Brown from Camp Carroll and, earlier, the U.S. Marine spotter team from Fire Support Base Alpha-2.

Neither Hambleton nor Clark nor even Walker received any treatment that would not have been afforded any other downed airman. Major Lunday at the JPRC explained it clearly: "I don't remember any discussion about him [Hambleton] being special," he said, "other than the fact that he was fifty-three years old."[38] But it was one of the Jolly Green pilots who said it best: "We did not go any further in trying to get these guys out than we would have gone for any others."[39]

The answer lies elsewhere, and it depends on whom you ask. To the ground warriors, these survivors were clearly not worth the cost, certainly not in the face of such a massive attack. They had thousands who were fighting, suffering, and dying. Their loyalty was to their own, those who were waging the ground battle. Why should one or two or three aircrews be so important? To them these downed airmen had just had the miserable luck of being caught up in a very messy ground battle.

Maj. Jack Kennedy of F Troop of the 8th Cavalry pointed out that ground commanders accepted the fact that land combat meant losses would be taken: it was the price of war. Operations could not be stopped for the sake of one person. Nothing about any individual—not his position or training or background—could place him above the value of the group or the accomplishment of the unit mission.[40] So naturally, the ground commanders and advisers would question the value of all of this.

But the air warriors would respond that certainly they were worth all of that. By 1972, after eight years of almost sustained combat operations in Southeast Asia, the only mission that still made any sense to the fliers was the rescue of their own. Yet the answer from the Air Force perspective is a bit more complicated and has several parts, some historic, institutional, and cultural in nature, and some very specific to the time and circumstance. To understand, we have to explore where the U.S. Air Force forces still in the war were mentally and emotionally in 1972.

13

★

A Long, Bitter, and
Frustrating War

AS IT HAD BEEN at the onset, by 1972 the American war in Southeast Asia was once again an air war. Most ground forces had been withdrawn. Other than the advisers, those ground units that remained were performing base-security duty while the ARVN fought the battles. The few remaining Americans still engaged in combat were fighting from the air

But American airpower was still considerable in the theater and was performing a rear-guard role as the United States disengaged. But even though the basic decisions to withdraw had been made in 1968, the actual period of withdrawal from 1969 to 1972 saw some of the greatest bloodletting of the war. This was due in part to the lavish use of airpower. By 1972 the question was how to withdraw the remaining forces while securing the return of American prisoners and leaving South Vietnam reasonably secure.[1] The order of these deeds suggest their priority. On the eve of the Easter Invasion, the airmen still in the war were a frustrated force. There were several reasons for this, some endemic to the way the United States chose to fight the war and some based on short-term events.

Since the halt of all bombing of North Vietnam in 1968, the Air Force, with some exceptions, had been involved in efforts to isolate the battlefield in South Vietnam by interdicting the flow of supplies from the North along the Ho Chi Minh Trail in Laos, South Vietnam, and Cambodia to its units in the South. The exceptions were usually raids of limited duration against specific targets in North Vietnam, as directed by orders from Washington. The intent was to build a shield of some form behind which Vietnamization could take place and South Vietnam could build a stable society.

This shield was necessary because of the strategic realities of the war. North Vietnam still held to its objective of uniting the two countries under Hanoi's control, and South Vietnam continued to resist. Increasingly, North Vietnam was using its main-force army to prosecute the war. Earlier in the war, North Vietnam had infiltrated forces and supplies into the South from ships at sea and through the ports and jungles of Cambodia. Both paths had been cut by decisive U.S. and South Vietnamese naval and ground campaigns. The remaining conduit for moving the soldiers south was the Ho Chi Minh Trail.

The Trail had its genesis in 1959, when North Vietnamese leaders made the basic political decision to fight in the South. Thereafter they sent troops who expanded it year after year, so that by 1969, it was a strategic corridor from North to South Vietnam. Early on, U.S. aerial forces attacked the Trail and the troops and vehicles on it. FACs began to patrol the roads on a daily basis, and electronic sensors, under a program called Igloo White, were dropped along the roads to report the passage of trucks.

Refitted A-26s, AT-28s, AC-47s, and A-1s from the Korean War sortied each day to attack what targets they could find; FACs assigned to the 23d TASS flying O-1s would spot for them. The larger F-105s and F-4s were also used, but the priority for them was the Rolling Thunder missions being flown against North Vietnam. B-52s flew many strikes against the early Trail, but their priority was ground support for troops in South Vietnam. All of that would change in 1968.

That year was the watershed year for the United States in the war. The debacle of Tet led to the demise of President Johnson, the end of the bombing of North Vietnam, and the strategy of withdrawal and Vietnamization under President Nixon. Upon taking office, President Nixon ruled against reinitiating airstrikes against North Vietnam. Instead, the planes sitting in abundance on airfields and aircraft carriers in Southeast Asia would be used to cover our withdrawal from the war. They would be used as the shield necessary to buy time for Vietnamization and withdrawal. President Nixon said at a press conference: "As far as air power is concerned, let me also say this: As we reduce the number of our forces, it is particularly important for us to continue our air strikes on the infiltration routes."[2] The plan was to attack the Ho Chi Minh Trail wholesale with airpower, using the two Ts of American military power: tonnage and technology.

The effort would be a series of campaigns called Commando Hunt I through VII, from November 1968 to March 1972. The Commando Hunt objectives were twofold: first, to reduce the logistical flow by substantially increasing the time needed to move supplies from the North to the South; second, to destroy trucks and supply caches along the roads and streams and in the truck parks and storage areas along the Ho Chi Minh Trail in Laos and along its tributaries into Cambodia and South Vietnam.[3]

The tonnage necessary for the endeavor was certainly available. Freed from missions against North Vietnam, several hundred fighter aircraft were readied to strike Trail targets. In October 1968, 4,700 sorties were flown against Steel Tiger, as that part of Laos was now designated. The next month that number increased to 12,800. By the time American participation in the war ended, Air Force, Navy, and Marine aircraft had dropped more than 3 million tons of explosives on Laos, with over half that amount dropped along the Ho Chi Minh Trail.

Planners also turned to technology for solutions. They noted the use of sensors along the Trail under the Igloo White project. They were also encouraged by the use of sensors in locating and destroying North Vietnamese units besieging Khe Sanh in 1968. Seizing upon the concept, they decided to use high-technology sensors and communications to replace soldiers on the ground. A whole series of electronic sensors was available. One was basically a microphone and would transmit whatever sounds it heard. Another sensor would pick up the vibrations of people or vehicles moving nearby. Building on Igloo White, Seventh Air Force implanted thousands more along the Trail. The sensors were then tied by relay aircraft to two huge IBM 360 computers at Nakhon Phanom. There the data could be analyzed and transformed into targeting information. Controllers there would then contact the orbiting command-and-control aircraft and have them respond to activations with airstrikes.[4] When fully operational, it was an extensive system. Controllers bragged that the enemy now had nowhere to hide. Said one Air Force officer, "We got the Ho Chi Minh Trail wired like a pin ball machine."[5]

To provide for around-the-clock and all-weather operations, the Air Force introduced several modifications to aircraft. It upgraded numerous F-4s and RF-4s with LORAN navigational gear, so that they could easily use the targeting data passed by the controllers. It also upgraded several Skyspot radar sites to allow them to guide fighters on blind strikes. Additionally, it introduced a vastly upgraded force of eleven B-57Gs with forward-looking radar infrared and low-light-level television and laser ranging devices.

It also upgraded its fixed-wing gunship force. Since the beginning of interdiction along the Trail, orbiting gunships had been used. Initially, they were old AC-47s firing .50-caliber machine guns. These were replaced by AC-119s and eventually by AC-130 Spectre gunships firing two 20mm Gatling guns, two 40mm Bofors cannons, and a 105mm Howitzer. Additionally, the gunships were equipped with sophisticated sensor systems that could see through foliage and then aim the heavy-caliber weapons. One device could sense truck engines when they were running. Given their ability to spend hours orbiting over the Trail, they rapidly became some of the most effective weapons against trucks and supplies.[6]

The fifteen Pave Nail OV-10s at Nakhon Phanom were initially modified to fight the Trail war. The squadron commander, Lieutenant Colonel Macleay, first commanded the squadron detachment at Ubon and field-tested the system in Cambodia. He built up a team of young, enthusiastic, and creative pilots and navigators to make the system work. They faithfully followed the procedures suggested by the various experts sent over from the States to explain its use. But very rapidly they discovered that the suggested techniques were impractical for combat use, and Lieutenant Colonel Macleay gave them free rein to develop any tactics that they felt would make the system most useful. They rapidly discovered that it had great flexibility and could be used day or night. Its only limitations were a lack of laser-guided bombs, bad weather, and a lack of creativity of those using it. In short order, these airmen had destroyed most targets in northern Cambodia worthy of a laser-guided bomb. Thereafter the Pave Nails began flying over the Ho Chi Minh Trail.

All of this technology was matched to the tonnage and applied to the Trail war. But given the unclear nature of this mission, it was difficult to measure success. Since the target was logistical, the mechanism decided upon was the number of trucks killed: figures and statistics became the name of the game. Dry statistical measures of success were institutionalized. As the campaigns evolved, the truck counts rose steadily and were daily reported to the leaders in Saigon and Washington. By Commando Hunt

V in 1971, almost twenty-one thousand trucks were reported destroyed or damaged.

However, the leaders were deluding themselves. CIA analysts estimated that only six thousand trucks entered Laos during that period. The discrepancy has several reasons: First, the North Vietnamese had become masters at deception. Second, there was no good way of assessing the effectiveness of airstrikes. Most bomb-damage assessment was done by the aircrews based on strictly visual results. Since large counts were sometimes the basis for awards, reports became unduly optimistic. Third, some vehicles were obviously bombed and reported destroyed numerous times. Fourth, aircrews considered their weapons to be more effective than they really were. In 1971 Seventh Air Force ran tests to determine the effectiveness of the gunships. Results indicated that kill reports were overstated and that accounting systems and campaign results had to be reevaluated.[7] We were fooling ourselves into thinking that we were winning.

Earl Tilford, in his book *Setup: What the Air Force Did in Vietnam and Why*, explained it: "Undoubtedly, gunships destroyed a large number of trucks while B-52s and fighterbombers wreaked havoc on the roads and jungles. Whatever tactical advantages were gained, however, paled beside the impact resulting from the enforcement of the managerial ethos that took over during Commando Hunt. In what came to resemble 'production line warfare,' success was assessed primarily on dubious statistics, the compilation of which became an end unto itself. Statistics, however, proved no substitute for strategy, and for all the *perceived* success in that numbers game, the Air Force succeeded only in fooling itself into believing Commando Hunt was working."[8]

The aircrews were not fooled. Even though they could not understand what life was like below, they could sense that trucks were getting through. In fact, anyone who spent any time at all in the air developed a solid respect for the troops below. As one pilot said, "Whoever was in charge [of the Trail] had his shit together."[9]

In contrast, comparing U.S. efforts with those of the enemy, one FAC said, "The effectiveness of our interdiction efforts along the Trail was piss poor."[10] And intelligence knew that there were whole segments of the Trail about which the United States knew nothing.[11]

Airpower was not the weapon to cut the Trail—not by itself, at least. In the effort, it was being wasted; the aircrews could intuitively feel it. One young pilot defined the dilemma of the Ho Chi Minh Trail thus: "A 500-pound bomb makes a hole five feet deep and ten feet across. With 50 coolies filling the hole and packing it with a battering ram, the road can be open again the next day."[12] That was it—the American statistical view matched by the raw human power of the enemy below. Those words were spoken in 1964; eight years later, the United States was still trying to do the same thing.

Gen. Creighton Abrams watched these events with dismay. He too had come to the conclusion that firepower alone would not stop the flow down the Trail. He proposed, and American and Vietnamese political leaders accepted, a bold plan to launch a strong conventional ground force of South Vietnamese armor and infantry to block the Trail and destroy NVA supplies. It would attack west into Laos along the old Route 9 from Khe Sanh, to cut the Trail as far as Tchepone. At the same time, it would destroy vast stockpiles that the NVA had been building next to the South Vietnamese border.[13] The operation would be called Lam Son 719.

This force of fifteen thousand entered Laos in early February 1971. Initially they were met by soldiers from the engineer and antiaircraft battalions who did not put up much of a fight. ARVN and Marine task forces fanned out and swept through several base areas and destroyed large quantities of trucks and supplies. Then the South Vietnamese forces were counterattacked by five regular divisions of NVA troops with heavy tanks and artillery. The fighting was some of the heaviest of the war.

U.S. and VNAF airpower responded to the needs of the troops on the ground. But the NVA covered their forces with antiaircraft guns and, in effect, achieved a level of air deniability against the attacking aircraft. The ARVN began to retreat. The retreat nearly became a rout, as the South Vietnamese forces pulled back into their homeland and licked their wounds.

Lam Son 719 was at best a partial success. Great quantities of supplies had been destroyed, and some NVA units had been mauled. But the Trail was not cut for any length of time. Most important, though, the North Vietnamese had showed that they would fight to hold southern Laos, the key ground of Laos and location of the Ho Chi Minh Trail. The additional antiaircraft guns brought in to cover the NVA counterattack stayed in place and supplemented the already frightening inventory of guns. The aircrews noticed it immediately and watched it steadily worsen.

By January 1972, the Trail was the hottest that it had ever been: there were guns everywhere. Worse yet, SA-2 SAM sites had been introduced into Laos and downed an AC-130 south of Tchepone on 28 March.[14] Additionally, the SAM sites protected the key passes at Mu Gia and Ban Karai. Because of this, the B-52s could not be used to keep them closed. The task fell to the tactical aircraft. But they could not continuously devastate the roads as did the bombers, and the supplies continued to flow. The massed guns along the Trail vastly decreased the effectiveness of the FACs and gunships. It can perhaps even be argued that the NVA had successfully challenged the United States for air superiority over portions of the Trail.

The air defenses were protecting the large troop and armor formations heading south. They were the wherewithal for the upcoming invasion. Commando Hunt had failed, and the air effort, while looking good on paper, had been wasted. The aircrews sensed this, and the generals at Seventh Air Force knew it. The United States and South Vietnam had lost the battle of the Ho Chi Minh Trail. It was a loss of huge proportions, because given the strategic realities of the theater, the Ho Chi Minh Trail was the North Vietnamese operational center of gravity. They fought tenaciously to protect it, for it was key to their strategy for defeating the South with modern, conventional forces, and they made it impervious to American and South Vietnamese airpower.[15] Perhaps in mute testimony, by the end of 1972, the Igloo White system was all but shut down. It had not been cost-effective. Over three billion dollars had been spent on the program, and the trucks were still rolling.[16] South Vietnamese soldiers and Marines from Quang Tri to An Loc would pay for that failure under the merciless pounding of the North Vietnamese artillery, rockets, and tanks. And all of this led to a bitter and cynical frustration among the American airmen still in the war.

The Seventh Air Force commander, Gen. John Lavelle, watched these developments with great concern. If he could not get at enemy forces in Laos, maybe he could get at them in North Vietnam before they disappeared into the endless jungles over the Trail. He decided to try to do something about it: use airpower more effectively.

Lavelle had taken over the previous summer as the commander of Seventh Air Force. Considered one of the brightest rising stars in the U.S. Air Force, his previous assignments as director of the Defense Communications Planning Group and vice commander of the Pacific Air Forces (PACAF) made him the ideal choice to command in Vietnam. He subsequently chose an old friend and career fighter pilot—Maj. Gen. Winton W. Marshall—to be his vice commander.[17] When Lavelle assumed command, Seventh Air Force was deeply involved in the Commando Hunt campaign against supplies, logistics facilities, and trucks along the Ho Chi Minh Trail. Strikes against North Vietnam had been stopped in 1968 as part of the informal "understanding" between the United States and the North to begin negotiations to end the war. As a quid pro quo, the North had agreed not to invade South Vietnam through the DMZ. The only U.S. flights over the North were reconnaissance flights and occasional protective reaction strikes against enemy defenses that attempted to shoot down the reconnaissance aircraft.[18] These attack sorties totaled 285 in 1969 and 1,113 in 1970.[19]

But by the end of 1971, General Lavelle was very concerned about the increased air-defense threat that had moved into Laos, and he initiated a Gun-Kill program to try to beat it down. Reconnaissance jets filmed likely gun sites. After the film had been analyzed and the sites marked, copies of the photos were provided to the FACs. They then called in aircraft that were equipped with laser illuminators, like the Pave Nails, which zotted the guns. Orbiting fighters then dropped the laser-guided bombs, which were highly accurate and destroyed quite a number of guns. The FACs and fighters did the same thing to SA-2 sites, when they could find them.

But, taking advantage of the restrictions against bombing the North, the North Vietnamese began moving their SA-2 sites right up next to the border to launch missiles against unwary aircraft over Laos. They did the same with long-range radars to provide control for their MiG fighters, which were beginning to fly over the Ho Chi Minh Trail. Their efforts were beginning to have some success, for in the last three weeks of 1971, they brought down ten American aircraft at a cost of thirteen aircrewmen lost.[20]

Concerned with the losses, the Joint Chiefs of Staff directed Seventh Air Force to be more aggressive in countering the threat and more flexible in using the "existing authorities" to protect American forces. They were also authorized to increase the size of strike flights detailed to protect reconnaissance aircraft. The existing authorities were, of course, the rules of engagement that dictated how American forces could be used in combat. Defined in large generalities to regulate the level of fighting to match the limited goals inherent in a limited war, they were designed so that civilian leaders in Washington could maintain strict control over the war against

North Vietnam. For the Air Force crews, the specific directive was 7AF Operation Order 71-17, published in the early stages of the war and updated on 6 December 1971. It was an extensive, detailed set of rules of which all aircrews, air liaison officers, mission controllers, and planners were supposed to demonstrate a thorough knowledge before assuming operational duties.[21]

For operations over the southern portion of North Vietnam, armed escorts could provide protection to manned reconnaissance aircraft that were attacked. In all cases, though, aircraft engaged in immediate-response strikes were not authorized to attack other unfriendly forces or installations except in response to a hostile action by them.

But there were conflicting interpretations of the rules. In August, just after he had taken over Seventh Air Force, General Lavelle was advised by General Abrams, his direct superior as commander of United States Forces, Military Assistance Command Vietnam, to make armed escort of sufficient force level to protect U.S. aircraft and achieve the impact desired for full punitive response to enemy air-defense tactics under the current rules. He went on to say, "Interlocking and mutually supporting NVN air defenses constitute an unacceptable hazard for aircrews attempting to identify a particular SAM/antiaircraft gun firing site" and it was "considered appropriate for escort forces to direct immediate protective reaction strikes against any identifiable element of the firing/activated air defense complex."[22] This message had the effect of broadening the interpretation of what could be done under existing authorities.

And this guidance seemed to follow the political rhetoric flowing out of Washington. Previously, in November

1970, Secretary of Defense Melvin Laird had said, "We will continue to take protective reaction as necessary to protect the pilots of our unarmed reconnaissance planes . . ." One month later President Nixon himself said, "If our airplanes are fired upon, I will not only order that they return the fire, but I will order that the missile complex around the site which supports it also be destroyed by bombing."[23]

In December 1971, after a joint Seventh Air Force, Pacific Air Forces, and JCS conference on the threat, Admiral McCain, Commander in Chief, Pacific, directed that reconnaissance escort flights could be enlarged and structured for increased protective reaction capability and that all efforts should be made "to so employ our current authorities as to maximize protective reaction against elements of the MiG threat."

The threat dictated this change, because intelligence had determined that the air-defense system in North Vietnam had been raised to a higher level of sophistication. The North Vietnamese had developed the ability to link their long-range early warning radars with the tracking radars of the individual SAM sites. This development meant that the SAM sites could receive tracking information on aircraft without turning on their individual radars, or could track an aircraft from one site while coordinating with and then firing on it from another site through a process called triangulation. These were tremendous tactical advantages for the North Vietnamese for two reasons: first, the American aircraft were equipped with warning devices that detected and hence warned of the SAM tracking radars, but not the long-range radars. Consequently, the SAM sites could remain undetected until they actually launched their missiles.

Thus reaction time was reduced, and the probability of being shot down was raised. This improvement was a serious threat to aircraft operating over North Vietnam or the border areas of Laos. Two aircraft were shot down by this new tactic.[24]

Second, the SAM (Fan Song) tracking radars used one signal for the radar and another for the missile guidance. Because the NVA could radiate the tracking signal and the guidance signal from different sites, U.S. pilots could become confused and react improperly to the missile. This increased the chances of being hit and downed.

The enhanced threat and these apparent liberalizations of the rules for protective reaction strikes gave some latitude for interpretation. But the basic written ground rules remained the same: such strikes were restricted to the threat below twenty degrees north with a few exceptions, and were only to be conducted as immediate responses to enemy fire or hostile actions that directly threatened U.S. aircraft.[25]

Yet General Lavelle gave these directives a very liberal interpretation. He assumed that any aircraft flying over the southern portion of North Vietnam were going to be shot at, thereby justifying a reaction. Therefore he determined to go after the continuously improving NVA air defenses and the truck convoys before they left North Vietnam and were lost along the Ho Chi Minh Trail. For reasons not clearly understood to this day, he began directing his fighter units under the guise of "protective reaction" to hit targets in North Vietnam and then apparently claim that the strikes had been a necessary response to hostile action.

In March 1972, a young airman in the intelligence section of the 432d Tactical Reconnaissance Wing at

Udorn Air Base, Thailand, complained about these questionable strikes in a letter to his senator.[26] The chief of staff of the Air Force, Gen. John Ryan, ordered an investigation of the claim. When the inquiry revealed that "some airstrikes had struck North Vietnam which exceeded the authorities granted [the] Command," he recommended to the secretary of defense that General Lavelle be relieved as commander of Seventh Air Force and retired as a major general.[27]

In retrospect, his actions had to be condemned because they were at variance with what the national leaders were trying to accomplish diplomatically. Indeed, as these raids were occurring, government officials were secretly negotiating with the North Vietnamese for a political settlement of the war, and military actions were being orchestrated to fit that process. General Lavelle's actions and rationale, had they been followed, could have led to the (apparently justified in General Lavelle's mind) unrestricted bombing of North Vietnam. That was not the U.S. government's policy. Unfortunately, the military leaders in Vietnam were not apprised of the nature or sensitivity or even the existence of these ongoing negotiations with North Vietnam, nor of the details of President Nixon's attempts to isolate North Vietnam from China and the Soviet Union. The generals were not given these critical pieces of the puzzle.[28]

Of course at the time, the aircrews did not know all of this; they only knew that their commander had been sacked, supposedly because he wanted to get at the enemy. Their leader was trying to help his men win the war and protect them at the same time. That made a lot of sense to those actually doing the flying and fighting. One of the pilots from Udorn, 1st Lt. Bill Dalecky, explained this dilemma from the perspective of the air-crews:

> The sense was that . . . [it was] an artificial limitation that was being done for a political reason and it was limiting extremely what we had to do. This [ground-fire reporting]was the solution. . . . I don't think that anybody ever had any sense that people were concerned about it. I mean even including the intel people, nobody said, "Well this didn't really happen, did it?" . . . and seemed taken aback by that. . . . Everyone felt a sense of collective frustration, I guess, at not being able to fly, to really get at the North Vietnamese where we really needed to. . . . There were fairly regular intel reports about the large amount of supplies being built up. It was obviously in preparation for [the invasion]. . . . There was collective sense that . . . lives were going to be at stake. . . . All of this materiel is going to be used to kill Americans and South Vietnamese if it gets down into the country.[29]

As General Lavelle abruptly departed, operations at Seventh Air Force continued: there was still a war to be fought. But Major General Marshall was aghast at the developments. He had nothing but the highest regard for General Lavelle; he held him as a man who had dedicated his life to national service and was one of the finest officers in his service. Since arriving at Seventh Air Force, already well versed in the war and how his nation had chosen to fight it, he had thrown himself into the job. He had monitored intelligence closely and constantly briefed General Abrams on the latest reconnaissance findings. And the developments in NVA air defenses had concerned him deeply, because they put his men at risk. The aircrews who had flown over the North and knew what the North Vietnamese were doing shared his frustrations and concerns. They knew that the NVA was preparing for big operations and vastly upgrading their air-defense capabilities.

But it was done, and the airmen in Southeast Asia had a war to finish. General Lavelle was replaced by Gen. John Vogt, another fine officer. But the Lavelle debacle had an immediate impact on the headquarters at Seventh: the younger staff officers felt betrayed by the whole incident. It was something they could not get off of their minds. Major General Marshall saw the effect it had on headquarters morale: "All of the guys really felt terrible about it. I wondered how it was going to affect our combat operations. Is a guy really going to press it when the commander, our commander, whom we have been 'yessirring' and saluting all of this time, is fired and there is a big question about how he was fired?"[30]

Very soon those staff officers would be called upon to make some very big decisions in response to the NVA Easter Invasion. Some of these decisions would have to do with the rescue of one man stuck in the middle of a ground battle between two Vietnamese armies.

The aircrews would be swept up by those same events. With dismay and concern, they watched the developments within North Vietnam and along the Ho Chi Minh Trail. They could see how the NVA air defenders were rapidly improving, both in types and volume of equipment, and in technical and tactical expertise. One mission debrief in particular highlights this neatly. While somewhat complicated and full of jargon, it demonstrates the level of sophistication the NVA missile crews had achieved by 1972.

> I had two Spoonrest radars and one Flat Face radar [both early warning] that I was jamming . . . I saw two small signals below the jamming signal that was on the Flat Face. . . . I recognized these as two B606 missile guidance signals . . . I called to the pilot, "SAM! Take her down!" . . . As the aircraft was going into the SAM break, I switched to UHF [communications radio] and called, "SAM uplink, vicinity of DMZ" . . . The pilot reported seeing SAM missiles detonating, at which time I called, "SAM visual, vicinity of DMZ" . . . At the bottom of the SAM break I dispensed 15-20 bundles of QRC-530 chaff. The two guidance signals B606s were up *together* from 10-15 seconds. I never had any indication of Fansong TWS [Track While Scan] signal . . .[31]

The engagement described here was reported by Maj. Ed Anderson, the EWO on Bat 22. It describes the engagement in which Bat 21 was shot down. The hapless crew of that EB-66 were the victims of the specific weapons and upgraded enemy tactics that most concerned General Lavelle. Waste, terrible waste. It only added to the bitterness and frustration.[32]

Whereas the war seemed without end or purpose, there was one mission with which every aircrew member could identify: the rescue of one's own. Indeed, by 1972 search and rescue was about the only mission that meant anything to the aircrews. One A-1 pilot stated: "This rescue business is the best, most rewarding operation of the entire war. And if nothing else does, getting a man out makes sense."[33]

Beyond the bitterness, there were several reasons for this. First of all, it should be noted that rescuing a fellow person in danger is a basic part of the human psyche. Regardless of the time or circumstance, rescue has always been one of the great human-interest stories. In crises people pull together as never before, often performing deeds far beyond the normal, and the beginnings of aerial rescue had well preceded this war.

Second, as the aircraft in its various forms was developed and used during the earlier wars of this century, the need and ability to rescue downed aviators was recognized and slowly developed. Its history has been recorded elsewhere. But certain key developments had a heavy impact on events in Southeast Asia. In World War II, future Air Force leaders realized the morale value of making efforts to rescue downed crewmen. After the war, they established units dedicated, trained, and equipped to do that.[34]

Some of those units deployed to Korea when U.S. and UN forces engaged and stopped the North Korean aggression in the early fifties. One unit, the 3d Air Rescue Squadron, using various fixed-wing aircraft and increasingly more sophisticated helicopters, rescued 254 U.S. and allied aircrew members from behind enemy lines.[35] It was the first unit in the conflict to be awarded the Presidential Unit Citation.[36] Tactically and organizationally, air rescue came of age in the Korean conflict. And some hard lessons were learned:

1. Fundamental to the successful accomplishment of the air-rescue mission was the air superiority gained by

friendly forces. It allowed the vulnerable rescue aircraft to operate without fear of enemy air attack.

2. Centralized command and control of assets located within the Joint Operations Center made for optimum use of resources.

3. Technology could be exploited. The use of the SU-16 (HU-16) amphibian and the improved helicopter vastly improved capabilities. The development of individual personnel survival equipment, especially the small hand-held radios, increased the chances of location and recovery.[37]

THIRD, MORE SUBTLY and perhaps more importantly, the idea had taken hold in the minds of the airmen that if they were hit and had to eject behind enemy lines, regardless of location or situation, their buddies would not abandon them and the rescue crews would make every effort possible to find them and get them out. It was a bond among the airmen. The young lieutenants and captains would bring these feelings back to the United States with them. In the not-too-distant future, they would be the leaders and commanders of other combat units that would go to war in another part of Asia, and they would take the bond with them.

Consequently, when the U.S. Air Force was sent to Southeast Asia to do battle with a new enemy, units of the renamed Aerospace Rescue and Recovery Service went with them. Indeed, even some of the units were the same. The now renamed and enlarged 3d Aerospace Rescue and Recovery Group, headquartered in Saigon, commanded all HC-130s and rescue helicopters in the region and had immediate call on whatever else it needed. The lineage was continuous.

But as the war dragged on and the nation slowly turned against it, SAR began to replace all others as the most critical mission. There were two reasons for this. First, for the United States, Vietnam was a limited war, worth an undetermined but limited investment. Historically, Americans had not been adverse to sacrificing great numbers of men when it was thought that the cause justified the cost. In the last year of the Civil War, the road from Washington to Richmond was paved with bodies clad in blue and gray. At places like Spotsylvania, Cold Harbor, and Petersburg, they were shot down by the thousands. It was a tragic and horrible price to pay, but the men wearing those uniforms felt that the preservation or independence of their nation was worth it. But the Vietnam War was not for national survival. And by 1972 Americans had exceeded the limited price that they were willing to pay in that limited war.

Second, Americans prefer to fight wars with equipment, technology, and firepower. This is because this great industrial nation has not had to fight a major, devastating war on its own soil in more than a century, and it has developed an economic base that can produce massive quantities of high-quality, high-technology weapons.[38] If a country can do that, why risk people? Firepower is better.

And America used those weapons in great quantities. Throughout Southeast Asia, the air forces of the United States and its allies dropped nearly 8 million tons of bombs, over twice the tonnage dropped by the Allied powers in World War II. That tonnage was delivered by more than 3.4 million air sorties, 90 percent flown by the United States.[39]

Essential, of course, for the operation of high-technology equipment were competent, highly trained crew-members. The equipment itself had no value unless highly trained personnel were there to operate it. The process of finding and training them was long and expensive, and this put a premium on the aircrews as resources and, in fact, as key components of airpower.[40] They had to be protected, especially because as the United States withdrew from the war, they were rapidly becoming the only ones still at risk.

These characteristics colored the U.S. approach to and development of search and rescue. Any technological advancement that could be applied to SAR found its way into the inventory. Communications equipment, laser-weapon advancements, they were all used. But perhaps the helicopter was the ultimate example; in fact, it came to represent rescue. The modern helicopter, essential to long-range rescue, was itself a child of and a testimony to high technology. It offered the ability to rescue anyone just about anywhere.

But helicopters were vulnerable to ground fire, so they had to be protected. And the United States had the fire-power to do that. Korea had shown that fighter aircraft could be linked to helicopters to form a task force that could protect the helicopter as it darted in to make the pickup. And of course all of this had to be organized. Americans, being innovative, built the 3d ARRG/Joker team. It became masterful at bringing it all together; it was the linchpin for melding the tonnage and technology.

All that was lacking was a reason or objective. But in SAR the objective was crystal clear: to save a fellow airman, a high-expense investment, who was down in enemy territory. Everyone could understand that, and in a war that became more and more confusing and apparently worthless from the American perspective, it was worth doing. It was the tactical expression of the U.S. strategy to bring home its troops. It was a perfect matchup of resources—tonnage and technology—to objective. It was all there. For all of these reasons, the concept of rescue, the idea of doing all for one, became part of the psyche of the airmen in the Southeast Asian war. SAR became the priority mission. The idea had set in early. Col. Jack Broughton, a Korean War veteran and F-105 strike flight leader early in the war, described these feelings. "One of the strongest fighter principles," he said, "is that if an airman goes down, you do everything within your power to divert your mission to Combat Air Patrol, which in our language is CAP. Your priority becomes flying cover, or CAP, and getting rescue forces on the scene."[41]

Colonel Broughton described vividly how this might happen. While leading a large strike flight toward a target in the Hanoi area in the summer of 1967, he heard that two aircraft of the Wild Weasel SAM-suppression flight, which had preceded him into the target area, had been shot down. Three aircrew members (Leo Thorsness, Harry Johnson, and Bob Abbott) were on the ground. Colonel Broughton described his actions: "Since I had the entire strike force only a few miles behind Leo, we had the world's greatest potential rescue effort set up for those guys. I spotted Leo and Harry and circled them as they descended in their chutes. We covered them for about three hours, and we had tankers standing by to the south to recycle us when we got low on fuel."[42]

In other words, Colonel Broughton diverted an entire

strike package designed and dispatched to destroy a target in the Hanoi area to CAP for the rescue of downed fellow airmen. It was a bold move, and it showed that the frustrations of this war and the preeminence of the SAR psyche had set in early. Yet the feelings of the crews reflected how the American people themselves were turning against the war. And as support for the war flagged, the SAR efforts grew. Post-1968, as it became clear that the United States was going to pull out of the war, SAR began to take on a life of its own, absorbing more technology and more firepower. Many of the rescues became, in fact, small individual battles. But these battles grew steadily in size, expenditure of resources, and intensity.

One such illustrative engagement took place on 17 January 1969. Stormy 02, an F-4, was shot down near Tchepone, in central Laos. Only the backseater, Stormy 02 Bravo, ejected. Over a period of several days, SAR and supporting forces battled enemy gunners before the survivor was rescued. In the process, several other aircraft were downed. One A-1 pilot was killed; the others were rescued. But the scope of the SAR was massive and dwarfed anything that had occurred up to this date: 70 A-1s were involved in the effort; 16 helicopters were utilized for the pickup attempts; 16 FAC aircraft directly participated, while many others supported the operations in some other way; 5 HC-130s were constantly on orbit to direct operations or refuel the helicopters. In all, 59 flights of fighters were put in to suppress ground fire and enemy activity. A total of 284 aircraft was involved.[43]

But it only took eleven months for this record to be eclipsed. On 5 December 1969, another F-4 was shot down just south of Mu Gia Pass on the North Vietnam–Laotian border near the former village of Ban Phanop. The aircraft, call sign Boxer 22, was the wingman in a flight of two F-4s out of Cam Ranh Bay. The aircraft were carrying special bombs used to mine roads along the Ho Chi Minh Trail. The area was well protected by NVA antiaircraft guns. As Boxer 22 rolled in for his bomb pass, he was hit by fire from a 23mm gun. The crew of Capt. Ben Danielson (Boxer 22 Alpha) and 1st Lt. Woody Bergeron (Boxer 22 Bravo) ejected. Over the next several days, rescue forces attempted to bring out the downed fliers, but they were trapped in one of the most heavily defended sections of the Ho Chi Minh Trail. In the ensuing melee, the pilot was killed. Yet the brave Sandy and Jolly Green crews prevailed, and after an unprecedented three days on the ground, 1st Lt. Woody Bergeron was rescued.[44]

But the cost was high. Numerous A-1s and helicopters were damaged so badly that they never flew again. One pararescueman was killed and several other participants were wounded. A total of 336 sorties were flown in the operation that ultimately saved Boxer 22 Bravo. It was a high price to pay for one person.[45]

By 1972, every flight lead was trained how to CAP a downed wingman and how to contact the rescue forces.[46] Flight leads routinely briefed that if anyone went down, the flight would automatically divert to SAR duties.[47] Every FAC was trained in what to do when an aircraft went down: he was the immediate link to the rescue forces and would immediately divert his mission to respond to a downed aircraft, as Bilk 34 did for Bat 21, Sandy 01 did for Nail 38, and Nail 21 did for Covey 282. As told in Thomas Yarborough's book *Da Nang*

Diary, one FAC briefed a flight of fighters one day, "If you get in trouble, your best emergency bailout is the high stuff [terrain] to the east. If you end up on the ground, stay cool, work with me, and I'll save your butt for mama!"[48]

The King HC-130 aircraft orbited to monitor Mayday calls and initiate rescue efforts. The entire SAR force existed for no other reason. Its commander in Saigon had his own command-and-control system and could have whatever assets he needed in the theater to prosecute a mission. Aircraft were modified to enhance the effort, and technology was applied when it helped. The Pave Nail OV-10s were initially designed to be used against the Trail as part of Commando Hunt, but their applicability to SAR was immediately recognized, and whenever it was necessary, they were refragged to SAR support.[49] SARs, when they occurred, would take on a life of their own. One of the Nail FACs described such efforts:

Once in a while you would have a good tactical mission. But it wasn't anything like saving a friend. . . . A SAR really put some value into what you were doing a lot more than just going out and looking for trucks and dropping bombs to see if you could get a secondary explosion. . . . A SAR really brought it home. It really made you feel like you were accomplishing something. It was very difficult to feel like you were really doing anything over there, other than flying your mission and doing a good job, but it was hard to see any direct impact on anything. I think the SAR was the thing that really . . . you know, everybody just dropped everything and . . . it became very personal and very re-

warding. Some of the SARs that we pulled off were just
amazing. The feeling you got when you get those guys
out. It's just . . . it must be like winning the Super
Bowl. You just get this tremendous high.[50]

In a war that was frustrating to those involved and that
by 1972 was largely seen as a "loser," SAR success was
easy to measure. The 3d ARRG kept a running total of
the number of aircrew members rescued. By the end of
the war, they logged 3,883 individuals rescued.[51]

These successes were rewarded. The various members
of the rescue forces were among the most highly deco-
rated U.S. personnel of the war. Between January 1966
and the beginning of 1971, they received more than
13,000 awards and decorations. During 1971 and early
1972, they received 1,760 more Silver Stars, Distinguished Flying Crosses, Bronze Stars, Air Medals, and
Commendation Medals.[52] During the rest of 1972 and
the first quarter of 1973, they received 1,808 awards and
decorations, including 3 Air Force Crosses and 67 Silver
Stars.[53] But the real motivation was personal. They did it
for one another.

Thus by 1972, SAR had become the quintessential air
mission. It was tonnage and technology with a purpose,
the ultimate expression of the American way of war, and
it brought Bat 21 Bravo, Nail 38 Bravo, and many others home.

But there was one factor in the rescue of Bat 21 Bravo
that made the Bat 21 SAR unique in the war. And it held
portents well beyond the life of just one man.

14

**There is nothing over here
which is worth an American life.**
Lt. Col. Lachlan Macleay

Disconnect

UNFORTUNATELY, BY 1972 most Air Force aviators did not consider those fighting on the ground
to be among "their own." Some of this was basic service
parochialism. Air warriors and ground warriors have always had different views of war, but by the time of the
Bat 21 Bravo SAR, for the most part, the men in the air
and those on the ground were of different nationalities
and races. Therefore the reasons were institutional, emotional, and cultural. They must be considered separately
to understand their full combined impact.

The emphasis on the Ho Chi Minh Trail war intensified an ugly side of the Air Force psyche. Since its separation from the Army in 1947, its aircrews had shown little

interest in land battle or in airpower's impact upon it.[1]
The training of its officers had focused on airpower and
how it could be used in battle, but its focus was narrow
and parochial. Training emphasized the primacy of the
air-to-air mission and strategic bombing, the two things
that made air forces distinct from ground forces and justified the act of separation.

With rare exceptions, air combat, unlike ground combat, was very impersonal. The aircrews moved above the
battlefield to deliver their weapons on targets they could
only vaguely see, for at best a few minutes, and then
returned to bases perhaps hundreds of miles away. They
left the battles into which they had intervened, battles
that had perhaps been going on for several days, and
returned to the comfort and safety of their bases unaware of the destruction that they had just wreaked on
those below. They did not hear the screams or smell the
burning flesh; they did not have to deal with the
wounded. They were not exposed to the results of their
actions. One F-4 pilot, Capt. John Waddell of the 366th
Tactical Fighter Wing at Da Nang, explained this point.
"It's almost impossible to relate to it [ground opera-
tions]," he said. "I don't think anyone here thinks about
blowing in and dropping bombs and killing a person.
It's all very impersonal. You don't hear the bombs. It's
all very abstract."[2]

Most airmen were taught very little about working
with ground forces or integrating with their operations.
The various strike units, fighters, gunships, and other
aircraft did not even have ground-liaison officers assigned to them to brief the crews on friendly ground
operations. What information they did receive was obtained through intelligence channels. But these channels

had other interests and priorities. The intelligence personnel were responsible for assimilating and calculating the bomb-damage assessment numbers of truck kills and road cuts to document the success of U.S. interdiction campaigns against the Ho Chi Minh Trail. And they were, at this stage of the war, more concerned with enemy air defenses and MiG operations than with the details of enemy ground operations or friendly troop movements. As the numbers of enemy guns and SAM sites increased throughout the theater, the aircrews became almost numb to the briefings.[3]

These institutional shortcomings provided fertile ground for the emotional and cultural reasons. Once U.S. ground troops began to depart Vietnam and the remaining air units were increasingly being transferred to Thailand—thus physically separating them from the battles—the chasm widened. There was, in some cases, open disdain for U.S. allies throughout the theater. One pilot who had bombed a friendly Laotian position in northern Laos stated after the war that he had "absolutely no regrets at all. Didn't give a shit. Just Asians were Asians, and they are all the enemy."[4]

These feelings also extended to the ARVN and were reflected in an incident that occurred with American ground troops near Hue on 12 April 1972, as Bat 21 Bravo was being brought out. Troops of the 196th Light Infantry Brigade were ordered to patrol outside of their perimeter because of possible NVA activity in the area. They refused to go. One soldier told reporters, "If there were GIs out there that needed protection, that would be different. But there ain't nobody out there except a bunch of Dinks."[5]

By this stage of the war, most aircrew members at the

rank of captain or above had been to Southeast Asia at least once. Since they had their career tickets punched, most did not want to come back and did not, unless involuntarily ordered.[6] But the young guys did not necessarily have that choice. Many of those graduating out of the pilot and navigator schools were pipelined to Southeast Asian assignments. As young lieutenants, they were perhaps only two years out of the universities; consequently, they knew the mood of the country. They knew that the nation was turning its back on the war.

When they arrived in the theater, they encountered ARVN allies who seemed for the most part content to sit back and let the U.S. Air Force do the fighting for them. Admittedly, many of the younger aircrews went over to the war not so much dedicated to a cause as seeking the adventure of it all. Yet in the grim reality of war, that soon wore off. They became stern professionals in the business of death, quickly realizing the costs. At the same time, they saw in the ARVN individuals who did not seem to be as committed to their own defense as were the Americans. This observation was very disheartening to many.[7] One officer dryly stated: "The colors in the South Vietnamese flag are certainly appropriate—most of the people are yellow, and the rest are red."[8]

What many of the young Americans could not understand or feel was the war weariness of the Vietnamese people. The Vietnamese had been surrounded by war in some form since the Japanese occupation of World War II, and it had devastated their homeland and families. They did not have the luxury of getting on a jet and flying away from the war forever. They had to live with it and see it through. Many ARVN soldiers were the sole providers for their families, and when families were threatened by the war, many soldiers left their posts to care for them. Americans saw this as cowardice. To the Vietnamese, it was survival. Cynically, the American aircrews had a bar song that captured this chasm:

> Hear the pitter-patter of little feet
> It's the goddamn ARVN in full retreat
> They're movin on, they'll soon be gone
> They're burning gas, they're hauling ass
> They're movin on.[9]

And on the helmets of the American soldiers who still remained, the fliers saw the initials UUUU, meaning "the unwilling, led by the unqualified, doing the unnecessary for the ungrateful."[10] It was all part of the same mosaic.

Consequently, American aircrews did not feel the loyalty to one's own for the South Vietnamese ground troops that the ground advisers felt for the southern soldiers and Marines. Their loyalty was reserved for their fellow airmen, comrades in the same lamentable cause. As one FAC supervisor briefed his new personnel: "Any pilot taking great risks in any action other than in direct support of U.S. [personnel] not only would not get any medals, he'd be in trouble with me." He concluded his pitch by giving them a father-to-son talk about getting killed for a debatable cause.[11] Like most of their countrymen still in the field with the Vietnamese combat units, they worked hard and tried to do a professional job. But few could find in the official explanations or in the actions of the Vietnamese whom they encountered a rationale for why they were fighting. So like the grunts, they adopted the slogan that summed up the war: "It don't mean nothing."[12]

The Americans were not alone in harboring ill feelings for their allies. Many Vietnamese were just as tired of the American troops and concerned about their impact on Vietnamese society. In fact, by early 1972 the Vietnamese populace was seething with anti-American resentment. Surveys taken among the South Vietnamese in late 1971 detailed deep bitterness against the Americans for the killing of innocent civilians.[13] Their concerns were well placed, for the Vietnamese people suffered horribly in that war. After it had ended, the U.S. Senate Subcommittee on Refugees estimated that civilian casualties in South Vietnam numbered 400,000 killed, 900,000 wounded, and 6,500,000 refugees. Including the soldiers, they estimated that 2,000,000 had been killed and about 4,500,000 wounded, about 10 percent of the Vietnamese population.[14]

The Vietnamese people also resented the defoliation and destruction of crops and burial grounds, the coercion of girls into prostitution, the drug smuggling and use, and the reckless driving. Some former governmental leaders also stated that careless spending by GIs had adversely affected local economies, inflated prices overall, and had a negative impact on the Vietnamese way of life. By 1972 we had become the "ugly Americans."[15] One young Vietnamese student, perhaps unknowingly, illustrated this feeling in an interview for the book *Fire in the Lake*. When the Americans arrived, he said, "They seemed so carefree, so strong, I was moved to think they would have come from so far away to die for something other than their own country." But as time passed, "I saw how they interfered at all levels in Vietnamese society. I read about the massacre of Vietnamese civilians in My Lai. I saw myself how the lives of city people were disrupted by the American presence. I began to feel that the American presence itself is the reason why the Communists continue the war."[16]

In many ways the United States, with its heavy-handed ways, overbearing culture, and extravagant use of almost unrestrained firepower, was as big a threat to the South Vietnamese as was the enemy from the North. Indeed, it was a favorite tactic of the Viet Cong and NVA to sneak into a village, set up a large-caliber gun, and shoot at a FAC. When he responded they would flee, knowing full well that he would call in an airstrike and level the village. It was used repeatedly to turn the people against the Americans and the South Vietnamese government.[17]

Of the almost eight million tons of bombs the United States dropped in Southeast Asia during the war, just about half was dropped on South Vietnam. In fact, South Vietnam is the most bombed nation in the history of aerial warfare. This does not include all of the artillery, mortars, and land mines used by ground forces, nor does it include the eighteen million gallons of chemical defoliants sprayed over nearly six million acres of the countryside, until the spraying was stopped in 1971.[18]

But the young Americans still in the war at the time did not know the magnitude of this reality. Therefore, South Vietnamese resentment was not understood, and it bothered a great many of the American soldiers, Marines, and airmen. The theme resonates clearly through the writings that have appeared since the war. Many Americans have a romantic view of their role in war, seeing themselves and their warriors as the good guys who go forth to do good deeds and dispense things that (they think) the rest of the world, naturally, wants. Many such military people came to South Vietnam (they thought) to help. Yet by 1972, the Vietnamese people clearly resented them, and many Americans wondered why they were still fighting. Regardless of the long, tired, political justifications put forth, by 1972 it was simple. "We fight for each other," said one young soldier. "We're really tight here. Nobody else cares for us."[19]

This bond has existed in armies in all wars. What was different in Vietnam was the fact that by 1972, the war for many Americans seemed pointless. And not only was the reason for being in Vietnam unclear at best, the United States's "allies" did not clearly desire the U.S. presence at all. Thus the Vietnamese, for the most part, were not included in the U.S. servicemen's bond.

Of course, not all American airmen felt this way. Maj. Dave Brookbank, the Air Force air liaison officer adviser assigned to the 3d ARVN Division, was one. He obviously developed a strong loyalty to the Vietnamese troops with whom he fought: their battle was also his battle. But Brookbank was clearly an anomaly, for he saw battle as very few Air Force officers have ever seen it. He was, in effect, a ground officer. His views replicate those of many of the last advisers to the ARVN and Vietnamese Marine ground combat units.

Many of the FACs who worked closely with various ground units harbored strong feelings for the guys on the ground. The Raven FACs assigned to special duty in Laos were this way. Even though they were all Air Force officers, when they went out into the field and got to know their "little guys," they bonded with them and went to great lengths to help them. To these FACs, at least, the cause was not debatable: the war was not just targets on the ground, but people whom they knew by name and cared for.

And there were fighter guys who hung it out for the guys on the ground, who made multiple passes on targets for Vietnamese or Laotian or Cambodian forces. But they were clearly in the minority, going against the grain, and, in some cases, liable to punishment by their superiors for doing so. To most Air Force crewmembers, the battles below were anonymous and, by this late date in the war, questionable in value, from an American perspective.

But rescuing another American was not a debatable cause. And that belief was passionately held by all still in the war.

With this mind-set, the U.S. Air Force responded to the Easter Offensive. When Bat 21 was shot down, the system reacted automatically for SAR operations. The FACs, who by this time had been disconnected from the ground forces, did what they were trained to do. So did the Sandys and Jolly Greens. Joker responded in the appropriate fashion, as it had for all SARs. But frustration and years of war by management interceded. The SAR snowballed and the effort was allowed to interfere with the ground battle, because almost all of the Air Force personnel involved did not understand and could not relate to what that battle was all about. Prejudices made concern for the American aircrews take precedence over other concerns. All of this was symptomatic of the U.S. frustration with that war.

So was he worth it? Years later Hambleton himself was asked that question. "I don't know," he said, "I don't know."[20] But what could he say? He did not ask for his dilemma; he was stuck with it. All he and Mark Clark and Bruce Walker could do was to hang on and hope. They had all worked on SARs for others, and they knew what to expect.

But others, whether they realized it or not, did answer that question. After watching Jolly Green 67 get shot down, Capt. Fred Boli, as Sandy 01 (responsible for the lives of all in the SAR task force) concluded that the survivors were not worth the lives of any others: he pulled the SAR task force out of the area. It was a difficult but pragmatic decision, based on the situation at hand. Lieutenant Colonel Harris felt the same way: the price was just too high for two men. Colonel Muirhead, the 3d ARRG commander, concurred with all of that. And when he dutifully reported the decision to Major General Marshall, the general also concurred—but then started the chain of events that eventually got Hambleton (and Clark, and may have gotten Walker) out through the ground rescue. The process was simple cost analysis. They found a "cheaper" way: the Anderson/ Norris team. Anderson, as previously explained, wanted his organization to be successful before it was disbanded. His intelligence officer, Capt. Bob Covalucci, put it this way: "[Anderson] had a fire burning in his belly, as we all did, to make a successful operation happen on our watch. . . . He saw that perhaps this was the last chance to do this. That is what drove Anderson. . . . He said, 'Hey, this is the last hurrah, guys. If we are going to do it, we are going to do it this time.[21]' "

With Norris, it was a bit more personal. He was incapable of walking away from a challenge. He and Anderson both analyzed it and felt that it was an achievable mission, that the guys were well worth the effort. Those two were the right people at the right place at the right time—Anderson as head of the JPRC, Norris to lead the team. It was Anderson's last mission before returning to the States, and it was the reason why Norris was in South Vietnam. He had volunteered for this second tour specifically because he wanted to rescue downed fliers.[22]

To the other aircrews, there was no question that Hambleton was worth it. The Blueghost crews did not have to go up there, but they did. The Jolly Green crews did not have to go up there, but they did. It was the bond. If asked or ordered, they would have gone in again, although years later, Lieutenant Commander Crowe of the Jolly Greens pointed out that had they been asked to go in again, they would have demanded much more from intelligence.[23]

If he had been given the order, Lieutenant Colonel Harris says that he would have questioned his superiors to make sure they understood the cost—but he would have carried it out. And he knew that the aircrews would have gone. A month later, when the 3d ARVN Division had been driven back to Quang Tri, his squadron was asked to fly five helicopters into the Citadel in the center of the town to rescue trapped American and Vietnamese personnel. When he called for volunteers, every member of his unit stepped forward.[24] The remaining combat aircrews knew that if ever they were downed, as long as they could maintain radio contact, the war would stop for them. This knowledge kept Woody Bergeron, Mark Clark, and the Blueghost guys going, and it kept Bruce Walker moving to the coast. As Hambleton said, "It has to make an American fighting man real proud to know that our government and our military will go to any length to save a fighting man's life."[25]

One of the most telling statements was inherent in the actions of Capt. Pete Chapman, the aircraft commander on Jolly Green 67 on 6 April. He flew even though it was not his turn, as a matter of honor. A few weeks before, he had flown a mission to recover a stranded U.S. Army reconnaissance team. As he was hovering over the team for the pickup, he took some ground fire. Believing that he was badly damaged, he pulled off and returned to Da Nang, and another helicopter recovered the team. But upon landing in Da Nang, Chapman discovered that his aircraft was hardly damaged at all. Chagrined and perhaps ashamed, he saw Bat 21 as his exoneration. He was willing to fly to show that he, as one of the Jolly Greens, could keep the faith. Because he knew that the rest of us believed—knew—that if our time ever came, the Jolly Green would be there.[26]

So that was it then. By April of 1972, the U.S. air units that were covering our nation's withdrawal from Vietnam were emotionally separated from their "allies" on the ground. There was no real bond or kinship, as still existed between many of the ground advisers and their units. When Mike 81, Bat 21, Blueghost 39, Blueghost 28, Nail 38, Jolly Green 67, and Covey 282 were shot down, the pilots and crewmembers acted automatically and responded to help their own. And the fully developed rescue system assisted them in that endeavor. It and they had been honed by years of practice in recovering downed comrades. In this case, that automatic response did interfere with the ground battle. That interference is hard to gauge, in light of all of the other factors involved in the ultimate loss and retaking of Quang Tri City and Province. Yet it did happen. No officially, not as an act of commission, but more subtl as an act of omission. The aircrew members were doing what they had been trained to do and what they expected of one another in that too-long, drawn-out war. Among the fliers, it was just understood. Those were the underlying passions and emotions that drove the young American fliers in the waning days of the war.

The fact remains that at that place and time, the priority, for a few days at least, was the shot-down aircrews— not officially, but certainly in the minds of the fliers, and they were the ones who were doing the fighting.

Yet the ground advisers saw the effects on the morale of the ground troops, those stuck with fighting off the massive NVA invasion. Thus they question the rescues to this day.

After Bat 21, hard questions were asked and lessons were learned. Colonel Muirhead at 3d ARRG conducted a post-action analysis and determined that numerous changes had to be made. Recalling that all aircrewmen had been taught basic escape-and-evasion procedures at the various survival schools, he directed that in some situations, survivors could very well be called upon to move to a safer environment for pickup. To facilitate such movement, survivors would not automatically be ringed with many types of ordnance, such as mines, to preclude capture; a "back door" had to be left in the protective field so that the individual could be safely moved. Because of the now-conventional nature of the fighting in South Vietnam, no-fire zones would no longer be used in rescue operations, and the rescue center would stay much more attuned to the ground battles through better coordination with intelligence and the other services.

The rescue forces accepted the fact that there were

situations in which conventional rescue would be impossible. The attempts could no longer be automatic; efforts had to be based on threat and location analysis. The helicopter attempts failed for one reason—the NVA air defenses were too tough. The fliers could not achieve enough localized air superiority for the vulnerable helicopters to even briefly dash in for the pickup. That lesson, so painfully learned in Korea, had been forgotten, at least in this case. But no rigid rules would be published regarding when a SAR effort should or should not be launched. Every situation would be considered on its own merits, and every element of tactical flexibility would be used to get guys back.

Colonel Muirhead then went out to all of the bases and briefed the wing commanders and crews of the combat units on these decisions. He explained that the United States would still do everything possible to get its guys. And he had good news to share: his analysts had discovered that if a crewmember had a successful ejection and could come up on his radio and establish voice contact, he had an 82 percent chance of being recovered by the SAR forces. But the blank check was gone: the tactical situation could very well dictate that nothing could be done. It was a hard thing to have to say to the crews, but everybody accepted it.[27]

Muirhead's direct superior, Brig. Gen. Richard Cross, the deputy director of air operations at Seventh Air Force, said the same thing more forcefully: "As airmen or soldiers or sailors, we should expect that there are times when as one person, we must be sacrificed for the overall."[28] It did not take long for that idea to be tested.

That spring, as the fighting intensified, Seventh Air Force fighters and bombers began hitting targets

North Vietnam. On 23 May, an F-4 from the 435th Tactical Fighter Squadron at Ubon Air Base, call sign Owl 14, was shot down on a night mission in southern North Vietnam. The pilot, Capt. Bill Byrns, was captured almost immediately. The backseater, Capt. Ray Bean, found what he thought was a good hiding place and hunkered down to wait for the rescue forces. But the area was so heavily defended that the only aircraft that even contacted him were "Fast FACs"—forward air controllers flying F-4s. They were the only aircraft that could survive in the area. For thirty-six hours they put in airstrikes around Bean in an effort to soften the area for the rescue forces to get in, but the defenses were too intense. No Sandys or Jolly Greens were committed. Finally Bean was captured. As he was being led away, he realized that the NVA defenses were so strong that he was literally in a trap. He could see now why the helicopters could not have been committed: they would have been blown out of the sky.

Captain Bean was released by Hanoi in early 1973. While in prison, he was told by some squadron mates captured after him that the day after his shootdown, they had wanted to make an attempt to get him out. Some of them had gone to Da Nang and talked to the Jolly pilots to find out why a pickup attempt was not being made, and they were told that the procedures had changed: attempts were no longer automatically made. When the fighter guys asked what had brought about the change, they were given a simple answer—Bat 21. Captain Bean was not bitter about this; he had seen what the NVA had waiting for the rescue forces.[29]

This non-SAR reflected the new pragmatism as the war intensified. As 1972 ran into 1973, few SARs were run into North Vietnam, and none was made around the densely populated and defended areas of the North.[30] There was one very notable and now famous exception to this; it involved an F-4 crew out of the 432d Wing at Udorn Air Base, Thailand.

On 10 May 1972, their aircraft, call sign Oyster 01, was shot down northwest of Hanoi. Only the backseater, Capt. Roger Locher, Oyster 01 Bravo, ejected. He evaded for several days as rescue forces tried to reach him, but the area was too heavily defended. It was obvious that a much larger force would be needed to get him out. The wing commander called Saigon, for the decision to commit such a large force had to be made by the new Seventh Air Force commander, Gen. John Vogt. He tells the story:

The Wing at Udorn called me and said they wanted to get him out. The problem was that it was going to involve a substantial effort. Choppers would have to be sent up there; they would have to have enough support to deal with the possibility that when they got up there around the air base at Yen Bai, the MiGs would come swarming in. There could be a major air battle, we might lose aircraft. I had to decide whether we should risk the loss of maybe half a dozen airplanes and crews just to get one man out. Finally I said to myself, "Damn it, the one thing that keeps our boys motivated is the certain belief that if they go down, we will do absolutely everything we can to get them out. If that is ever in doubt, morale would tumble." That was my major consideration. So I took it on myself. I didn't ask anybody for permission. I just said, "Go do it!"[31]

The strike force put together for the rescue was larger than the initial strike flown against North Vietnam on 10 May. In fact, on the day of the rescue, all other operations against North Vietnam were canceled. But after twenty-three days in enemy territory, Capt. Roger Locher was successfully rescued and brought back to a tumultuous and tearful welcome.[32] General Vogt's actions dovetailed with Major General Marshall's earlier actions for Bat 21 Bravo.

In those last years, U.S. airpower performed a rearguard role as the United States disengaged from that war. All of the aircrews knew that it was just a matter of time. Nobody wanted to be the last loss. The dilemma was how to withdraw the remaining forces while securing the return of American prisoners and leaving South Vietnam reasonably secure. Airpower was the only weapon left, and the key to its use was the morale of the aircrews. They fought for one another. Both of the generals knew that.

Vogt's logic was clearly understood at the other end of the combat chain of command. As one of the Jolly Green pilots said: "The reason we did so much for those guys was because they were there to have it done for them. We all hoped that if the role was reversed that he would do for us what we were trying to do for him. I think that is about all there is to that."[33]

In 1972, just outside of the revetted area in which the 37th ARRS parked its helicopters at Da Nang, there was a large billboard. On it was a picture of the Jolly Green Giant—the hijacked symbol of the rescue forces. Underneath were written four words: That Others May Live. Every American taking off to do battle with the enemy could see it, and they all understood what it meant. It would not be there much longer, and, ominously, it was not written in Vietnamese.

That was unfortunate, because with the failure of the 1972 North Vietnamese offensive, the United States would bring its troops home, leaving behind a "peace treaty" that did not bring peace. Emotionally, with the return of the POWs, the United States was done with the war. Yet the strategic formula "Saigon's infantry + American firepower > VC + NVA" was just as valid. The "peace" left to South Vietnam was based on the promise of continued American aid and the implied threat of a return of American airpower. But the American people were finished with the war, and its congressional leaders sensed this. They took away from President Nixon the authority to use American forces in Southeast Asia, and then they voted to reduce aid to South Vietnam. With those two severe actions, the disconnection was complete.

Meanwhile, North Vietnamese leaders had watched closely. When they had decided that America no longer had the will to act and their growing strength and South Vietnam's growing weakness had tipped the strategic equation in their favor, they decided to once again attack, in late 1974. The campaign was relatively quick: by April 1975, their army had overrun the South and it was all over. The flag that Maj. Dave Brookbank saw waving over the DMZ now flew over all of the newly reunited Vietnam.

So was Bat 21 worth it? Of course he was, from our perspective. The young Americans who flew and fought to save Bat 21 Bravo and all the others who were shot down were ultimately expressing the larger national desire to bring home the troops and get out of the war.

But there was a higher price. The partial abandonment of the battle to go and rescue Bat 21 did affect that particular battle. America repeated those actions on a larger scale when it abandoned its allies to disengage from that war, the ultimate symbol of which was the return of the POWs.

When the colonel said, "There is nothing over here which is worth an American life," he said more than he knew. He was really expressing the feelings of the nation. The bond between the fliers reflected the one between the American people and their men in Vietnam. Gen. Fred Weyand, the last American commander in Vietnam, explained this concept: "Vietnam was a reaffirmation of the peculiar relationship between the American Army and the American people. The American Army is really a people's Army in the sense that it belongs to the American people who take a jealous and proprietary interest in its involvement. When the Army is committed the American people are committed, when the American people lose their commitment it is futile to try to keep the Army committed."[34]

The general was slightly short of the mark: it was not just the Army, but all of the military forces that basked in the warmth of that "peculiar" relationship. It was the bond between a people and their sons. It ultimately did not apply to our allies.

The United States is a consensus-oriented society that is served rather than dominated by its defense establishment. That establishment responds to the political leaders, who respond appropriately to the people of the nation. The United States lost in a contest of wills against the Communist forces in Southeast Asia. They outlasted the Americans on the battlefield, until the frus-

trated and disillusioned American people, tired of the
war, forced their elected representatives to bring the
troops home and leave South Vietnam, Laos, and Cambodia to their own devices. The American people
wanted a quick, American-style (i.e., high technology,
lots of firepower) victory. In microcosm, that is what
SARs were. And perhaps it can be argued that the two
climactic Linebacker operations in late 1972 were the
ultimate SARs, because they brought the POWs home.
The analogy to Bat 21 Bravo is not perfect, but the
events are parallel, for the emotions and passions behind
them are the same. And war is about passions and emotions.

But SARs don't win wars, and in the larger struggle,
the American military could not deliver that kind of victory. This war, like most, was ultimately a struggle between two peoples. The North Vietnamese and their
allies wanted to win more than we and our allies did, and
the North Vietnamese were willing to pay the price.[35]
Ultimately, in what the United States saw as a limited
war, we had exceeded the limited price that the American people were prepared to pay. There was nothing
more over there worth an American life—except another
American. And that bond was the value of that one
American's life.[36]

So that is the story of Bat 21. And it is almost legend
now. The struggle of the one survivor, Lt. Col. Iceal
Hambleton, is a classic story of what one man can do
against the most terrible of odds, and it serves as a deep
inspiration to us all. But he was a lucky man, because his
story is one of the fortuitous combination of many historic, cultural, and immediate forces at one place and
time. Yet perhaps, more ominously, it is also a warning

about the dangers of alliances and the pitfalls of coalition warfare in wars that are too drawn out with objectives not clearly defined. But for Lieutenant Colonel Hambleton, at least, the story had a happy ending. He lives in retirement now, under the warm skies of Arizona.

As they get further and further away from a war
they have taken part in, all men have a tendency
to make it more as they wish it had been
rather than how it really was.

Ernest Hemingway, Men at War:
The Best War Stories of All Time

POSTSCRIPT

IT IS ALL FAR behind them now, and the years have
been good to most. The memories are still there. They
are vivid for some, but for most they remain as pictures
or logs in a forgotten corner somewhere. Life has gone
on, as it has for the nation.

After the SARs and battles of April, others followed.
The Marine advisers fought with their units until they
were withdrawn not too many months afterward. They
still take great pride in being the last covans with the
Vietnamese Marines; the Army advisers preceded them
home.

Lt. Col. Gene Hambleton returned to his unit at
Korat, but he did not fly again. Instead, he gave a series

of briefings and returned to the States. He was welcomed home as a hero. Likewise, First Lieutenant Clark returned to his unit up at Nakhon Phanom. He also had no desire to get back in an OV-10. But after a long and serious discussion with his squadron commander, he returned to the OV-10 and flew for several more months in Vietnam and Laos. He also got back in the SAR business, but not as a crewmember. He helped plan the successful rescue of his namesake, 1st Lt. Woody Clark, Cosmic 16 Bravo, who was shot down several months later near Mu Gia Pass in North Vietnam.

After the destruction of the 3d ARVN Division at Quang Tri, Maj. Dave Brookbank was assigned as an adviser down in the Delta region south of Saigon. He finished his tour there. Lt. Tom Norris went back to STDAT 158 and worked with the Vietnamese sea commandos. On 31 October he was a member of a small team that infiltrated behind enemy lines to capture a prisoner and gather intelligence. They were supposed to be inserted near the old naval base at the mouth of the Cua Viet River. Instead, they were put ashore eight kilometers north, near an enemy base camp. They were detected and a gun battle ensued. Norris was grievously wounded in the head, and his assistant, Michael Thornton, engineman second class, helped him swim for more than two hours back to their recovery boat. For his actions, Thornton was awarded the Medal of Honor. Because of his wounds, Norris was medically retired from the Navy.

But in early April 1976, he had occasion to put his uniform back on when the president of the United States wanted him to visit the White House to receive the Medal of Honor for his rescue of Hambleton and

Clark. Tom thought it over and decided to show up. As part of the deal, he was told that he could bring four guests to the ceremony. He made his plans. But just a few days before the big day, a White House aide called him and said that he could only bring three. Tom said that was impossible: he had made his plans. The aide explained that this was a ceremony involving the president, and some changes had to be made. Tom said that changes were fine, but he was bringing his four guests. The aide insisted, but he did not realize whom he was dealing with. Norris stated flatly that if he could not bring his four guests, he wasn't coming! The aide was flabbergasted. But he had run square into Norris's stubborn streak. When Tom made a decision, he didn't back down from anybody, not the North Vietnamese Army, not the White House. Reason prevailed: he had four guests at the ceremony. After that, Tom went through several more years of tedious and often painful medical rehabilitation. Today he works for another governmental agency and lives in the West, near the mountains.[1]

Many of the other participants left the military right after their time in Southeast Asia. Several of the pilots went on to careers as airline pilots; quite a few retired in the seventies and went on to new lives. Dave Brookbank left the Air Force as a lieutenant colonel, bitter about the turn of events during April. He still feels strongly that the U.S. Air Force sold out the Vietnamese during that April and ultimately abandoned them to a terrible fate.

Iceal Hambleton retired very soon after his return to the States. When he is not enjoying to the fullest his retirement in Arizona, he occasionally travels and speaks of his exploits as Bat 21 Bravo. But a strange and unexpected thing happened that day over Cam Lo, Sou

Vietnam: Iceal Hambleton ejected from the aircraft, but Bat 21 Bravo landed on the ground. His whole persona changed—and remains. The memories are still very much with him, and he thinks about his rescue almost every day. He is acutely aware of the cost and still feels the pain of the losses incurred. Whether he was worth all that he still does not know, and he still wonders why him.

But the larger forces that propelled this biggest of all SARs of that war are still with us, an ingrained part of the American psyche. And they occasionally resurface.

Many years after Bat 21 Bravo had been rescued, gruesome scenes appeared on televisions throughout the world. The pictures were too familiar: Americans shot down and surrounded by enemy forces in a tightening circle. High-technology helicopters hovered overhead, pouring massive firepower down on the hostile troops. Desperate men trying to perform desperate actions in desperate situations. But this was not a movie about Vietnam. It was real events involving young American fighting men in Mogadishu, Somalia, on the eastern Horn of Africa. It was October 1993.

Once again, American troops had been dispatched on a military mission that appeared to be going wrong. The objectives were ill-defined, and the American people wanted their sons (and now daughters) brought home. But before it was done, one debacle would lead to the death of seventeen soldiers and the serious wounding of seventy-seven others.

The previous October, American forces, as part of a UN force, had entered Somalia to provide humanitarian relief to its starving population. Seven months later most Americans departed, as the UN forces took full control

and changed the mission to one of 'nation building."
Unfortunately, though, that bedeviled nation was controlled by fractious warlords who felt threatened by the
efforts of the United Nations. The various factions, most
notably those of Mohammed Farah Aidid, began to fight
back. For those Americans still there, the mission began
to creep beyond humanitarian aid toward something re-
sembling real combat.[2]

American soldiers started suffering casualties. Taking a
risky action, the secretary of defense ordered U.S. Army
Rangers and supporting helicopter forces to Somalia to
capture Aidid. On 3 October the Ranger commander
received intelligence of Aidid's location. He ordered his
highly trained troops into action. Initially the mission
proceeded according to plan: the Rangers surprised the
Somalis and captured twenty-four of Aidid's lieutenants.
Then the Somalis reacted, and one of the supporting
Army MH-60 Blackhawk helicopters was downed by
ground fire. It crashed in an open street. Immediately
Army Rangers began to form a perimeter around the site
to protect and rescue the crew. The hostile Somalis
pressed ever tighter.

Then another MH-60 was downed. Rangers could not
get to it, and some of its crew were killed, some captured. But for several hours, the Rangers and their supporting helicopters surrounded themselves with a
cauldron of fire until a relief ground convoy could rescue
them all.

The outcry in the United States was loud and ugly
Americans had not realized that their troops were in
volved in a war; they thought that they had been sent
Somalia to help distribute food to a starving populat'
Their political leaders had not prepared them for a c

ening military involvement. Revolted by the turn of events by an almost two-to-one margin, they turned against any further U.S. military involvement in Somalia.[3] One citizen wrote to his local paper, "I believe we should send in more troops to rescue the troops that we have there now. . . . When that has been accomplished, I believe we should pull our troops out."[4]

Pundits began to compare it to the quagmire of Vietnam. Senator John McCain, a former Vietnam POW, said that there was no clear military mission in Somalia. "Someone ought to tell [the president] . . . it's time to bring the troops home."[5] The *Cincinnati Enquirer* opined: "Escalating casualties and fighting are wasting U.S. lives in Somalia."[6] The *New York Times* was more blunt. Their lead editorial read "Somalia: Time to Get Out."[7] None of this was lost on the troops, who could see that they were once again stuck in harm's way without any clear national purpose or will.

Although shorter in duration, the rescue in Mogadishu was a replay of the rescue of Bat 21 Bravo. Like warriors of any age, the Americans who were stuck in Somalia fought for one another. And they did it the American way, with lots of high-technology weapons and firepower. Later, as the postmortems were taking place, one soldier reflected, "If you can't take comfort in the higher calling of the mission, then you do it for your buddies."[8]

The passions and emotions were the same, and war is all about passions and emotions. It is a link that continues.

By the time of Somalia, though, the nation had forgotten the now long-distant Vietnam War. But the families whose lost had not forgotten. They waited as relations improved between the United States and Vietnam to the point where search teams could return to the battlefields of 1972. Patiently, the teams culled old records and battle reports for likely locations of our downed airmen and soldiers. Their steady patience paid off as the sites were located and carefully combed for remains of those lost.

Not long after the Somalia debacle, the remains of Blueghost 39 were recovered and returned to the United States for burial in Arlington National Cemetery. On an overcast morning in April 1994, family and friends met in the old chapel for a service to honor the common remains of the crew. Unfortunately, Gene Hambleton, Bat 21 Bravo, could not attend, but several other veterans of the battle did. Col. Rich Atchison (Ret.) was there from the Nail FACs. Mr. Mike Austin, another Blueghost pilot, was there. So were Tim Sprouse and Chuck LeCelle, the F Troop gun team who flew so many of the missions during that time and searched for Blueghost 39 after they were lost. They mixed easily with the others from F Troop of the 8th Cavalry who wanted to be there to welcome home their troops.

The casket was loaded onto the caisson for the slow journey into the cemetery itself. At graveside, the group gathered again for final prayers and the presentation of the flags as a lone soldier played taps from under a majestic oak tree.

Three years later, in November 1997, that caisson was called up once again to perform its somber task. Th[...] time, it was the crew of Jolly Green 67. Like the Ar[...] crew, their remains had been located and recovered [...] combined U.S. and Vietnamese search team. An[...]

Blueghost, their final resting place would be in Arlington.

So another group of family and friends gathered in northern Virginia. Veterans of the mission came from all parts of the United States. Jay Crowe, Don Morse, Rick Atchison, and Mark Clark met with the families of the lost crew and told them the story of the rescues and the loss of Jolly Green 67. It was a very emotional event but the families appreciated it. As one family member said afterward, "We never knew what really happened up there until now."[9]

The next morning, over three hundred people gathered for the ceremony. They followed the horse-drawn caisson as it carried the remains. The Air Force Ceremonial Band escorted them and played "On Eagles Wings" as the caisson arrived at the burial site.

As the music ended, everyone could feel the low pulsing thump of beating blades as two MH-53J "Pavelow" helicopters from the 20th Special Operations Squadron—the direct descendants of the Jolly Greens—made a dramatic flyby to honor the crew. As they passed, they trailed green smoke as a salute to their comrades.

Several veterans of the actual missions then stepped forward to speak. Jay Crowe, resplendent in his Coast Guard uniform, spoke as a representative of all who could not attend. He prayed that the crew of Jolly Green 67 would rest easy now, knowing they were home among friends.

Dave Mullinex spoke next. He was supposed to be the pilot on Jolly Green 67 that day but had swapped with n Call. He was there to welcome his crew home.

l Prebble, a pararescueman with the 37th ARRS, next. He was filling in for Dave Young, who was supposed to speak but had missed his flight to Washington. Bill talked about closure and the honor of knowing such men.

Gene Hambleton, Bat 21 Bravo, could not attend due to a previous engagement, but he sent a letter that was read by another pararescueman from the 37th ARRS, Dan Manion. In the letter Hambleton said of the crew:

[They] were doing what they had been trained to do and doing exactly what they were sent to SEA to do. April 2 [*sic*], 1972, was the most terrible day that I had ever lived through in all my fifty-three years. I had to sit there and watch six young men lose their lives in the effort to save mine. Heroes? You bet they are! They deserve all the accolades and honors that we, the living, can bestow upon them. . . . Please add my prayers to all during the Memorial. I will be there in spirit and for the entire crew, praying.[10]

Mark Clark, Nail 38 Bravo, spoke next. His words were simple and eloquent. He addressed the families:

For those of us who were in Vietnam during that era, those memories will live with us forever. In flying a rescue mission against frankly impossible odds, your sons and brothers were honoring their commitment to themselves and their country, a value that is very important today and that we need here in Washington particularly. Their actions embodied honor and commitment. Have no doubt that each of those men wer heroes. From a personal perspective I want the fam members to please accept my gratitude. Each of played a unique role in forming the character of

men who were willing to pay a very dear price to help
people like me get out of the jungle of Vietnam. It is
frankly impossible for me to share the sorrow that you
have felt for these twenty-five years. You have my deepest sympathy. You and these six brave men are in my
prayers daily and will continue to be so. As we honor
these men today, I hope that you can take some comfort in the fact that in the divine plan some good comes
out of every loss and tragedy. After twenty-five years,
that good may not be evident to all of us, but it is there,
and for me this memorial is an integral part of that
goodness that has come out of it because it has brought
us together.[11]

Lt. Gen. David Vesely attended as the official representative of the U. S. Air Force. But before he could step to
the podium, one more veteran wanted to say something.
It was Dave Young. He had caught a backup flight to
Baltimore, jumped in a taxi and sped to Arlington. He
entered the cemetery as the helicopters passed overhead.
As Mark Clark was concluding, he walked up to the
chaplain and announced that he would speak next. His
words were simple but deeply moving. He was supposed
to be one of the pararescuemen on Jolly Green 67 that
morning but was switched to the high bird at the last
moment. He said, "It wasn't any surprise to us what we
were getting into and it took exceedingly brave guys to
volunteer and get on that helicopter to do what they did
that day. These men have my deepest respect and admi-
ration."[12] He tried to continue but the words would not
come.

Then General Vesely spoke. He had served in Vietnam

as a helicopter pilot in that same 20th Special Operations
Squadron and was well familiar with the rescue. He said:

> As an airman who flew helicopters in Vietnam, I take
> special pride in their courage and their sacrifice. . . . In
> Southeast Asia, every American airman knew that wher-
> ever he might be down, such men as those we honor
> today would give everything to rescue them. . . .
> There are those who have asked whether it makes sense
> to risk so many lives to save one or two. All of us who
> have flown in harm's way know what a difference it
> makes to believe that every effort will be made to res-
> cue us if we are down. In Southeast Asia, our rescue
> people saved thousands of lives and encouraged all of us
> who were there. Today while we count the high cost,
> we should also count ourselves fortunate to be the ben-
> eficiaries of these, the best of men—men who gave their
> lives "so that others may live."[13]

As the general presented the flags to the families, it
occurred to many that a moment of closure had arrived.
The events of twenty-five years ago in that corner of a
country that no longer existed were complete: the SARs
were finally over. Numerous veterans, many wearing
their well-decorated uniforms, walked up to the casket.
Some saluted or touched it. Several placed well-worn
POW bracelets on top. And one affixed a Jolly Green
sticker to it. It was hard not to notice that most seemed
to have just a little problem with misty eyes.

Looking around at the assembled crowd, it all seemed
so right. These aged warriors had come for the Jolly
Green because they remembered a time when the Jolly
Green would have come for them. It was the bond, and
it is timeless.

NOTES

The story of Bat 21 is discussed in part in numerous previous works. The book *Bat 21,* by William Anderson (New York: Bantam, 1980) is the most specific, but it deals with the story really only from the perspective of the one survivor, Iceal Hambleton. Numerous works tell the story of the Easter Offensive in northern South Vietnam. The most comprehensive among them are Col. G. H. Turley (Ret.)'s *The Easter Offensive: The Last American Advisors, Vietnam, 1972* (Novato, Calif.: Presidio Press, 1985) and the more recent *Trial by Fire,* by Dale Andrade (New York: Hippocrene Books, 1995).

But to actually recreate the story, I had to refer to primary-source documents, logbooks, letters, and various messages. These (and all secondary sources) are documented in the notes.

The following individuals graciously agreed to be interviewed for this work:

U.S. Air Force
Col. Ed Anderson (Ret.), Lt. Col. Gerald Bauknight (Ret.), Col. Ray Bean, Lt. Col. Woody Bergeron (Ret.), Col. Tim Brady, Lt. Col. Dave Brookbank (Ret.), Col. Mike Carlin, Mr. Marty Cavato, Col. Mark Clark, Col. Bill Dalecky, Col. Mickey Fain, Mr. Gary Ferentchak, Col. Arnie Franklin, Lt. Col. Iceal

Hambleton (Ret.), Col. Bill Harris (Ret.), Mr. William Henderson, Lt. Col. John Hurst (Ret.), Lt. Col. Bill Jankowski, Lt. Col. Jim Kempton (Ret.), Col. Lachlan Macleay (Ret.), Lt. Gen. Winton W. Marshall (Ret.), Col. Cecil Muirhead (Ret.), Lt. Col. Mark Schibler (Ret.), Lt. Col. Ted Sienicki (Ret.), Mr. Rocky Smith, Col. Earl Tilford (Ret.), M.Sgt. Daryl Tincher (Ret.), Lt. Col. Jack Tullett (Ret.), and Gen. John Vogt (Ret.).

U.S. Army
Sp5c. Jose Astorga (Med. Ret.), Brig. Gen. Thomas Bowen (Ret.), Lt. Col. Bill Camper (Ret.), Col. Bob Covalucci (Ret.), Lt. Col. Augustus Greyhosky (Ret.), Col. Jack Kennedy (Ret.), Gen. Frederick J. Kroesen (Ret.), Mr. Chuck LaCelle, Col. Don Lunday (Ret.), Col. Bill Lozier (Ret.), Col. Donald Metcalf (Ret.), Mr. Ben Nielsen, Lt. Col. Mike Rosebeary (Ret.), Maj. Tim Sprouse (Ret.).

U.S. Coast Guard
Capt. Joseph "Jay" Crowe (Ret.).

U.S. Marine Corps
Lt. Gen. D'Wayne Gray (Ret.), Mr. Jack Matthews, Col. Gerald Turley (Ret.), Col. Regen Wright (Ret.).

U.S. Navy
Mr. Steve Keibler, Lt. Tom Norris (Med. Ret.), Mr. Dennis Sapp, Mr. Mike Warde.

Civilians
Mr. Paul Mather, Mr. Douglas Pike.

Chapter I. Hide and Seek
   1. Lewis Sorley, *Thunderbolt General Creighton Abrams and the Army of His Times* (New York: Simon and Schuster, 1992), 235.
   2. Ibid., 262.

3. Douglas Pike, *PAVN: People's Army of Vietnam* (Novato, Calif.: Presidio Press, 1986), 227.

4. Ibid., 219–20, 229.

5. "How Hanoi Calculated the Risk," *London Times,* 12 Apr. 1972.

6. David K. Mann, *The 1972 Invasion of Military Region I: Fall of Quang Tri and Defense of Hue* (Maxwell AFB, Ala.: Project Checo Report, 15 Mar. 1973), 4.

7. "How Hanoi Calculated the Risk."

8. *Airpower and the 1972 Spring Invasion,* U.S. Air Force Southeast Asia Monograph Series, vol. 2, monograph 3 (Washington, D.C.: U.S. Air Force, 1976), 4, 9.

9. Mann, *1972 Invasion,* 11.

10. Lt. Gen. Ngo Quang Truong, *Indochina Monographs: The Easter Offensive of 1972* (Washington, D.C.: U.S. Army, 1980), 19, 22.

11. Interview with Lt. Col. Bill Camper (Ret.), 3 Mar. 1993.

12. Truong, *Indochina Monographs,* 19.

13. Col. G. H. Turley, *The Easter Offensive* (Novato, Calif.: Presidio Press, 1985), 30.

14. Truong, *Indochina Monographs,* 16.

15. Interview with Col. Jack Kennedy (Ret.), 5 May 1994; and interview with Mr. Ben Nielsen, 15 May 1994.

16. *Airpower and the 1972 Spring Invasion,* 12, 14, 26–27.

17. Interview with Lt. Gen. D'Wayne Gray (Ret.), 25 June 1993.

18. *SAR Operations in Southeast Asia, 1 Apr. 1972 to 30 June 1973* (Maxwell AFB: Project Checo Report, USAF), xii, 1.

19. *Airpower and the 1972 Spring Invasion,* 12.

20. Interview with Col. Mickey Fain, 18 May 1990.

21. Interview with Mr. Rocky Smith, 17 May 1990; and interview with Col. Lachlan Macleay (Ret.), 1 Feb. 1993.

22. *SAR Operations,* Project Checo Report, 26. Also interview with Mr. William Henderson, 27 Apr. 1993.

23. Mann, *1972 Invasion,* 18, 34.

24. Brookbank interview.
25. Capt. Joseph G. Meeko, *Vietnamization of the Tactical Air Control System* (Maxwell AFB: Checo/Corona Harvest Division, Operations Analysis Office, HQ PACAF, 23 Sept. 1974), 40.
26. Turley, *Easter Offensive,* 44.

Chapter 2. The Battle

1. Turley, *Easter Offensive,* 45.
2. Truong, *Indochina Monographs,* 24.
3. Interview with Col. Mickey Fain, 7 Nov. 1992.
4. Camper interview.
5. Turley, *Easter Offensive,* 49.
6. Mann, *1972 Invasion,* 14.
7. Turley, *Easter Offensive,* 71.
8. From 31 Mar. through 30 Apr. 1972, Capt. Harold Icke, an O-2 pilot assigned to the 20th TASS, sent a series of letters and a tape to his wife describing the missions that he was flying in support of the rescues. Colonel Icke sent this narrative to me in Dec. 1992.
9. Turley, *Easter Offensive,* 73.
10. Letter from Capt. Tim Sprouse of F Troop of the 8th Cavalry to his parents, 4 Apr. 1972.
11. Turley, *Easter Offensive,* 82, 111, 116.
12. Mann, *1972 Invasion,* 25.
13. *Air War: Vietnam* (Indianapolis: Bobbs-Merrill, 1978), 124.
14. Truong, *Indochina Monographs,* 27.
15. Turley, *Easter Offensive,* 114.
16. Ibid., 107.
17. Truong, *Indochina Monographs,* 29.
18. 3d ARVN Division Tactical Operations Center (TOC) Log, MACV Advisory Team 155, 2 Apr. 1972, item 17. National Archives, Suitland, Md.
19. Turley, *Easter Offensive,* 118–20.
20. Ibid., 120. At this time, the gun line consisted of the USS *Buchanan* (DDG-14), the USS *Strauss* (DDG-16), th

USS *Waddell* (DDG-24), the USS *Anderson* (DD-786), and the USS *Hamner* (DD-718).

21. Turley, *Easter Offensive,* 123.

22. Ibid., 126.

23. After-action report, Lt. Col. Louis C. Wagner Jr., senior adviser to the 1st Armor Brigade, n.d., 5.

24. Turley, *Easter Offensive,* 140.

25. Ibid., 141, 143.

26. Maj. David E. Thomasson, *An Analysis of USAF Combat Damage and Losses in SEA, Apr. 72–Mar. 73* (Maxwell AFB: HQ 7AF, 30 June 1973), 69.

27. Icke narrative.

28. *History of the 37th Aerospace Rescue and Recovery Squadron, 1 Apr.–30 June 1972* (Maxwell AFB: Da Nang AB, SVN), 14.

29. MACV Command Center Log, 2 Apr. 1972, item 42, 1023Z. National Archives. Also deck log of the USS *Hamner,* DD-718, 2 Apr. 1972. Washington, D.C., Naval Historical Center.

30. 3d Division TOC Log, 2 Apr. 1972, items 56, 65.

31. David Fulghum and Terrence Maitland, *South Vietnam on Trial* (Boston: Boston Publishing Company, 1984), 140.

32. Interview with Maj. Tim Sprouse (Ret.), 11 Apr. 1994; and interview with Mr. Chuck LaCelle, 24 Apr. 1994.

33. Brookbank interview.

34. Truong, *Indochina Monographs,* 30.

35. Turley, *Easter Offensive,* 171. The story of the evacuation from Mai Loc is one of unbounded heroism in the face of incredibly difficult conditions.

36. Message/DTG 021400Z from I-DASC Da Nang to 7AF. Subject: BDA (bomb-damage assessment) report of 0600H–2000H 02 Apr. 1972. The strike coordinates were YD 24136108—exactly on the north end of the bridge. National Archives.

37. 3d Division TOC Log, 2 Apr. 1972, items 54, 55.

38. Fulghum and Maitland, *South Vietnam on Trial,* 139. See also John G. Miller, *The Bridge at Dong Ha* (Annapolis,

Md.: Naval Institute Press, 1989), which well describes the operation for which Captain Ripley received the Navy Cross.

39. Turley, *Easter Offensive*, 163.

40. Message/DTG 021400Z from I-DASC Da Nang to 7AF, BDA report, 02 Apr. 72.

41. Miller, *Bridge at Dong Ha*, 160.

42. Turley, *Easter Offensive*, 165.

43. Miller, *Bridge at Dong Ha*, 162.

44. 3d Division TOC Log, 2 Apr. 1972, items 88, 93, 97, 99.

Chapter 3. The Shootdown

1. Interview with Lt. Col. Iceal Hambleton (Ret.), 1 Feb. 1993. The EB-66s were old aircraft, grossly underpowered for the loads they were being forced to carry. Hence the nickname.

2. Interview with Lt. Col. Ed Anderson (Ret.), 8 Dec. 1993. EWOs preferred the E model over the older C model: the electronic systems were newer and more automated. But more important, the EWO ejection seats fired upward in the E as opposed to downward in the C model.

3. Message (declassified) from 366TFW, Da Nang AB SVN, to HQ PACAF, Hickam AFB, Hi., 170640Z Apr. 1972. Subject: Evasion and Recovery Report for Lt. Col. Iceal Hambleton. Washington, D.C., Bolling AFB. Also *History of the 42d Tactical Electronic Warfare Squadron (TEWS), 1 Apr.–30 June 1972* (Maxwell AFB: Korat AB, Thailand).

4. Ibid. Also E. Anderson interview.

5. Statement by Maj. Ed Anderson concerning the shootdown of Bat 21, taken at Korat AB, Thailand, 2 Apr. 1972. Dept. of Defense, Freedom of Information Act.

6. Icke narrative.

7. Evasion and Recovery Report for Lt. Col. Iceal Hambleton. Bat 21 was an EB-66C, tailnumber 54-466. Crew: Alpha pilot, Maj. Wayne Bolte; Bravo navigator, Lt. Col. Iceal Hambleton; Charlie EWO, Maj. Henry Serex; Delta EWO, Lt.

Col. Anthony Giannangeli; Echo EWO, Lt. Col. Charles Levis; Foxtrot EWO, 1st Lt. Robin Gatwood.

8. Technical Order 1B-66(E)B-1, Flight Manual, 31 Mar. 1969, Fig. 1-7. Air Force Academy Library, Colo.

9. Evasion and Recovery Report for Lt. Col. Iceal Hambleton. Also Hambleton interview.

10. Interview with Lt. Col. Jimmy D. Kempton (Ret.), July 1990.

11. Interview with Lt. Col. Bill Jankowski, Aug. 1990. Maj. A. J. C. Lavelle in the U.S. Air Force Southeast Asia Monograph Series, vol. 2, monograph 3, *Airpower and the 1972 Spring Invasion,* erroneously identifies Jim Kempton as an OV-10 FAC who spots Hambleton, follows him down, and initiates the SAR. As these two interviews indicate, this is obviously incorrect. Jim Kempton has always been bemused by this version of events. He thinks that possibly Major Lavelle was at Bluechip when word of the shoot-down came in and may have his facts mixed up. The error is also repeated in Anderson's *Bat 21* and in several other publications.

12. All crewmembers carried a survival radio that could operate in two modes—beeper or voice. In the beeper mode, it transmitted a loud, piercing tone, easily identifiable as an emergency. But while the radio was transmitting the beeper, it could not be used for voice communication. Consequently, when a crewmember got shot down, he would activate his beeper for several seconds and listen in the voice mode to see if anybody was responding to his emergency signal. Hence the standard line, "Beeper, beeper, come up voice!"

13. Jankowski interview.

14. Ed Anderson interview.

15. Jankowski interview.

16. Hambleton interview.

17. Jankowski interview.

18. Ibid.

19. Interview with Lt. Col. Dennis Constant (Ret.), 28 Sept. 1993.

20. Jankowski interview.

Chapter 4. Cavalry to the Rescue

1. Sandy statement for the SAR for Bat 21 Bravo by Capt. Donald Morse, Sandy 07, 2 Apr. 1972. Sandy statements are all included in the 56th Special Operations Wing History, Apr.–Jun. 1972, Maxwell AFB.

2. Interview with Lt. Col. Donald Morse (Ret.), 16 May 1993.

3. Verbatim testimony of witnesses given to Board of Inquiry, 23 Apr. 1972. Convened by the 196th Infantry Brigade to determine circumstances surrounding the loss of Blueghost 39. National Archives.

4. Nielsen interview.

5. Testimony of witnesses given to Board of Inquiry.

6. Witness statement of Sp5c. Jose Astorga. Included on a biographic computer printout of Sp5c. Ronald P. Paschall, dated 27 Feb. 1989, from the Casualty Division of the Joint Casualty Resolution Center. DOD, Freedom of Information Act. Also, interview with Sp5c. Jose Astorga (Med. Ret.), 24 May 1994. Sp5c. Astorga was held prisoner by the NVA and released in 1973. The others were listed as missing in action.

7. "And War Beat Goes On," *Pacific Stars and Stripes,* 5 Apr. 1972, 7. Also testimony of witnesses given to Board of Inquiry, and *History of the 37th Aerospace Rescue and Recovery Squadron, 1 Apr.–30 June 1972,* 15.

8. Sandy statement, Capt. Donald Morse, 2 Apr. 1972.

9. Sprouse letter.

10. Morse interview.

Chapter 5. Decisions in Saigon

1. 7th AF Regulation 64-2, 5 Apr. 1967, Para. 5. Washington, D.C., Bolling AFB.

2. John Morrocco, *Rain of Fire: Air War, 1969–1973* (Boston: Boston Publishing Company, 1985), 104–5.

3. Series of telephone interviews with Lt. Gen. W. W. Marshall (Ret.) between Nov. 1992 and Mar. 1993, and taped interview on 20 Mar. 1993.

4. 7th AF Manual 64-1, 1 Mar. 1968. Also *History of the 3d Aerospace Rescue and Recovery Group, 1 Apr.–30 Jun. 1972* (Washington, D.C., Bolling AFB).

5. Interviews with Col. Cecil Muirhead (Ret.), 22 Nov. 1992 and 23 Feb. 1993.

6. Interview with M.Sgt. Daryl Tincher (Ret.), 26 June 1993.

7. Muirhead interviews.

8. Interview with Maj. Gen. John T. Carley (Ret.), 24 Aug. 1993.

9. 3d Division TOC Log, 2 Apr. 1972, item 100.

10. Constant interview.

11. 3d Division TOC Log, 2 Apr. 1972, item 103.

12. Ibid., item 104.

13. Turley, *Easter Offensive,* 176.

14. Maj. Charles D. Melson and Lt. Col. Curtis G. Arnold, *U.S. Marines in Vietnam: The War That Would Not End, 1971–1973* (Washington, D.C.: History and Museums Division, Headquarters USMC, 1991), 61. Also Gray interview.

15. Gray interview.

16. 3d Division TOC Log, 2 Apr. 1972, items 105, 106, 108, 109.

Chapter 6. Heavy Action

1. *Airpower and the 1972 Spring Invasion,* 137.

2. Interview with Mr. Gary Ferentchak, 24 Apr. 1993.

3. Constant interview.

4. Ferentchak interview.

5. 3d Division TOC Log, 3 Apr. 1972, items 4, 8.

6. Ibid., items 9, 11, 26.

7. Hambleton interview.

8. Smith interview, Henderson interview.

9. Interview with Col. Mark Clark, 5 Jan. 1993.

10. Smith interview.

11. Maj. Rick Atchison, USAF Oral History Program, Maxll AFB, 16 Jul. 1975, 41. To *zot* meant to fire a laser beam at

the position. The onboard computer would then "talk" to the Loran to determine the actual coordinates.

12. *Airpower and the 1972 Spring Invasion*, 138.

13. Smith interview, Henderson interview.

14. Interview with Lt. Col. Mark Schibler (Ret.), 40th ARRS 1972, 30 Oct. 1992.

15. Interview with Capt. Jay Crowe (Ret.), USCG, 1 Apr. 1993.

16. Sandy statement, 1st Lt. Glen Priebe, 3 Apr. 1972.

17. Sandy statement, Capt. Donald Morse, 3 Apr. 1972.

18. Sandy statement, 1st Lt. Glen Priebe, 3 Apr. 1972.

19. Crowe interview.

20. Henderson interview.

21. Interview with Col. William Harris (Ret.), 3 Feb. 1993.

22. Sandy statement, Capt. Robert Burke, 6 Apr. 1972. Also Harris interview.

23. Harris interview.

24. Crowe interview.

25. Statement of 1st Lt. Larry D. Cheek, asst. aviation officer, HHD, 37th Signal Battalion, 12 Apr. 1972. Obtained From the U.S. Army Intelligence and Security Command, Fort George Meade, Md. Also MACV Command Center Journal, 4 Apr. 1972, item 3. National Archives.

26. "The U.S. CH-3 Helicopter," *Quan Doi Nhan Dan*, in Vietnamese, Hanoi, 3 Dec. 1970, 2. Indochina Archives, University of California at Berkeley, Calif.

27. Ibid.

28. "Shooting Down Pilot Rescue Helicopters," *Quan Doi Nhan Dan*, in Vietnamese, Hanoi, 3 Apr. 1971, 3. Indochina Archives.

29. Harris interview.

30. Sandy statement, Capt. Robert Burke, 6 Apr. 1972.

31. Capt. Fred Boli, "Report on Jolly Green 67, 6 Apr. 1972," dated 18 Apr. 1972. Given to author by Colonel Boli.

32. Clark interview, Henderson interview.

33. Henderson interview.

34. Ibid.

35. Sprouse letter.

36. Boli report, "Jolly Green 67." Also Sprouse interview, LaCelle interview, Nielsen interview.

37. Evasion and Recovery Report for 1st Lt. Mark N. Clark, 56th Special Operations Wing, APO SF 96310, 24 Apr. 1972, Maxwell AFB. Also Clark interview.

38. Henderson interview.

39. After-action report, Lt. Col. Louis C. Wagner Jr., 5.

40. 3d Division TOC Log, 3 Apr. 1972, item 33.

41. Icke narrative.

42. Atchison oral history.

43. Henderson interview.

44. Truong, *Indochina Monographs,* 31.

45. Boli report, "Jolly Green 67."

46. Icke narrative.

47. Crowe interview.

48. Morse interview.

49. Sandy statement, Capt. Donald Morse, 4 Apr. 1972.

50. Morse interview.

51. Boli report, "Jolly Green 67."

52. Crowe interview.

53. 3d Division TOC Log, 3 Apr. 1972, items 12, 17, 20, 35, 40, 41, 42, 43.

54. Boli report, "Jolly Green 67."

55. Personal flight log of and interview with Col. Mike Carlin, HQ USAF, 30 Oct. 1992.

56. Ibid.

57. *The USAF Response to the Spring 1972 NVN Offensive: Situation and Redeployment* (Maxwell AFB: Project Checo Southeast Asia Report, HQ PACAF, 10 Oct. 1972), 39, 41.

58. Ibid., 54.

59. *Air War: Vietnam,* 114, 125.

60. Radio intercept, Hanoi VNA, 5 Apr. 1972, no. 72-063, "Bagging a B-52 Over Vinh Linh." Indochina Archives.

Chapter 7. Flight of the Jolly Green

1. Evasion and Recovery Report for 1st Lt. Mark Clark.
2. 3d Division TOC Log, 3 Apr. 1972, items 26, 29.
3. Boli report, "Jolly Green 67."
4. Schibler interview.
5. Crowe interview.
6. Harris interview. Also *History of the 3d Aerospace Rescue and Recovery Group*, 58.
7. Boli report, "Jolly Green 67."
8. Schibler interview.
9. Boli report, "Jolly Green 67."
10. 3d Division TOC Log, 6 Apr. 1972, item 34.
11. Boli report, "Jolly Green 67."
12. Ibid.
13. Tape recording of the rescue attempt by Jolly Green 67.
14. Boli report, "Jolly Green 67."
15. Ibid.
16. Ibid. Also Sandy statements, Capt. Donald Morse and Capt. Fred Boli (Sandy 01), 6 Apr. 1972.
17. Boli report, "Jolly Green 67."
18. History of the *History of the 3d Aerospace Rescue and Recovery Group*, 58. This history states that the call sign for the downed helicopter was Jolly Green 65. According to the Southeast Asia Data Base for this time period, Jolly Green 67 is correct.
19. Schibler interview.
20. Boli report, "Jolly Green 67."
21. Harris interview.
22. 7th AF Manual 64-1, para. 3–9, and Muirhead interview.
23. 3d Division TOC Log, 6 Apr. 1972, items 37 and 38
24. Evasion and Recovery Report for 1st Lt. Mark Clark. Also Clark interview.
25. Interview with Lt. Col. Iceal Hambleton (Ret.), cite Lt. Col. Stanley Busboom, "Bat 21: A Case Study," Army War College, Carlisle Barracks, Pa., 2 Apr. 1990,

26. 3d Division TOC Log, 6 Apr. 1972, items 40, 41, 42, 43.

Chapter 8. More Bad News

1. Letter from Col. Fred Boli to author, 9 May 1990.

2. Icke narrative.

3. 3d Division TOC Log, 7 Apr. 1972, numerous items.

4. After-action report, Lt. Col. Louis C. Wagner Jr., 7.

5. Findings of fact and supporting documents concerning the status of Marine first lieutenant Larry F. Potts, procured from the National Personnel Records Center, St. Louis, Mo. Form DD-1300, "Report of Casualty" for First Lieutenant Potts, states, "Numerous reports have been received indicating Potts was captured and subsequently died of a leg wound." First Lieutenant Potts was officially declared dead on 31 Jan. 1979.

6. Interview with Lt. Col. Dave Talley (Ret.), 9 Feb. 1993.

7. Thomasson, *Analysis of Combat Damage,* 70.

8. Southeast Asia Combat Area Casualties Current File, National Archives, Washington, D.C., 6 Oct. 1991. It shows his date of death as 8 Apr.; Potts's twenty-fifth birthday was on 7 Apr. Also Talley interview.

9. Statement of Lt. David P. Throop, included in the findings of fact and supporting documents concerning the status of U.S. Marine first lieutenant Larry F. Potts, National Personnel Records Center.

10. Ibid

11. Message from COMUSMACV to CJCS, 21 Apr. 1972, 2356Z. DOD, Freedom of Information Act.

12. Talley interview.

13. Atchison oral history, 59.

14. Ibid., 58.

15. "Pilots Tell of Raids on SAM Sites," *New York Times,* 9 1972, 5.

Ibid.

"On Da Nang Flight Line, GIs Work and Sweat," *New ꞏimes,* 8 Apr. 1972, 5.

18. Personal undated notes of Col. William Losier (Ret.), G3 adviser, 3d ARVN Division, Apr. 1972. Provided to author.

19. Maj. David A. Brookbank, "VNAF TACS and the Fall of Quang Tri," special report (declassified), 31 Jul. 1972, 8.

20. Atchison oral history, 60.

21. Hambleton interview, Clark interview.

22. Interview with Col. Don Lunday (Ret.), 4 Dec. 1994. Also, interview with Col. Bob Covalucci (Ret.), 3 Jan. 1995.

23. "New Air Chief in Vietnam," *New York Times*, 18 Apr. 1972.

24. Hambleton interview.

Chapter 9. Bright Light

1. Charles F. Reske, *MACV-SOG Command History, Annex B, 1971–1972*, vols. 1 and 2 (Sharon Center, Ohio: Alpha Publications, 1990), 473. MACSOG is referred to as MACV-SOG by some writers. My research indicates that MACSOG appears to be more common.

2. Ibid., 479.

3. Thomas Yarborough, *Da Nang Diary* (New York: St. Martin's Press, 1990), 263–67.

4. Interview with Lt. Col. Jack Butcher (Ret.), 27 Mar. 1993.

5. Yarborough, *Da Nang Diary*, 267. Also Reske, *MACV-SOG Command History*, 489.

6. Reske, *MACV-SOG Command History*, 10.

7. Covalucci interview.

8. Lt. Col. Andrew E. Anderson (Ret.), "Narrative of Action," 12 Dec. 1989 comments to director of Marine Corps Histories and Museums regarding *U.S. Marines in Vietnam The War That Would Not End, 1971–1973*. Also Muirhead interview.

9. Muirhead interview, Marshall interviews.

10. Letter from Col. Fred Boli to author, 9 May 199[?]

11. Atchison oral history, 62.

12. Anderson narrative. Also Atchison oral history,

13. Clark interview. Col. Lachlan Macleay (Ret.), commander of the 23d TASS, created this message for First Lieutenant Clark based upon Mark's previous tour of duty at Mountain Home AFB, Idaho.

14. Hambleton interview.

15. Anderson, *Bat 21.*

16. Icke narrative.

17. Message From COMUSMACV to CJCS, 21 Apr. 1972, 2356Z.

18. T. L. Bosiljevac, *SEALs: UDT/SEAL Operations in Vietnam* (New York: Ivy Books, 1990), 165. Also interview of Lt. Tom Norris (Med. Ret.) by Mr. Dale Andrade, 17 Mar. 1990.

19. Undated mission narrative by Tom Norris. Given to author by Norris in Jan. 1993. Also interview with Norris, 21 Jan. 1993. See also Kevin Dockery, *SEALS in Action* (New York: Avon, 1991), 200.

20. Norris interview.

21. Norris narrative.

22. Norris interview.

Chapter 10. Battles— Large and Small

1. Gen. Donn A. Starry, *Armored Combat in Vietnam* (New York: Merrill, 1980), 209. Also 3d Division TOC Log, 9 Apr. 1972, items 13, 18, 24, 40, 45, 46.

2. Icke narrative.

3. Turley, *Easter Offensive,* 206–9.

4. 3d Division TOC Log, 10 Apr. 1972, items 14, 15.

5. Atchison oral history, 46.

6. 3d Division TOC Log, 9 Apr. 1972, item 54.

7. Anderson narrative.

8. Ibid.

9. Norris narrative, Norris interview.

10. Clark interview.

11. Norris narrative.

12. Ibid.

13. Clark interview.

14. 3d Division TOC Log, 11 Apr. 1972, item 18.

15. Norris interview by Andrade.

16. Norris interview.

17. Anderson narrative, Icke narrative.

18. 3d Division TOC Log, 11 Apr. 1972, items 31, 32, 33, 34, 35.

19. Norris narrative.

20. Notes provided by Mr. Chuck Rouhier. At the time, he was a flight engineer with the 37th ARRS.

21. Icke narrative.

22. Norris narrative.

23. Ibid.

24. Operation report of Gunnery PO Nguyen Van Kiet, Camp Pendleton, Calif., 13 July 1975. Given to author by Tom Norris.

25. Norris narrative.

26. Icke narrative.

27. Interview with Mr. Denny Sapp, 12 Jan. 1993.

28. Brady interview, Hambleton interview.

29. Norris narrative. Also 3d Division TOC Log, 13 Apr. 1972, items 12, 17, 18, 20.

30. "Dramatic Rescue of Two Crewmen Cost Seven Lives." *Pacific Stars and Stripes,* 23 Apr. 1972, front page.

31. Harve Saal, *MACV Studies and Observations Group,* vol. 3, *Legends* (Ann Arbor, Mich.: Edwards Brothers, 1990), 568.

32. Norris narrative.

33. End-of-tour report of Col. Cecil Muirhead, commander of the 3d Aerospace Rescue and Recovery Group and director of Aerospace Rescue, 7th AF, 14 Jan. 1972 to 9 Jan. 1973, Maxwell AFB, 7.

34. Paul D. Stevens, *The Navy Cross: Vietnam* (San Francisco: Sharp and Dunnigan, 1987), 332.

35. *The Congressional Medal of Honor Library Vietnam: The Names, The Deeds* (New York: Dell, 1984), 167. First Lt. Mark Clark had to write a corroborating witness statement to the Navy to support the award submission. He concluded his remarks by saying: "I personally would not have gone into that area to save myself if I didn't have to. I simply would not have

done it. That to me is the heroism of Tom Norris. . . . If there is a hero to be had here, it has to be Tom Norris for the actions that he did and probably to some extent [Lieutenant] Colonel Anderson . . . who masterminded this and brought it all together. But Tom Norris has clearly got to be the guy who made it happen . . . you can't say any more than that."

Chapter 11. Bruce Walker

1. 3d Division TOC Log, 14 Apr. 1972, item 14.

2. Fain interview.

3. CNA Loss/Damage Data Base, Chief of Naval Operations, OP-5W, p. E-12. The crew was Lt. John G. Greenleaf, pilot; Lt. Clemie McKinney, radar intercept officer (RIO). The North Vietnamese later admitted that Lieutenant McKinney had been captured alive but died in captivity. His remains were returned in 1985. See also message (date, time, and group obscured) from OL A 3ARRGP Son Tra AB, Republic of Vietnam, to CTG 77.7. Subject: Linfield 203 Mission.

4. Norris interview.

5. Personal logbook of Col. Mickey Fain, and interview.

6. Message from COMUSMACV to CJCS, 21 Apr. 1972, 2356Z.

7. Message/DTG 200753Z Jul. 1992 CJTF-FA Det Two Bangkok Thailand. Subject: Field Investigation Report concerning Case 1820 (Walker and Potts). DOD, Freedom of Information Act.

8. Tape recording of Lacey flight received from Col. Gene Taft (Ret.).

9. Ibid.

10. Message/DTG 200753Z, Field Investigation Report concerning Case 1820 (Walker and Potts).

11. Fain interview. Also Icke narrative.

12. Message from COMUSMACV to CJCS, 21 Apr. 1972, 2356Z.

13. Charles F. Reske, *MACV-SOG Command History,* 440. Also Norris interview.

14. Truong, *Indochina Monographs,* 36, 38, 39.

Chapter 12. Controversy

1. Turley, *Easter Offensive*, 176, 178, 217, 222.

2. Morrocco, *Rain of Fire*, 107. The specific ARVN officers are not named and the remark is not footnoted.

3. Muirhead end-of-tour report, 6.

4. Lunday interview.

5. Brookbank special report, 7. The size of the no-fire zone is controversial to this day. The records clearly show that the 3d ARVN Division received the message. But neither Colonel Muirhead nor Master Sergeant Tincher remember declaring such a large area. While they were almost always used for SARs, no no-fire zones had ever been that size. Additionally, when questioned about it, 7th AF rapidly agreed to reduce the size. I surmise that the original directive may have been a typographical error.

6. Turley interview.

7. Turley, *Easter Offensive*, 178. Also Turley interview. Colonel Turley did not know the exact location of the survivors until shown by the author during our interview. But his best guess, carried these twenty-one years, was only five hundred meters off.

8. Douglas Kinnard, *The War Managers* (New York: Da Capo Press, 1991), 92.

9. Turley, *Easter Offensive*, 175–76.

10. Brookbank special report, 7.

11. Turley interview.

12. Mann, *1972 Invasion*, 23.

13. Muirhead end-of-tour report, 7.

14. Atchison oral history, 42, 45–46.

15. Brookbank interview.

16. Turley interview.

17. Marshall interview.

18. Morse interview.

19. Melson and Arnold, *U.S. Marines in Vietnam: The War That Would Not End*, 61.

20. Camper interview.

21. "Liberation Storm Rolls over Quang Tri," Giai Fong Press Agency, Hanoi, 6 Apr. 1972. Indochina Archives.

22. "Big Victory on Quang Tri—Thua Thien Front," Giai Fong Press Agency, Hanoi, 3 Apr. 1972. Indochina Archives.

23. *Collection of Sketches of Battles: Course Supplement, History of Military Arts* (Republic of Vietnam: Ministry of Defense, 1986. Trans. Mr. Robert J. Destatte, Dec. 1990).

24. Mann, *1972 Invasion,* 51. The specific statement is: "The extended SAR no-fire-zones which hampered ARVN efforts to counter NVA movements and firepower."

25. After-action report, Lt. Col. Louis C. Wagner Jr., 5.

26. Col. Donald J. Metcalf, "Why Did the Defense of Quang Tri Province, SVN, Collapse?" U.S. Army War College, Carlisle Barracks, Pa., 23 Oct. 1972, 12.

27. After-action report on the Battle for Quang Tri, Gen. Frederick J. Kroesen (Ret.), n.d. Also, interview with Gen. Frederick J. Kroesen (Ret.), 12 Nov. 1990.

28. "South Vietnamese Brace After First Test," *Christian Science Monitor,* 13 Apr. 1972.

29. Lunday interview.

30. Quoted in Sorley, *General Creighton Abrams,* 320.

31. Michael Lee Lanning, and Dan Cragg, *Inside the VC and the NVA* (New York: Fawcett Columbine Books, 1992), 171.

32. Richard M. Nixon, *No More Vietnams* (New York: Arbor House, 1985), 151.

33. Stephen T. Hosmer, Konrad Kellen, and Brian M. Jenkins, *The Fall of South Vietnam: Statements by Vietnamese Military and Civilian Leaders, R-2208-OSD* (Arlington, Va.: Rand, 1978), 62. The actual quotation reads "Saigon's infantry + American firepower > NLF's Army." The NLF's Army consisted of the better known Viet Cong and North Vietnamese Army.

34. Anderson, *Bat 21,* 51, 59.

35. Clark interview.

36. Hambleton interview.

37. Rosebeary interview.

38. Marshall interview, Muirhead interview, Morse interview, Lunday interview.

39. Crowe interview. The *London Times*, in an article titled "Rescue of Radar Plane Man Costs Seven Lives," 22 Apr. 1972, stated:

The EB-66 contains highly secret electronic equipment designed to jam the radar guidance devices of the North Vietnamese missiles. The fact that it was shot down at all sent shock waves through the Pentagon. The Americans were determined that its navigator should not fall into Communist hands.

It may be that they were worried about all of this in Washington, but to the airmen out on the flightline who had to try and rescue him, it did not make any difference.

40. Kennedy interview.

Chapter 13. A Long, Bitter, and Frustrating War

1. Earl H. Tilford, *Setup: What the Air Force Did in Vietnam and Why* (Maxwell AFB: Air University Press, June 1991), 215.

2. *New York Times*, 13 Nov. 1971, front page.

3. Tilford, *Setup*, 173.

4. Ibid., 173, 177.

5. "The Air Force's Secret Electronic War, *Indochina Chronicle*, 15 Oct. 1971, 2–6.

6. Tilford, *Setup*, 179.

7. Ibid., 184.

8. Ibid., 185.

9. "Bombing the Ho Chi Minh Trail," *Air Power History*, winter 1991, 4.

10. Ferentchak interview.

11. Eduard Mark, *Aerial Interdiction: Air Power and the Land Battle in Three American Wars* (Washington D.C.: Center for Air Force History, 1994), 372.

12. "Laotians to Let U.S. Planes Bomb Ho Chi Minh Trail," *New York Times*, 21 Dec. 1964, 1.

13. Keith W. Nolan, *Into Laos: The Story of Dewey Canyon/Lam Son 719, Vietnam 1971* (New York: Dell, 1986), 30.

14. Mann, *1972 Invasion*, 11.

15. Tilford, *Setup*, 218, 220. Also *The Ho Chi Minh Trail* (Hanoi: Foreign Languages Publishing House, 1985).

16. "Resounding Success or Costly Failure?" *Philadelphia Inquirer*, 14 Dec. 1972.

17. Marshall interview.

18. "USAF Operations Against North Vietnam, 1 July 1971–30 June 1972," Maxwell AFB, Project Corona Harvest, 8 June 1973, 8.

19. Guenter Lewy, *America in Vietnam* (New York: Oxford University Press), 1978, 406–7.

20. Morrocco, *Rain of Fire*, 104.

21. "Rules of Engagement, Nov. 1969–Sept. 1972" (declassified), Maxwell AFB: Project Checo Report, 1 Mar. 1973, 2.

22. Ibid., 31, 40.

23. "Why the Bombing Had to Start," *London Times*, 11 Apr. 1972, 14. Also untitled article on Secretary Laird from the *New York Times*, 24 Nov. 1970. Indochina Archives.

24. "Rules of Engagement," 41.

25. "USAF Operations Against North Vietnam," 21.

26. Morrocco, *Rain of Fire*, 105.

27. "Laird Says He Backed Gen. Lavelle's Removal," *Wall Street Journal*, 17 Apr. 1972.

28. U.S. Congress, Senate Committee on Armed Services, Hearings: John D. Lavelle for appointment as lieutenant general on retired list of U.S. Air Force, and matters relating to authority for certain bombing missions in North Vietnam between Nov. 1971 and Mar. 1972. 11–15, 18, 19, 22, 28 Sept. 1972. U.S. Government Printing Office, 1972, 125.

29. Interview with Col. Bill Dalecky (Ret.), 29 Jan. 1994.

30. Marshall interview.

31. Statement by Maj. Ed Anderson concerning the shoot-down of Bat 21.

32. Marshall interview. Also interview with Mr. Marty Cavato, 25 Jan. 1994, and author's personal recollections.

33. Richard S. Drury, *My Secret War* (Fallbrook, Calif.: Aero Publishers, 1979), 50.

34. L. B. Taylor, *That Others May Live* (New York: E. P. Dutton and Co., 1967), 73. See also Earl H. Tilford, *Search and Rescue in Southeast Asia, 1961–1975* (Washington, D.C.: Office of Air Force History, 1980), 8.

35. Tilford, *Search and Rescue in Southeast Asia,* 13.

36. Ibid., 14.

37. Robert F. Futrell, *The United States Air Force in Korea, 1950–1953* (New York: Duell, Pearce, 1961), 543.

38. Allan R. Millett and Peter Maslowski, *For the Common Defense: A Military History of the United States* (New York: The Free Press, 1984), xii.

39. Tilford, *Setup,* 282. Also Thomas C. Thayer, *War Without Fronts* (Boulder, Colo: Westview Press, 1985), 82.

40. Col. John A. Warden III, *The Air Campaign Planning for Combat* (Washington, D.C.: National Defense University Press, Fort Lesley J. McNair, 1988), 49.

41. Col. Jack Broughton (Ret.), *Going Downtown: The War Against Hanoi and Washington* (New York: Pocket Books, 1988), 65.

42. Ibid., 149.

43. *USAF Search and Rescue, Nov. 1967–June 1969* (Maxwell AFB: Project Checo Report, HQ PACAF, 30 July 1969), 42–46.

44. Interview with Lt. Col. Woody Bergeron (Ret.), 7 May 1993.

45. Tilford, *Search and Rescue in Southeast Asia,* 119.

46. Almost every Air Force and Navy officer interviewed for this work, from lieutenants to generals, stated unequivocally that it was "understood" that "everything would be done to get you out if you went down." This was an act of faith among the fliers. A notable exception was Maj. Dave Brookbank, b

consider where he was. Being on the ground with the 3d ARVN Division, he saw the war as few airmen do. His loyalty transferred to his cohorts on the ground.

47. Cavato interview.

48. Yarborough, *Da Nang Diary*, 206.

49. End-of-tour report of Col. Lachlan Macleay (Ret.), commander 23d TASS, Maxwell AFB, 15, 16.

50. Macleay interview.

51. Tilford, *Search and Rescue in Southeast Asia*, 155.

52. *Search and Rescue Operations in Southeast Asia (Unclassified), 1 Jan. 1971–31 Mar. 1972* (Maxwell AFB: Project Checo Report, HQ PACAF), 39.

53. *SAR Operations in Southeast Asia, 1 Apr. 1972 to 30 June 1973*, 31.

Chapter 14. Disconnect

1. Tilford, *Setup*, 284.

2. "Pilots Tell of Raids on SAM Sites," *New York Times*, 9 Apr. 1972, 5.

3. Brady interview.

4. Christopher Robbins, *The Ravens: The Men Who Flew in America's Secret War in Laos* (New York: Crown Publishers, 1986), 191.

5. "U.S. Troops Refuse Patrol Duty in Vietnam," *London Times*, 13 Apr. 1972, 1.

6. Tilford, *Setup*, 216.

7. Clark interview.

8. "How Good Is Saigon's Army?" *Time*, 17 Apr. 1972, 37.

9. Author's personal recollections.

10. Cincinnatus, *Disintegration and Decay of the United States Army During the Vietnam War* (New York: W. W. Norton, 1981), 27.

11. Lt. Col. Richard L. Brown (Ret.), "The Forward Air Controller," *Vietnam Combat*, no. 2, 1988, 8.

12. Christian G. Appy, *Working Class War* (Chapel Hill, N.C.: University of North Carolina Press, 1993), 208.

13. "Secret Surveys Reveal Viet Hatred," *Washington Post,* 25 Jan. 1972, B11.

14. Loren Baritz, *Backfire: A History of How American Culture Led Us to Vietnam and Made Us Fight the Way We Did* (New York: Morrow and Company, 1985), 344.

15. "Secret Surveys Reveal Viet Hatred," B11.

16. Frances Fitzgerald, *Fire in the Lake: The Vietnamese and the Americans in Vietnam* (Boston: Little, Brown and Co., 1972), 419.

17. Tilford, *Setup,* 75.

18. Ibid., 282. See also Thayer, *War Without Fronts,* 82.

19. Appy, 242.

20. In Busboom, "Bat 21," 82.

21. Covalucci interview.

22. Sapp interview.

23. Crowe interview.

24. Harris interview.

25. In Busboom, "Bat 21," 81.

26. Harris interview.

27. Muirhead interview.

28. Tilford, *Search and Rescue in Southeast Asia,* 119.

29. Interview with Col. Ray Bean, 11 Feb. 1993.

30. Tilford, *Search and Rescue in Southeast Asia,* 121.

31. Jeffrey Ethell and Alfred Price, "Man on the Run," *Air Power History,* fall 1989, 45.

32. Ibid.

33. Crowe interview.

34. Summers, Col. Harry G., Jr. *On Strategy: The Vietnam War in Context* (Carlisle Barracks, Pa.: U.S. Army War College, 1981), 7.

35. Stuart A. Herrington, *Peace with Honor? An American Reports on Vietnam, 1973–1975* (Novato, Calif.: Presidio Press, 1983), 199. See also Stuart A. Herrington, *Silence Was a Weapon* (Novato, Calif.: Presidio Press, 1982), x.

36. This is a controversial point, but it is still with us. Santoli, in his book *Leading the Way: How Vietnam Veter Rebuilt the U.S. Military, an Oral History* (New York: Bal

tine Books, 1993), documents how this dichotomy was still a factor in the Persian Gulf War. Santoli interviewed Air Force lieutenant general Buster Glosson and Marine lieutenant general Walter Boomer, both of whom were senior commanders in the Gulf and had been young veterans during the last years in Vietnam. Following are a few of the comments they made that pertain to this issue:

Boomer: A major lesson I learned from having been an adviser in Vietnam was how to deal with other cultures. The coalition approach was essential to our success. We simply couldn't ride roughshod over our allies. We had to deal very carefully [p. 214].

Glosson: I [as a flight commander in Southeast Asia] was responsible for eight F-4 fighters with twelve front and back seaters—pilots and weapons systems officers.

I remember feeling that no one higher up cared enough to explain to us about what they were asking us fighter pilots to do. Or how we fit into the overall scheme.

In the Gulf, to make sure that no fighter pilot had those same feelings, I personally visited every fighter squadron in the 14th Air Division . . . I told the fighter pilots everything. . . . I expressed my wish to see all of the pilots at similar meetings after the war ended. I told them, "There is not a damn thing in Iraq worth dying for until the first soldier or Marine crosses the border."

Around the middle of February, approximately one week before the land campaign started, I sent the following message to every fighter wing. I made it mandatory reading for every fighter pilot before he flew his next mission: "All of you heard me say earlier that 'Not one thing in Iraq is worth dying for,' and that was true. Sometime next week, there is going to be a lot worth dying for in Iraq. We call them American soldiers and Marines. When I said I want a minimum loss of life, we nnot draw distinctions between Americans who die. If a Marine dies or a soldier dies, it's the same to me as one of you dying. For that reason, there will be no restrictions placed on you by anyone [p. 205]."

Postscript

1. The citation for Tom Norris's Medal of Honor reads:

For conspicuous gallantry and intrepidity in action at the risk of his life above and beyond the call of duty while serving as a SEAL advisor with the Strategic Technical Directorate Assistance Team, headquarters, U.S. Military Assistance Command, Vietnam. During the period 10 to 13 April 1972, Lieutenant Norris completed an unprecedented ground rescue of two downed pilots deep within heavily controlled enemy territory in Quang Tri Province. Lieutenant Norris, on the night of 10 April, led a five-man patrol through 2,000 meters of heavily controlled enemy territory, located one of the pilots at daybreak, and returned to the Forward Operating Base(FOB). On 11 April, after a devastating mortar and rocket attack on the small FOB, Lieutenant Norris led a three-man team on two unsuccessful rescue attempts for the second pilot. On the afternoon of the 12th, a Forward Air Controller located the pilot and notified Lieutenant Norris. Dressed in fishermen disguises and using a sampan, Lieutenant Norris and one Vietnamese traveled throughout that night and found the injured pilot at dawn. Covering the pilot with bamboo and vegetation, they began the return journey, successfully evading a North Vietnamese patrol. Approaching the FOB, they came under heavy machine gun fire. Lieutenant Norris called in an air strike which provided suppression fire and a smoke screen, allowing the rescue party to reach the FOB. By his outstanding display of decisive leadership, undaunted courage, and selfless dedication in the face of extreme danger, Lieutenant Norris enhanced the finest traditions of the United States Naval Service

2. "The Making of a Fiasco," *Newsweek*, 18 Oct. 1993, 34–35.

3. "Enthusiasm Wanes," *Washington Times*, 8 Oct. 1993, 6.

4. "Reader Feedback: Should the United States Continue to Keep Troops in Somalia?" *Boston Globe*, 8 Oct. 1993, 16.

5. "Escalating Casualties and Fighting Are Wasting U.S. Lives in Somalia," *Cincinnati Enquirer*, 6 Oct. 1993, 8.

6. Ibid.

7. "Somalia: Time to Get Out," *New York Times*, 8 Oct. 1993, 34.

8. "In Divided Mogadishu, GIs Recall Losses," *Washington Post*, 26 Nov. 1993, 1.

9. Author's personal recollections.

10. Letter from Lt. Col. Gene Hambleton (Ret.) to Mr. Dan Manion, 11 Nov. 1997. Graciously given to the author by Mr. Manion.

11. "Jolly Green Funeral Ceremony," HQ USAF TV Center, 11th Communications Sq., Pentagon, Washington D.C., 25 Nov. 1997.

12. Ibid.

13. Ibid.

GLOSSARY

ABCCC Airborne Battlefield Command and Control Aircraft, a C-130 that orbited over certain areas of Southeast Asia and coordinated air actions. Used call signs such as Cricket, Hillsboro, Alleycat, and Moonbeam.

ANGLICO Air and Naval Gunfire Company. Unit of U.S. Marines that provided individuals to coordinate naval gunfire and airstrikes with ground units.

APC Armored personnel carrier.

AVRN Army of South Vietnam.

CAP Combat air patrol.

CBU Cluster bomb units, a type of aerial dispenser that opens and disperses numerous smaller bomblets over a wide area. There were many different types.

CDU Cluster dispenser units, similar to CBUs.

CINCPAC Commander in Chief, Pacific Forces.

COMUSMACV Commander United States Forces, Military Assistance Command, Vietnam. At this stage of the war, it was U.S. Army general Creighton Abrams.

DAR Director of Aerospace Rescue, the individual at 7th A. Force who was responsible for all aerial rescue in Southe Asia.

DCPG Defense Communications Planning Group.

ELINT Electronic Intelligence. Intelligence data that indicates how electronic weapons and components work.

EW Early warning, a type of long-range radar that initially detected aircraft.

EWO Electronic warfare officer. A crewmember assigned to several different types of aircraft, who was specially trained in electronic warfare and could operate the various types of equipment designed for that purpose.

FAC Forward air controller.

GCI Ground-controlled intercept radars, long-range radars used to track enemy aircraft and vector friendly aircraft to intercept them.

GUARD Emergency radio frequency, 243 MHZ. Most aircraft in Southeast Asia had radios with a second receiver that was pretuned to this frequency.

JCS Joint Chiefs of Staff, located in Washington, D.C.

JOLLY GREEN Call sign for rescue helicopters.

JPRC Joint Personnel Recovery Center in Saigon.

JSARC Joint Search and Rescue Center, call sign Joker, located in 7th Air Force headquarters, Saigon.

KING Call sign for the HC-130 command-and-control aircraft. Earlier in the war, they also used the call sign Crown.

LETTERS Military operations depend upon the flow of information of all kinds. Much of this information is passed verbally through either electronic lines or electronic radio signals. Both channels are subject to interference, which means that signals can sometimes get garbled. Many letters (E, G, C, etc.) sound the same, especially when things are confused or happening quickly. It is called the Fog of War. To prevent confusion with letters, the military has created a monster called the phonetic alphabet. Each letter is replaced by a word that begins with that letter. The words are clear and distinct.

A—Alpha	D—Delta
B—Bravo	E—Echo
C—Charlie	F—Foxtrot

G—Golf	Q—Quebec
H—Hotel	R—Romero
I—India	S—Sierra
J—Juliet	T—Tango
K—Kilo	U—Uniform
L—Lima	V—Victor
M—Mike	W—Whiskey
N—November	X—X-ray
O—Oscar	Y—Yankee
P—Papa	Z—Zulu

LORAN Long-range navigation system, carried by many aircraft in Southeast Asia. It allowed for fairly precise navigation and target location and identification.

MACV Military Assistance Command, Vietnam.

MACSOG Military Assistance Command, Vietnam, Studies and Observations Group. Also referred to as MACVSOG or MAC(V)SOG by some writers.

NAD Naval Advisory Detachment, one of the naval subunits of MACSOG.

NVA North Vietnamese Army.

PACAF Pacific Air Forces.

PJ Pararescuemen. Enlisted specialists assigned to the rescue squadrons. They were trained to, if necessary, go down from the rescue helicopters and recover downed airmen.

REDCROWN A U.S. Navy ship on patrol in the Gulf of Tonkin. It monitored NVA air defenses and called warnings to American airmen.

RESCAP Rescue combat air patrol.

RHAW Radar homing and warning gear, carried by many aircraft in Southeast Asia. It gave the crews warning that they were being tracked by various types of enemy radar.

SAM Surface-to-air missile. There were different kinds: SA-2s were large missiles, guided by radar. SA-7s were smaller ones, guided by infrared homing on aircraft engine exhaust.

SANDY Call sign for the A-1 rescue aircraft.

SAR Search and rescue.

SEA Southeast Asia.

STD Strategic Technical Directorate, the South Vietnamese equivalent of MACSOG.

STDAT Strategic Technical Directorate Advisory Team.

TACC Tactical Air Control Center, call sign Bluechip. It was the 7th Air Force command center, located in Saigon.

TACS Tactical air control system, consisting of Air Force and Army personnel, designed to coordinate the actions of air and ground units in combat.

TASS Tactical Air Support Squadron.

TEWS Tactical Electronic Warfare Squadron.

TFS Tactical Fighter Squadron.

TFW Tactical Fighter Wing. Usually controlled numerous types of subordinate squadrons.

VNAF (South) Vietnamese Air Force.

INDEX

The Naval Institute Press is the book-publishing arm of the U.S. Naval Institute, a private, nonprofit, membership society for sea service professionals and others who share an interest in naval and maritime affairs. Established in 1873 at the U.S. Naval Academy in Annapolis, Maryland, where its offices remain today, the Naval Institute has members worldwide.

Members of the Naval Institute support the education programs of the society and receive the influential monthly magazine *Proceedings* and discounts on fine nautical prints and on ship and aircraft photos. They also have access to the transcripts of the Institute's Oral History Program and get discounted admission to any of the Institute-sponsored seminars offered around the country.

The Naval Institute also publishes *Naval History* magazine. This colorful bimonthly is filled with entertaining and thought-provoking articles, first-person reminiscences, and dramatic art and photography. Members receive a discount on *Naval History* subscriptions.

The Naval Institute's book-publishing program, begun in 1898 with basic guides to naval practices, has broadened its scope in recent years to include books of more general interest. Now the Naval Institute Press publishes about 100 titles each year, ranging from how-to books on boating and navigation to battle histories, biographies, ship and aircraft guides, and novels. Institute members receive discounts of 20 to 50 percent on the Press's nearly 600 books in print.

Full-time students are eligible for special half-price membership rates. Life memberships are also available.

For a free catalog describing Naval Institute Press books currently available, and for further information about subscribing to *Naval History* magazine or about joining the U.S. Naval Institute, please write to:

Membership Department
U.S. Naval Institute
118 Maryland Avenue
Annapolis, MD 21402-5035
Telephone: (800) 233-8764
Fax: (410) 269-7940
Web address: www.usni.org